SOFTWARE ARCHITECTURE

ORGANIZATIONAL PRINCIPLES AND PATTERNS

ISBN 0-13-029032-7

90000

9 780130 290328

WWW.WWISA.ORG

The Worldwide Institute of Software Architects (WWISA) is a non-profit professional organization dedicated to establishing a formal profession of software architecture and providing information and services to software architects and their clients—analogous to the formation of the American Institute of Architects roughly 140 years ago. The essential tenet of WWISA is that there is a perfect analogy between building and software architecture, and that the classical role of the architect needs to be introduced into the software construction industry.

The architect, whether designing structures of brick or computer code, forms the bridge between the world of the client and that of the technical builders. This critical bridge has been missing from the software industry, resulting in a decades-long software crisis. Entire software structures are dysfunctional or have been scrapped entirely—before seeing a single "inhabitant." We have simply been building huge, complex structures without architects, and without blueprints.

WWISA was established in 1998 and now has over 1,000 members in 37 countries. Membership is open to practicing and aspiring software architects, professors, students, CIOs, and CEOs. Members participate to promote training and degree programs, develop architectural standards and guiding principles, and work toward creating a standard body of shared knowledge. We are our client advocates; clients are our driving force. We hope to become the clients' bridge to successful software construction by helping them leverage the full range of technology.

SERIES VISION

Software technology is critically important to the world's businesses and human society. However, software engineering remains a chaotic, immature discipline, unable to systematically deliver successful systems. What's missing is software architecture. But, many questions about software architecture, going much deeper than academic discussions, remain unresolved. In particular, how do we apply software architecture on real-world projects and across business enterprises?

At the same time, many successful practitioners of software architecture know how to answer these questions from experience. From among these practitioners our series authors are carefully selected. Often they work in companies that rely upon software system success as their core business model (e.g., business systems, telecommunications, and financial services). These innovative software architects have developed systematic disciplines for doing work that consistently surpasses the industry averages for on-time, on-budget deliveries that meet users' needs and expectations. Some of these experts utilize published standards and patterns for software architecture. Others can share unique lessons learned through professional experience. We have discovered significant commonalities in practical software architecture knowledge which can be useful across most software applications. Together, the joint knowledge of innovative software architects represents the next generation of practice for leading technologists in the software discipline.

The mission of the Software Architecture Series is to publish a common body of knowledge for the software architecture discipline. Software architecture is a specialty distinct from software engineering, programming, and project management. A software architect balances and resolves design forces from many perspectives, including system stakeholders and system developers. Software architects are responsible for a much wider and more interesting range of issues (technical, intuitive, and human factors) than we typically associate with project management. Software architects create technical plans that coordinate the work of groups of programmers, resolving significant systemwide risks and project/technical inefficiencies. The software architect role is an important career path for lead programmers and other IT professionals, as an alternative to project management.

In this series, our goal is to establish the knowledge base for the software architect career path. We hope to share the comprehensive knowledge of successful software architects in a way that fundamentally changes how people develop software, to show better ways of working, and to develop individuals (such as yourselves) into world-class professionals drawing from the acquired knowledge of a wide range of peers in the software architecture profession. We share these goals with a nonprofit organization, the Worldwide Institute of Software Architecture (WWISA), a co-sponsor of this book series.

In conclusion, knowledge is power, particularly for software architects. We are giving to you—the next generation of software architects—the best of our knowledge in the hope that you will fundamentally change the software profession, through your individual practices, toward a mature discipline, which achieves systematic success in the development of software systems. We hope that you as software architects derive all of the benefits and professional recognition that is due to you. In this transition, we do not expect your personal career to be trouble-free and easy. But we do know that software architecture is one of the most exciting fields of endeavor, and we welcome you into our worldwide community!

THOMAS J. MOWBRAY, PH.D.
SERIES EDITOR

SOFTWARE ARCHITECTURE SERIES

Thomas J. Mowbray, Ph.D., Series Editor

SOFTWARE ARCHITECTURE

ORGANIZATIONAL PRINCIPLES AND PATTERNS

DAVID M. DIKEL

DAVID KANE

JAMES R. WILSON

PRENTICE HALL PTR
UPPER SADDLE RIVER, NJ 07458
WWW.PHPTR.COM

Library of Congress Cataloging-in-Publication Data available

Editorial/Production Supervision: *MetroVoice Publishing Services*
Acquisitions Editor: *Paul Petralia*
Marketing Manager: *Bryan Gambrel*
Editorial Assistant: *Justin Somma*
Cover Design: *Anthony Gemmellaro*
Cover Design Direction: *Jerry Votta*
Buyer: *Maura Zaldivar*
Project Coordinator: *Anne Trowbridge*

PH
PTR

© 2001 Prentice Hall PTR
Prentice-Hall, Inc.
Upper Saddle River, NJ 07458

Prentice Hall books are widely used by corporations and government agencies for training, marketing, and resale.

The publisher offers discounts on this book when ordered in bulk quantities.
For more information, contact Corporate Sales Department, phone: 800-382-3419;
fax: 201-236-7141; e-mail: corpsales@prenhall.com
Or write: Prentice Hall PTR
    Corporate Sales Department
    One Lake Street
    Upper Saddle River, NJ 07458

Printed in the United States of America
10 9 8 7 6 5 4 3 2 1

ISBN 0-13-029032-7

Prentice-Hall International (UK) Limited, *London*
Prentice-Hall of Australia Pty. Limited, *Sydney*
Prentice-Hall Canada Inc., *Toronto*
Prentice-Hall Hispanoamericana, S.A., *Mexico*
Prentice-Hall of India Private Limited, *New Delhi*
Prentice-Hall of Japan, Inc., *Tokyo*
Pearson Education Asia Pte. Ltd.
Editora Prentice-Hall do Brasil, Ltda., *Rio de Janeiro*

DEDICATIONS

David M. Dikel

I would like to dedicate this work to my wife, Margaret; my children Aaron and Ilana; my parents, Joyce Quintana and Samuel S. Dikel (deceased); and to my Guru, Satguru Sivaya Subramuniyaswami. I am deeply grateful for Margaret's encouragement and for her substantive contributions as an editor and as an expert on music, and for Aaron and Ilana's working around my book schedule so that we could spend precious time together.

David Kane

I would like to dedicate this book to Jordi for her encouragement and patience throughout this endeavor. I would also like to dedicate this book to my parents, Bill and Diane, who helped me find a path of my own.

James R. Wilson

I would like to dedicate this book to Dr. Carolyn A. Wilson, my noble wife, and our sons, Nathaniel and Avery. My family observed and supported this book-writing venture that coursed across several summers and many weekends—time that would otherwise be cordoned for lacrosse, walks in the park, and other essential family fun. Care, Nate, and Avery—thank you. You are the lift under my wings.

Contents

7   Simplification: Clarifying and Minimizing   *169*

PREFACE

Building software has almost always involved fitting together products and organizations as well as developing code. Software architecture is fundamental to both activities, especially today. For example, an ordinary business transaction will traverse many layers of software architecture, leveraging shared platforms such as the Internet, client browsers, Web servers, business logic components, security systems, and back-end databases. In this environment, many partners must not only agree on a core set of interfaces and standards, but they must also agree on how to use those standards. Partners must also agree on the value they will add and receive for their contribution. All these agreements must remain workable and stay in place in the face of rapid changes in technologies, re-alignments of partners, shifts in business goals and requirements, as well as the ever-present mergers and acquisitions. If these agreements do not remain in place, the product and its architecture may fail, causing pain for developers and customers, as well as their managers and sponsors.

This book focuses on the interrelationship between software architecture and the organization. Software architecture serves as a framework that defines and orders not only the technical interactions needed to develop and implement a product, but also group and personal interactions. The ability of software architecture to fulfill this role over time relies on organizational factors.

It has long been observed that the structures of architectures and the organizations that build and use them influence one another. A close look reveals an extensive and complex relationship. Real-life architecture often is far removed from the intended structure, including hidden chunks of software, odd connections, hard-coded "shortcuts," missing pieces, and other irregularities. The same types of surprises come from an organization's culture, its people, their beliefs, abilities, and behaviors. In practice, architecture and organization form a sensitive and highly volatile matrix. Done right, organization and architecture can deliver great value; failure can melt the core of the enterprise.

We have written this book to help people who have a critical stake in the success of software architecture understand and overcome the challenges of architecture and organization. These stakeholders form a large interdependent group that is getting larger as software products cross more organizational boundaries in their development and use. This group includes people who manage, develop, implement, maintain, acquire, and use software architecture. Each stands to benefit from a better understanding of how software architecture and organization interact. For example, partnering skills can decrease the time it takes for developers to find out about changes to a release of an architecture or platform, and increase the chances that they can negotiate to restore features that are critical to their continuing use of the architecture. Without these skills, the architect would soon lose customers; the customers would soon be maintaining a lot more code and creating a lot less product.

Our book is based on more than five years of research within some of the country's best-known large-scale software development organizations and numerous workshops, as well as our work architecting product lines and implementing architectures for small, medium, and very large organizations. We also drew on work in other disciplines, especially organizational development. Our research yielded a model composed of five organizational principles that affect software architecture success—Vision, Rhythm, Anticipation, Partnering, and Simplification (VRAPS). We call this the VRAPS Model.

Together, the VRAPS principles provide a model you can use to get your arms around what to do and to improve your personal and corporate ability to get lasting value from products and ventures that depend on software architecture. The VRAPS model will help you to organize and interpret your observations and relate them to practices and patterns that others have used successfully. You can also use the model and principles to identify strengths and weaknesses, to communicate insights, and to encourage actions across roles, boundaries, and levels within and external to your organization.

You can take several paths through our book:

▶ You can get a quick overview of the book in Chapter 1. Then go to Chapter 8 to find a case study that illustrates how the VRAPS principles worked within Allaire Corporation, as it grew from a small startup to become a leading provider of tools for building Internet applications.

▶ You can find out more about each VRAPS principle in Chapters 3 through 7. After defining and describing the principle, these chapters provide criteria to help you gauge how well your organization applies the principle. Patterns, stories, and antipatterns provide practical guidance about what to do and what not to do to benefit from the principle.

▶ You can get a detailed understanding of the VRAPS model and how it relates to other work in Chapter 2. Chapter 9 provides a real-world illustration of how to use the model, along with nine specific templates, tools, and guidance you can use to assess your organization and compare it with others. We describe how the templates were used in a commercial benchmark.

We invite you to read on and visit our Web site at www.VRAPS.com.

David M. Dikel
David Kane
James R. Wilson

ACKNOWLEDGMENTS

We would like to thank the many people and organizations without whom this book would not have been possible.

The following individuals have served as advisors and collaborators, helping us to scope our research objectives, define our research protocol, develop the VRAPS model, and evaluate the results. We would like to express special appreciation to Bill Loftus and Steve Ornburn who were partners in our research and whose insights, ideas, and innovations made a lasting impression on our work.

Jeremy Allaire

J.J. Allaire

Robert M. Beckman
 (deceased)

Grady Booch

Barbara Bowers

David Bristow

Linda Brown

Marcia Carlyn

Lynn-Robert Carter

Robert Charette

David Chao

Francios Coallier

Patricia Cornwell

John den Otter

Glenn Dillard

John Foreman

John Garman

Connie Gersick

Ramses Girgis

Tom Goodall

Ron Grace

Kuan-Tse Huang

Bill Loftus

Ruth Malan

Joe Maranzano

Jean Mayrand

Susan Mohrman

Geoffrey Moore

Jim Moore

Burgess Oliver

Steve Ornburn	Bill Saunders	George C. Wilson
Mike Pait	Bob Savely	Jim Withey
Rick Peebles	Simeon Simeonov	Smith T. Wood
Stan Rifkin	Mike Sonneman	John Woodfin

We are also deeply grateful to those in the patterns community who introduced us to patterns, and shaped our first efforts in their roles as co-authors, shepherds, or mentors:

Brad Appleton	Neil Harrison	Don Olson
Mike Beedle	Christy Hermanson	Bill Opdyke
Charles Crowley	Raphael Malveaux	Linda Rising
David Delano	Tom Mowbray	

The following individuals helped us to shape this work by critiquing the VRAPS principles and associated patterns, participating in the research or providing feedback on our book:

John Artim	Terry James	Tim Niesen
Glen Adams	Ralph Johnson	Bill Opdyke
Steve Berczuk	Mary Kane	Eric Price
Adam Berrey	Tony Kram	Bob Rizzo
Dana Breedemeyer	Susan Lilly	Ralph Roland
Ben Cantlon	Mike Lombardi	Adam Satcowitz
Steve Cichinski	Doug Lowe	Jordana Schmier
David Coyle	John Lund	Michael Smith
Gitika Dalla	Brian Lyons	Ken Song
Karen DeChino	Raphael Malveaux	Patrick Steranka
Martine Devos	Priya Marsonia	George Stern
Margaret Dikel	Charles McKay	Charles Teague
Steve Drucker	Jim Moore	Carol Terry
Steven Fraser	Tom Mowbray	Sarah Tilman
Steve Green	April Morris	Kim Walker-Borst
Neil Harrison	Sadhunathan Nadesan	Dave Watts

In addition to individuals, we are thankful to the organizations and their business units that sponsored or participated in case studies and benchmarks that provide the foundation for this book:

Allaire Corporation

Andersen Consulting

AT&T

Bell Canada

Defense Advanced Research Projects Agency (DARPA)

Defense Information Systems Agency (DISA)

Electronic Data Systems

Hewlett-Packard

Lucent Technologies

National Aeronautics and Space Administration (NASA)

Nortel Networks

PECO Energy

Texas Instruments

U.S. Air Force Reuse Center

U.S. Air Force Space and Warning Systems Center

U.S. Army Communications–Electronic Command

U.S. Navy Air Warfare Center

U.S. Navy Surface Warfare Center

Last, but not least, we thank our sponsors and champions at Prentice Hall, including executive editor Paul Petralia, and his colleagues Justin Somma, Ann Trump Daniels, Jeffrey Pepper, and Judith Brief, as well as senior technical reviewers Jeff Barr and Linda Rising. We would also like to thank our current companies, SRA International and Cyberserv for their encouragement and support. We are thankful for the many fruitful years of business, professional, and intellectual relationships that we have experienced while on our journey toward writing this book. We hope that this work will make a useful contribution to the practice of software engineering. In writing this book, we have each grown as architects, engineers, managers, and executives. We are deeply grateful for the opportunity.

CREDITS

WHAT YOU CAN'T SEE
COULD HELP YOU

Architecture is frozen music.

—Madame de Staël, in
Ralph Waldo Emerson, Letters and Social Aims

In September 1993, while preparing a Department of Defense (DoD) Reuse Plan that was later submitted to Congress, one of the authors, David Dikel, was introduced to Ron Grace, a program manager for Hewlett-Packard's Software Reuse Initiative. Dikel's goal was to incorporate and adapt the best commercial practices into the DoD plan. Grace said that when he first moved to the initiative, he thought that his primary challenge would be to engage and sharpen his software engineering knowledge and skills. He said that he was surprised that much of his work involved social science, rather than state-of-the-art technology.

Grace said, for example, that when a business unit asks for help to learn software reuse, "We insist their key people take a workshop on partnering first." Grace's statement triggered an "Of course!" in Dikel's mind. Dikel had seen so many cases in which reuse programs fizzled not for the lack of the latest repository or classification technology (the then-current trends), but for the lack of basic consideration of what reuse would mean to the organization. It was suddenly clear that requiring a partnering workshop would bring to the surface and help resolve many of these issues.

WHAT THIS BOOK IS ABOUT

This book maps out the intersection of software architecture and the organization. Software architecture increasingly serves as a framework that defines and orders technical and business interactions. Systems development is moving from "stovepipe" solutions to systems built on shared architectures. Similarly, organizations that develop and deliver business products and services are engaging a greater number and variety of people and groups. While the opportunities offered by these shifts are undeniable, the organizational factors involved with sharing software architectures present dangerous pitfalls to stakeholders. The pitfalls don't just affect people in organizations implementing or using architectures, they also affect their suppliers, partners, and customers.

The book is designed to complement the outstanding work in software architecture that exists today. It is written for everyone who is a stakeholder in the success of software architecture, from developers to executives. The content in this book is organized in a model, which is built around five principles—Vision, Rhythm, Anticipation, Partnering, and Simplification (VRAPS). The VRAPS Model is based on over five years of research applying grounded theory concepts, including several case studies, a commercial software architecture benchmark, numerous workshops, and our work as architects. We use patterns and antipatterns to illustrate how the principles can be put into practice. The VRAPS Model also draws on work in other disciplines, especially organizational development.

Not long ago, the word "software" was rarely mentioned in executive suites. Now few executives can overlook the strategic advantages brought about by software and software architecture.

Software Architecture's Growing Importance

A number of trends are dramatically increasing the importance of an organization's capabilities to develop and utilize software architecture and to cooperate across organizational boundaries. Not long ago, the word "software" was rarely mentioned in executive suites. Now few executives can overlook the strategic advantages brought about by software and software architecture—both are critical to their personal, professional, and corporate survival. To stay competitive, companies are replacing monolithic, stovepipe information systems by using Web technologies, outsourcing, and a variety of off-the-shelf products.

Software architecture makes it possible to combine the wide variety of supporting products and services necessary to keep up with these trends. A shared architecture allows implementers to break up the problem at hand, identify which parts of the problem to address in-house and select the best mix of products and services to fill the gaps. Before, monolithic solutions were largely under the control of one organization. Now, you can have more attractive solutions that take advantage of the strengths of many groups within and outside of your company. However, to realize the benefits enabled by shared architecture, your product team, architecture group, and entire company may need a new set of organizational skills.

Sharing software architecture across a product line brings a core set of knowledge and assets to the development process. Using a common architecture across a software product line can significantly reduce the cost of developing and maintaining code and can streamline production, documentation, training, and marketing [Jacobson97] [Dikel97a]. There are other advantages. Customers become unhappy when features from the same vendor and product line do not act the same way. Integrators lose patience and trust when application program interfaces (APIs) require dissimilar technologies. Legacy system—yesterday's killer products—are far more difficult to migrate or encapsulate in new technology. Product line architecture can remedy or prevent these situations.

For Some, the News They are Stakeholders Comes Too Late

Creating viable software architecture requires a deep grasp of technology, excellent cognitive and communication skills, and a lot of hard work. However, getting value from software architecture is not just a matter of technology and sharp engineers. Success often depends on organizational factors that an executive, manager, or practitioner may not be looking at.

As an example, Nortel's[1] leadership in digital switch architecture enabled the company to capture U.S. and international markets. After the 1984 breakup of AT&T, only Nortel could provide Bell operating companies with the capability to offer customers equal access to long-distance carriers. The company's high product quality allowed it to become the first digital switch supplier in Japan.

After nearly 20 years of successful use, however, Nortel's digital switch architecture began to show signs of needing renewal. It had grown large and complex. One engineer remarked that the architecture "required half the people in Canada with an IQ over 140 to maintain." In the late 1980s, the company considered a major restructuring of the architecture, but the CEO decided to wait—the architecture underlay significant profits, and change entailed costs and risk.

The decision to wait had severe consequences. Product quality dropped and the length of release cycles tripled. Nortel later attributed these problems to architecture breakdown [Ziegler93]. Nortel took action (which included a

---

[1] Nortel, or Northern Telecom, succeeded Bell Northern Research; all are subsidiaries of BCE.

change of CEOs) and rebounded. After reporting an $878 million dollar loss in 1993, Nortel posted earnings of $408 million in 1994, increasing to $829 million in 1997 (see Figure 1.1).

Of course, other factors contributed to Nortel's performance. However, as a result of this event, the CEO who lost his job and a range of others realized that architecture affected them in a very direct way.

Software architecture and the organization are sometimes viewed as two very different entities, or they are not separated at all. Architecture is "something the architect does"; organization is "something executives and HR deal with" (see Figure 1.2). In some large bureaucracies, architecture is confused with organization. In this case, the identity of an architectural component has little or nothing to do with its functionality or interface and everything to do with the project responsible for the component.

Stemming back to 1968, people began to recognize that organization and architecture were interrelated [Conway68]. Today's architectures support and require the involvement of many different groups within and outside a company or agency (see Figure 1.3). To deal effectively with today's architectures, you must look at how these architectures interact with the organizations they support.

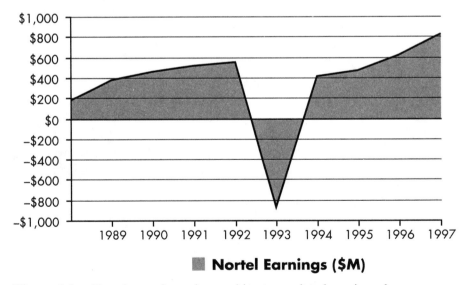

■ Nortel Earnings ($M)

Figure 1.1   Nortel experienced an architecture related earnings decrease, and rebounded.[2]

---

[2] Earnings data ("Earnings (loss) before extraordinary items") from Northern Telecom 1996 and 1997 annual reports.

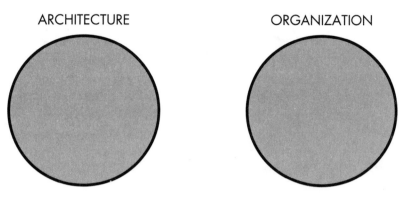

Figure 1.2   Some view architecture and the organization as separate.

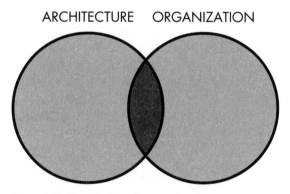

Figure 1.3   Today, the overlap between
architecture and organization is undeniable.

When you do look at how organization and architecture interact, you begin to see how many people within an organization affect its survival. If you are an executive, the effects of architecture may not be in plain view (see Figure 1.4). As a result, a seemingly harmless commitment to support a proprietary application program interface (API) could require the architecture team to make fundamental changes to the architecture that lead to incompatibility with other vendors' products. If you are a practitioner, the effects of organization may be hidden (see Figure 1.5). If you don't take the business goals of your organization into account, you might use an open source component, whose licensing terms are in conflict with the company's business model, exposing the company and its customers to substantial risk.

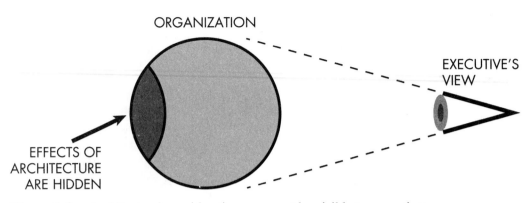

Figure 1.4   Architectural considerations may not be visible to executives.

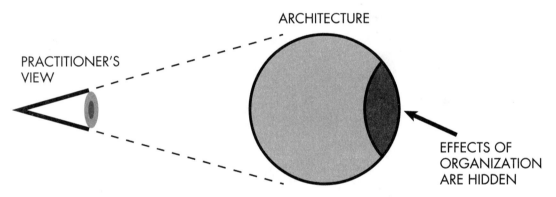

Figure 1.5   Organizational considerations may not be visible to practitioners.

We believe that using this book to focus on the intersection can shift the perspectives of practitioners, managers, architects, and executives, enabling them to "see" what they need to see to jointly make the architecture and organization succeed (see Figure 1.6).

Figure 1.6   VRAPS shifts both executive and practitioner perspectives to provide a more balanced view of architecture and organization.

PRINCIPLES REVEAL THE HIDDEN

Focusing on the VRAPS principles can make hidden risks and opportunities of software architecture visible.

This book examines five principles that serve as a common frame of reference for addressing these challenges. We organized the principles—Vision, Rhythm, Anticipation, Partnering, and Simplification—into what we call the VRAPS Model. Focusing on the VRAPS principles can make hidden risks and opportunities of software architecture visible. A brief description of each principle is listed here along with a related example of an aspect of architecture which is often hidden. The principles are examined in more detail in the later chapters.

Vision

The source of architecture vision is sometimes hidden. The vision principle describes how to project a coherent, compelling, and flexible picture of the future to architecture stakeholders. Architects may not catch the idea that the architecture vision they are developing derives its life from the business vision of one or more people. This is more likely to happen in a large organization when several levels separate the architect and visionary. Not surprisingly, the architecture vision they build doesn't align itself with the company's business goals.

Rhythm

The consequences of late deliveries are sometimes hidden. The rhythm principle describes an organization-wide confidence that work products will be regularly exchanged with predictable tempo, content, and quality. Sometimes executives become so focused on getting a killer feature to market that they hold back the release even when customers are counting on significant, albeit more pedestrian fixes or features in the next release. Sometimes developers spend so much time perfecting the details, they drive right past the release gate.

Anticipation

Assumptions about the future are sometimes hidden. The principle of anticipation balances astute efforts to predict the future with testing and adapting to what is found. Sometimes the lead architect's technical predictions are right on the mark. Yet customers decide that compatibility with an emerging product or standard is more important than meeting the specifications the lead architect is working to meet. Without testing both technical and business assumptions, the architect can be unpleasantly surprised.

Partnering

The needs of partners are sometimes hidden. The principle of partnering calls for strong cooperation as well as clear, fair contracts between individuals and groups. Swept up by the flurry and fanfare of a new architecture initiative, some lead architects seek and obtain the "buy-in" of visible product team leaders without working out a clear understanding. Details such as how the product team will participate in platform development are glossed over. The lead architect gets his or her funding released and product team leaders get recognition. However, when it's time to incorporate the architecture team's work, everyone is surprised—the architecture team hasn't learned about critical requirements, and the product teams have found other ways to deliver architecture features.

Simplification

The drivers of complexity are sometimes hidden. The principle of simplification calls for clarifying and minimizing both architecture and the organizations that build and use it. Consider the architect who, seeing the overlap of components built by two groups, specified a single component that could be shared. Soon after making a recommendation, the architect listened to good reasons why each team was uniquely capable of building the single component. It wasn't long before each group had a variation of the "simplified" design. The end result was more complexity, not less. Not only did each team's products become more complex, but part of the rationale is now hidden, since teams often don't document their actions to preserve turf. The architect was blindsided by organizational issues, which made his contribution negative rather than positive.

Taking Action With Principles

These five principles not only help you to see hidden or not-so-hidden risks, they allow you to measure how well your organization has implemented each principle and help you to determine what to do next.

The next section provides an illustration of how a newly hired architect of an Internet startup sought to apply these principles to tame a chaotic, albeit not uncommon, situation.

ORGANIZATIONAL PRINCIPLES AT WORK: THE ARCHITECT'S NEW JOB

The architect's job, when he arrived at the Internet startup, entailed a software product line that had no architecture. As a test, he asked each of the developers to draw a picture of the architecture. The pictures were muddled; each was different and not very clear. The brilliant CEO, who was the founder, chief visionary, and lead investor, had an intense vision of what the product line should be and the wealth it would generate, *only if* it was realized. The young company's history had been problematic. Substantial sums were invested in a technology that bottomed out and lost money. Two prior product line executives with whiz-kid résumés had either been fired or left in frustration. Venture capital investors watched the company with both interest and concern.

To understate matters, pressure for success was above average. The software code base, many tens of thousands of lines on instantiation, resembled a BIG BALL OF MUD "[a] haphazardly structured, sprawling, sloppy, duct-tape and bailing wire, spaghetti code jungle" [Foote99].

The architect was terrified by his new job.

On the plus side, the product developers were enthusiastic and smart, the Web product marketplace was highly promising, the CEO was committed to discovering and doing the right thing, and the company had good collateral revenues from other segments.

A searing question for the architect was, "What should I do?" He called a trusted colleague, and the duo drew up a risk list:

► What could go wrong?
► What's the worst that can happen?
► What can you do about it?

They looked at the product line goals:

► Where do you want to be?
► Who are the stakeholders?
► What do they want and need?

The architect piled much of this into a project task list. The project task list, explicit and shared across the product line organization, would eventually prove to be an essential mechanism for success.

Rhythm

Each day—or every few days—yielded a new build of the product that was placed in the lead customer's hands, a "live" beta site. Version numbers flew by like the digits on Steve Austin's machmeter.[3] This concerned the architect. He read, in one of our earlier works, about a seasoned engineer who said: "Rhythm: That's the best thing we ever did" [Dikel95]. So, the architect calibrated his project Gantt charts to show a stair-step release cycle. The engineers applauded—they had a defense against daily churn.

Painful surprises turned up on the architect's doorstep like dead chipmunks from his cat.

But that was *not* the answer: Painful surprises turned up on the architect's doorstep like dead chipmunks from his cat, and he sat red-faced before his boss in weekly project management meetings, looking at inaccurate but regular Gantt charts. The architecture was too much a "ball of mud" to respond to a simple rhythmic schedule. He had read about the rhythm principle, but the architect applied it in a context that didn't fit. He instituted a regular tempo of deliveries before his team was able to ensure content or quality (see Figure 1.7).

---

[3] Steve Austin: Readers may remember him as the soon-to-be-bionic "Six Million Dollar Man" on the television show (1973–1978), spiraling down in his experimental flight vehicle to a horrific, end-over-end tumbling crash.

Figure 1.7
Demanding regular deliveries without ensuring content or quality caused more harm than good.

To learn more about the rhythm principle, how and where it works best, see Chapter 4: "Synchronizing and Maintaining Rhythm."

Vision

No, the big "ball of mud" the architect inherited didn't dance very well. His challenge was to cut the Gordian knot and resolve the mess (Figure 1.8). The architect considered page-by-page code inspection, along with coaching the

Figure 1.8   How do you cut the Gordian knot of a lost vision?

programmers to rewrite their modules. He did this in a few places—picking areas of attack in triage mode and selecting programs and components based on technical or business criticality. But the spot fixes were labor intensive and still not embedded in a sound overall architecture.

He spoke with his boss, the CEO mentioned earlier, about where the product line was headed and what the customers wanted—he received an earful, an overabundance of what the product *should* do and how successful it *would* be. The visionary was an extraordinary motivator, even captivating, but the architect saw that the vision was not translating effectively into a product line that could win and hold ground for the long term. It took quite a while—and many lessons—to align the vision and the architecture. But when this was done, the company arose and began to grab markets and headlines with its Web applications.

To learn more about vision, and how executives and architects can resolve and build one that works, see Chapter 3, "Projecting and Unifying Vision."

Simplification and Anticipation

With his head bowed, the architect went into "deep-think" mode. He drew a lot of pictures. He built some prototypes. He downloaded and re-read copies of the Software Engineering Institute's Capability Maturity Model, and thumbed through his textbooks. He recognized that his company was not like the "classical" software shops he had read about, one that followed a cookbook model. No, the company was vibrant and its technology base—the Internet—was changing at warp speed. Rulemaking would not fit this organization. The VRAPS principles seemed to be more useful abstractions.

One principle, *simplification*, seemed particularly relevant. The architect reflected that what he had was complex, fat, and muddled. The question was "How do you make the complex simple, the difficult easy?" The architect drew more pictures. He was convinced that in order to win, anything he did would have to involve as little coding as possible. The programmers were very talented, but the rate of change and growth of requirements were so great and the Web market so new, that anything committed to code would quickly become legacy. Let the architecture handle as many problems as possible, he thought.

The architect had enough dead chipmunks. He became obsessed with simplification. He vetoed projects where there was already something pretty good available off-the-shelf, as well as projects that were merely consulting or did not contribute to the product line. He investigated other departments' work, to see if steps could be eliminated. He looked closely at the work of competitors.

While the visionary pressed for delivery dates, the architect ruminated. After about two months of long nights, worrying and ingesting everything he could learn, from requirements to new languages and technology, the architect proposed and prototyped a family of interface components that incorporated *everything* from navigation, data coupling, inheritance, and security to appearance, art, and beauty, all by using a core of less than two dozen programs and six tables. This was the new base, the architecture on which to build a product line.

The architect introduced the architecture to the organization's developers and partners by reviewing models, code samples, and functional prototypes. Folks stuck their hands on the architecture and pushed and pulled against core components, and they made suggestions on how to improve it. The architecture was revised and grew to accommodate the stakeholders' insights. Some initially violated the architecture and "broke the rules." Some of these errors were caught and fixed; others made it into the product baseline and had to be rooted out over time. Not everything was perfect, but the organization learned and grew as it moved its legacy product line to the new base and began to effectively sell and deliver its technology to large, multibillion dollar organizations. The architecture became embedded and the concept of a repeatable, adaptable Web application product line took root.

To learn more about simplification, including insight on how to preserve the core and cut the junk, see Chapter 7, "Simplification: Clarifying and Minimizing." To learn more about anticipation, including maintaining an architecture's value in a rapidly changing technological environment, see Chapter 5, "Anticipation: Predicting, Validating, and Adapting."

Partnering

As the new architecture was delivered, the architect became somewhat less focused on building new technology himself and spent more time as a coach and a messenger, helping programmers to use the architecture and to see their roles and the roles of others in building new components. He also spent time defending the architecture and working to help win market share so that new applications lived within and strengthened the architecture. As the company grew, the architecture became a "team sport." Research and Development, Client Support, Marketing, and external suppliers gathered around the architecture and its products. Interestingly, with its software existing in a rapidly changing marketplace, the company learned that a considerable amount of architecture knowledge was required to effectively sell and support the Internet technology.

To learn more about partnering, including helping component owners to work together and improve the architecture and strengthening lateral integration among corporate divisions, see Chapter 6, "Partnering: Building Cooperative Organizations."

The preceding story is a quick capsule. In Chapter 2, "The VRAPS Reference Model," we show how the principles fit together and describe how the model relates to other bodies of knowledge. In Chapters 3 through 7, we cover each principle in depth, describing and providing examples of the principles and their components. Chapter 8, "Principles at Work: The Allaire Case Study," and Chapter 9, "Case Study: Building and Implementing a Benchmark Using VRAPS," are the capstones of *Software Architecture: Organizational Principles and Patterns*, examining the principles at work in a fast-paced Internet startup and providing a guide to assess how well your organization is using the principles.

PRINCIPLES ON THE WEB

In this book, we examine the principles at work in a Web startup, Allaire Corporation. Allaire relies upon architecture to develop a highly competitive product line that is itself an architecture used by its customers to deliver Internet applications. Allaire's flagship products are ColdFusion, JRun, Allaire Spectra, and Homesite, Web server middleware and application development products. Started by J.J. Allaire in his Minneapolis apartment in 1995, the company followed venture capital to Cambridge, Massachusetts, in 1997. There, it grew from twelve to several hundred employees in less than two years. Allaire went public in January 1999 and saw its valuation soar to a half billion dollars.

Allaire is a provider of Internet software products and services for companies building their business on the Web. Allaire provides an architecture that spans JRun (Java) and ColdFusion Web application servers, packaged applications (Allaire Spectra), and visual tools. As of publication, Allaire counted more than 70,000 application server installations and a community of over 500,000 developers. Among its many customers, Allaire counts online companies Autobytel, Lycos, FAO Schwartz, and Williams-Sonoma, as well as the industrial firms Bank of America, Boeing, Kodak, Siemens, and United Parcel Service.

Summary

While technologists—highly capable software engineers—are often leery of organizational behavior, and management does not often understand how to guide a software product line architecture, we believe that this book provides a comfortable, tangible, and effective meeting place for stakeholders across the venture. Our experience is that the organizational principles make the complex and often frustrating organizational and technical components of a software product line work—and work quite well.

T W O

The VRAPS Reference Model: How the Pieces Fit Together

All models are wrong; some of them are useful.[1]

—George Box [Box99]

Overview

The model described in this book presents five interrelated principles that make a critical difference in software architecture success. The book provides examples of how each of the principles has helped executives, managers, and practitioners sort through complex situations to find solid answers. The principles are meant to be used together, applying a single principle without regard to the others can do more harm than good. Consider the architect whose startlingly accurate predictions and platform ideas always seem to get swallowed up by hidden political conflicts. In this chapter, we unite the principles of *Vision*, *Rhythm*, *Anticipation*, *Partnering*, and *Simplification* into a model we call VRAPS. This model can sharpen your ability to recognize, diagnose, and heal harmful conditions, but the model works best when it is internalized and integrated with your own experiences and observations. Once digested, you can use the model to gain insights and identify which areas within your organization need improvement and which elements should be left as they are.

---

[1] This quotation was originally stated as, "Models of course, are never true, but fortunately it is only necessary that they be useful." [Box79]

Our model describes how organizations develop, deploy, and use software architecture to build a family of products or product lines. Because software architectures are shared across organizational boundaries, an understanding of organizational considerations is important for long-term success. Unlike general models of organizational development, our model is focused on the investment, development, and use of software architecture.

This reference model also organizes the concepts presented in this book. The model not only describes the relationships of the principles to each other, but also explains how the elements of the book—criteria for assessment, patterns, and antipatterns—fit together.

Why Models are Important

Models are valuable for understanding complex information. This value can be illustrated through the game of chess (Figure 2.1). Chase and Simon conducted an experiment with three subjects, a chess Master, a Class A player, and a beginner.[2] Each was shown a position—a chessboard with game pieces on it—for five seconds. Shortly afterwards, each was asked to recreate the position from memory. The subjects were shown positions with random placement of pieces on the board and positions that would logically occur during a game. The experienced chess players were better than the beginner at recalling positions that simulated game play. However, when the pieces were placed randomly, the beginner performed as well as, and in some cases better than, the expert players. When the experienced players were able to use their inter-

Figure 2.1
Models, such as those in chess, are valuable for understanding complex information.

---

[2] A Master player has a rating of 2200 to 2399. A Class A player has a rating of 1800 to 1999. A player rated 100 points higher than another would be expected to win 5 out of 8 games. The beginner is a player who has never played in a rated tournament and has a rating of 0 [USCF99].

nalized model of the game, they performed much better than when they tried to recall the position as a collection of disconnected information [Chase73].

The experiment illustrates how a model can help to organize information and improve the efficiency of information recall and recognition. Even though the dynamics of organizations are much more complex than the game of chess, and leading an organization is more difficult than remembering the position of pieces on a chessboard, organizations can also be better understood through models. Metaphors of machines, organisms, brains, and cultures, to name a few, have all been used to understand organizations. There are also models that use abstract metaphors for understanding social systems, such as envisioning organizations as continuous transformations [Morgan86]. Using these models, organizations can be assessed, analyzed, and understood.

The VRAPS Model

The VRAPS model focuses on the organizational aspects of implementing and evolving software architecture. We chose to focus on organizational principles because we observed that the primary obstacles to software architecture are very often organizational rather than technical. Creating viable software architecture requires a deep grasp of technology, excellent cognitive and communication skills, and a lot of hard work. However, succeeding with software architecture is not just a matter of technology and sharp engineers. Success often depends on organizational factors that an executive, manager, or practitioner may not be looking for. Or, they may take for granted that these factors are present when they are not. All too often, technically excellent architectures fail because organizational factors were not adequately addressed. This model differs from other organizational literature in that it focuses on software architecture and can be more easily understood and applied by practitioners in this field.

The following sections describe the model. The first section provides the context, which describes the situations where the model applies. The second section describes the five principles that comprise the core of the model. The third section describes a conceptual framework that explains how the model fits with other models for understanding and improving software development. The fourth section describes how the principles can be applied, including criteria for assessing the principles, as well as patterns and antipatterns to guide their implementation. The fifth section describes the history of this model, including a description of the research upon which the model is based.

CONTEXT

*Software archi-
tecture is the fun-
damental
organization of a
system embod-
ied in its compo-
nents, their
relationships to
each other and
to the environ-
ment and the
principles guiding
its design and
evolution.*

The focus of the model is on organizations that develop and use software architecture to build a set of products or product lines. The context of the model includes not just the team that builds and deploys the architecture, but also those who build products or product lines using the architecture and the customers who use these products. The context also includes the architecture itself. The Institute of Electrical and Electronics Engineers (IEEE) defines software architecture as "the fundamental organization of a system embodied in its components, their relationships to each other and to the environment and the principles guiding its design and evolution" [APG00].[3] Software architecture is not static, but can change over time reflecting changes in customers, standards, technology, business direction, and organization. A software product line architecture is a software architecture that is shared across more than one system, product, or family of products [Parnas76]. Sharing a common software architecture across a product line brings a core set of knowledge and assets to the development process. Product line architecture not only reduces the complexity and cost of developing and maintaining code, but also streamlines the production of documentation, training materials, and product literature [Dikel97a] [Jacobson 97].

Another important element is the suppliers who provide part or all of the software architecture. In some situations, one person or organization can occupy both roles of architecture supplier and customer simultaneously. For example, we have observed cases where one person is responsible for a layer of an architecture that is shared by a number of products and is also responsible for a product release that itself incorporates other layers in the architecture. Figure 2.2 illustrates the primary focus of the VRAPS Model and the other important participants.

The context of the VRAPS Model can be better understood by examining what it means for a particular organization. Consider the case of Allaire as illustrated in Figure 2.3. The ColdFusion, JRun, and Allaire Spectra tools are core to Allaire's enterprise Web application development. The architecture incorporates components from other providers to provide services such as application server security, which are bundled with some of Allaire's products. They also provide interfaces for their customers to incorporate components from other providers and interfaces so that their customers can develop sharable components themselves. There are Web application developers and

---

[3] From IEEE Std 1471-2000. Copyright © 2000 IEEE. All rights reserved.

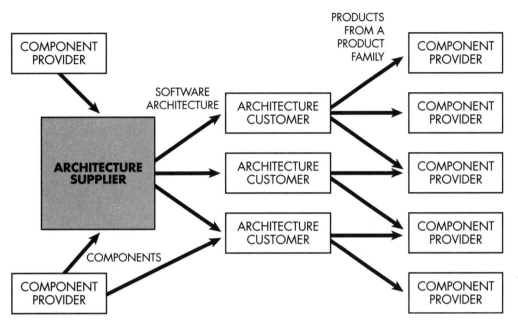

Figure 2.2 The primary focus of the model is the architecture supplier for a product line, but the other participants are critical for success as well.

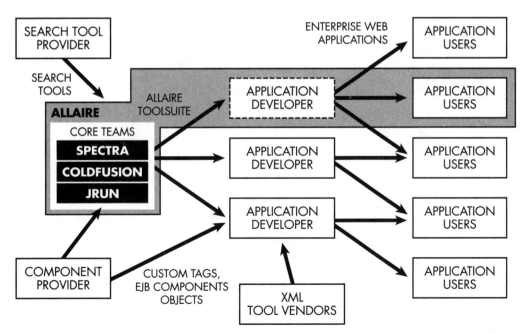

Figure 2.3 ColdFusion, JRun, and Allaire Spectra are at the heart of Allaire's software architecture.

users inside Allaire, but most of the developers deploying these tools are in other organizations, Allaire's direct customers. Enterprise application developers use this architecture based on ColdFusion, JRun, and Allaire Spectra to develop and deploy enterprise-wide applications over the Web. Figure 2.4 depicts Allaire's view of their architecture and how this view maps to the roles in our model.

While the focus of the VRAPS Model is software product line architecture, many of the concepts are applicable to smaller scale software development. These other situations can be envisioned as a compressed version of the above description in which a single organization plays several roles. For example, an organization might not have a distinct architecture provider, but might incorporate third-party components to provide one or more products, as illustrated in Figure 2.5.

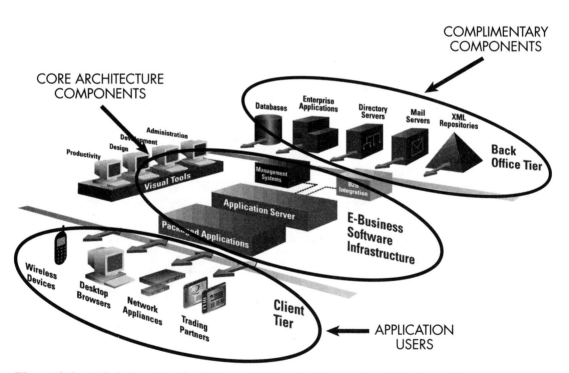

Figure 2.4   Allaire's enterprise Web application development architecture relies on components from both Allaire and other vendors.

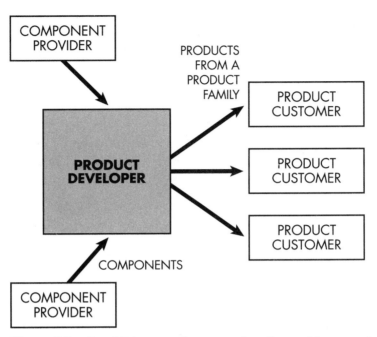

Figure 2.5   In addition to software product-line architecture, the VRAPS Model may be applied to other, simpler situations.

ORGANIZATIONAL PRINCIPLES FOR SOFTWARE ARCHITECTURE

The core of the VRAPS model is built around five principles: *Vision*, *Rhythm*, *Anticipation*, *Partnering*, and *Simplification* (Table 2.1). Each principle is actionable, experience-base, and explanatory.

- ► *Actionable:* Each principle can be acted upon. To take action, skills are required. To put a principle in practice, your organization may need to improve its skills. The principle suggests what your organization must do, but without requiring specific techniques. While patterns and antipatterns are provided to illustrate how to take action on a principle, they are not intended to be prescriptive.
- ► *Experience-Based:* Each principle is grounded in the experience of both successful and unsuccessful software architectures. The principles have been developed through direct experience building software architectures as well as through conducting and analyzing hundreds of inter-

views with software architecture practitioners, managers, and executives from many leading companies.

▶ *Explanatory:* The principles help make sense of experience. Sometimes, when you begin to feel the architecture is headed for trouble, stopping to ask, "How are we doing at partnering?" or, "How well are we doing at rhythm?" can help you step out of the mire and see what to do next. However, the principles yield the most insight when viewed in combination rather than individually. Once you gain an understanding, the principles can help you relate your insights to others. As such, the principles can align people's vision and action within groups and across layers of an organization.

The Role of Principles

We believe that this principle-based approach to a model for organization and software architecture is valuable for several reasons. It is broad enough that it can be used to understand software architecture in a wide range of contexts, from shared information systems development in large corporations to the world of open source software development. This flexibility has enabled the VRAPS Model to provide guidance to software architects and their managers, to conduct benchmarks comparing organizations, and to provide a basis for conducting structured case studies. The VRAPS Model reflects hard-won experience, and so in addition to being broad and flexible, it also communicates very practical knowledge. Finally, the model enables the reader to relate findings and insights from other disciplines, such as organizational development and process improvement, in a systematic way.

It is worth pointing out that our use of the term *principle* to describe organizational concerns differs from how some others use the term. The IEEE definition of software architecture refers to principles that are specific to one or more architectures, describing high-level goals or constraints [APG00]. Dana Bredemeyer describes a process for software architecture in which principles for the architecture are defined. These principles describe the high-level orientation of a specific architecture [Bredemeyer00]. For example, one of the driving principles behind the architecture of Allaire's product line is that of "democratizing the Web." That is, the tools created should be easy to use and leverage existing skills. The principles in the VRAPS Model focus on the organization, not the architecture alone, and are not specific to a particular architecture.

Vision

Vision shapes an architecture's future, providing context and motivation for its successful use. For the vision to be successful, it must map the value it delivers to customer constraints. The vision must also be *clear, compelling, congruent,* and *flexible* so that it can be understood and used effectively by its stakeholders.

Sharing the vision of the architecture among the stakeholders can be challenging. Often a software architect enters the scene after the vision has been initially established. In larger organizations, layers of management may separate the project architect and the executive who maintains the product vision. This distance can add complications, especially when communication is poor. To overcome these challenges, establishing a strong, positive relationship—and a shared and active vision—between the executive and architect is crucial.

Rhythm

Rhythm enables software architectures to be developed and used across organizational boundaries. Since many of the groups involved in developing and using an architecture are autonomous, it is not possible to coordinate the groups from the top down. Rhythm provides a temporal framework that allows groups to synchronize activities and expectations. With rhythm, participants know when and on which activities to focus. Not only can planned activities be coordinated, but rhythm also helps coordinate informal yet critical activities such as inter-group communication. Participants just know when and when not to request information or support.

Anticipation

Organizations must be able to anticipate and react to change in order for long-term investments in a software product line to pay off [Jacobson97]. To achieve that payoff, the organization must make sure that the architecture meets the needs of many applications, including those that may have not yet been envisioned when the architecture was designed. The architecture must be able to adapt to new technologies, standards, markets, and competitors. This longevity has several implications for architecture. Assumptions found true when the architecture was initially devised may not be valid years later even though the architecture is still in use. This requires that the organization must be able to anticipate and evolve the architecture.

Partnering

Partnering is essential for the success of an architecture because the participation of so many different groups is critical to architecture development, implementation, and use. These groups cross all sorts of organizational boundaries: teams, locations, divisions, even companies. Each group critical to the architecture must see how using and working to improve the architecture serves its own interests. The principle of partnering addresses how to identify who is essential to the success of the architecture, and how to secure support of those partners.

Simplification

Simplifying software architecture is deceptively easy in concept, but in practice it requires a tough-minded focus on value, combined with an understanding and the support of the organization in which the architecture lives. The architect must understand the minimal essential characteristics of the architecture. Simplification also requires a concerted effort to communicate these characteristics to each member of the team implementing the architecture.

TABLE 2.1   *Summary of Principles*

Vision	Vision is the mapping of future value to architectural constraints as measured by how well the architecture's structures and goals are clear, compelling, congruent, and flexible.
Rhythm	Rhythm is the recurring, predictable exchange of work products within an architecture group and across their customers and suppliers.
Anticipation	Anticipation is the extent to which those who build and implement the architecture predict, validate, and adapt the architecture to changing technology, competition, and customer needs.
Partnering	Partnering is the extent to which architecture stakeholders maintain clear, cooperative roles and maximize the value they deliver and receive.
Simplification	Simplification is the intelligent clarification and minimization of both the architecture and the organizational environment in which it functions.

Principles Interact

No one principle stands alone. Figure 2.6 illustrates how the principle of *Vision* interacts with the other principles. *Vision* establishes the overall direction that enables the coordination expressed by *Rhythm* to occur. A good *Rhythm* allows organizations to provide incremental progress towards the goals established by *Vision*. The assumptions that underlie the *Vision* are tested under *Anticipation* and can be validated. As the architecture evolves, changes in the environment can be recognized and incorporated into the

Vision. The *Vision* helps create the criteria used to select partners and to understand the value each brings to the architecture. The constraints of these partners are key components of a well-crafted *Vision*. The *Vision* also contributes to *Simplification*. The projected value is interpreted and applied to architecture decisions that in turn help focus the *Vision*.

It is not just *Vision*, but all of the principles interact with one another. For example, the coordination described in *Rhythm* is impossible to achieve without *Partnering*. *Rhythm* helps focus on the *Simplification* because of the attention to the minimal essential requirements of each cycle. Figure 2.7 illustrates the interactions of all of the principles.

As interrelated as the principles are to one another, each can be isolated as a skill set. For example, you can assess how well a team has learned to partner, and you can build a team's partnering skills. Nevertheless, if the team's simplification skills are not mature, others will not attempt to be their partners because doing so could become a complex and onerous commitment.

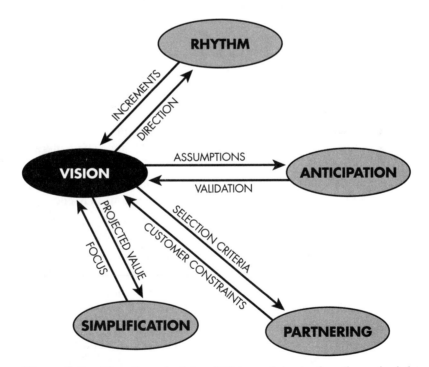

Figure 2.6   How the principle of Vision relates to the other principles.

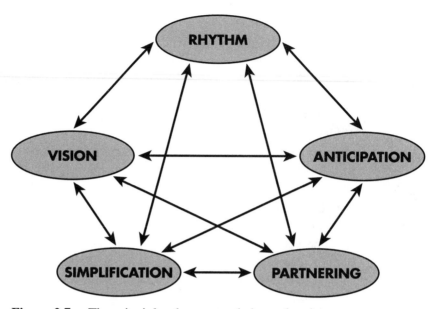

Figure 2.7   The principles do not stand alone; they interact.

CONCEPTUAL FRAMEWORK

Patterns describe solutions. Antipatterns describe pitfalls.

In order to make VRAPS more useful, we complement descriptions of each principle with criteria, patterns, and antipatterns. The criteria are used to determine how well each principle is implemented. The patterns describe solutions to recurring problems that may be found when developing or using a software architecture. Patterns help organizations improve one of the principles. The antipatterns describe pitfalls that organizations may encounter.

The criteria, patterns, and antipatterns listed for each principle are not exhaustive. In some cases, there are patterns or antipatterns that have already been written and published that can be applied. We identify and reference a number of these patterns and antipatterns in a "Related Patterns and Antipatterns" section of each pattern and antipattern. There is a more comprehensive table at the end of each principle chapter that contains patterns and antipatterns related to the principle as referenced in Linda Rising's *The Pattern Almanac* [Rising00]. Each principle chapter also has a table of antipatterns drawn from William Brown and colleagues' *Antipatterns* [BrownW98]. The criteria listed here are not exhaustive, but they represent the most broadly applicable ones. We have observed organizations that developed good metrics or heuristics for determining how well they were doing with a principle, but other groups may not be able to easily apply them. For example, everyone we interviewed in a telecom products organization drew the same basic picture of the architecture regardless of role or level. However, when we asked members of an organization that built accounting software to do the same, both the pictures and perspectives varied greatly.

Criteria

It is often easier to grasp the principles than it is to apply them to a specific situation. To put principles into practice, actionable specifics are needed. Criteria translate the broad principle into specifics that determine whether and how well the principle is being practiced (see Figure 2.8). In each chapter describing a principle, we identify three criteria for assessing a principle. The criteria described in this book are not intended to be comprehensive, but illustrate how the principle can be measured.

For example, the criteria for the principle of vision assess the extent to which:

► The architect's vision aligns with what its sponsors, users, and end customers are trying to accomplish
► Developers trust and use the architecture
► Tacit knowledge about architecture and components is visible and accessible to users

These criteria can be used in a number of ways. They can be used by managers as a list of indications to watch for when they develop or use software architecture. They can also be used as the basis for benchmarking the performance of organizations. Lastly, they can be used as diagnostic tools when things are not going well with an architecture.

For accessing a principle we encourage you to rely on your own experience to identify additional criteria that could be useful in your own organiza-

Figure 2.8   Criteria are used for assessing a principle.

tion. One manager we spoke with used the simple heuristic of finding out whether all of his engineers could draw the same picture of the architecture as an indicator of whether the vision of the architecture was shared across the engineering team. While this informal measure does not work for all organizations, it proved to be a useful tool for the manager to sustain an architecture over many years.

Patterns

Each principle in this book is accompanied by a collection of patterns for solving problems encountered when putting the principle into practice (see Figure 2.9). Unlike the principles, which broadly apply to software architecture, the patterns are more narrowly focused on solving problems in specific situations.

There are many different ways to describe patterns. Christopher Alexander, who originated the notion of patterns in the field of building (i.e., brick and mortar) architecture described patterns as a recurring solution to a common problem in a given context and system of forces [Alexander77]. Others have offered descriptions of patterns that highlight other characteristics. A pattern is also a named "nugget" of instructive insight, conveying the essence of a proven solution to a recurring problem in a given context amidst competing concerns. A pattern is also a literary format for capturing the wisdom and experience of expert designers [Appleton97]. The most widely read book on software patterns is *Design Patterns,* which focuses on solving software design problems [Gamma94]. Jim Coplien's BUFFALO MOUNTAIN pattern (see Figure 2.10) was the first to address organizational problems in software development [Cunningham99][Coplien00].

Figure 2.9   Patterns describe solutions to problems encountered when putting the principles into practice.

Figure 2.10   Jim Coplien's BUFFALO MOUNTAIN pattern was inspired by Buffalo Mountain in Colorado [Coplien95]. Source: Brad Odekirk.

This pattern was first published in Coplien's seminal paper, "*A Development Process Generative Pattern Language*" [Coplien95].

Antipatterns

Antipatterns provide further depth for understanding the principles (see Figure 2.11). Antipatterns describe what *not* to do, or solutions applied in the wrong context. In 1996, Michael Akroyd published the first work on antipatterns [BrownW98][Akroyd96]. Sometimes antipatterns occur when one of the architecture principles is pursued to the neglect of one or more of the others. Antipatterns can also result if the presence of a principle in an organization is only superficial. They may also result when otherwise good solutions are applied in the wrong situation.

Antipatterns have proven somewhat controversial. Some have asked, why bother documenting solutions that do not work? Others have suggested that there is nothing that can be described in an antipattern that cannot be suitably described with a pattern format. We believe that antipatterns are useful because they are written in a manner that emphasizes the problem, allowing them to be easily recognized when problems occur. In addition, we believe

Figure 2.11   Antipatterns may be good solutions applied in the wrong context.

patterns and antipatterns complement different learning styles, and that antipatterns can be especially valuable as complements to patterns in the role of providing named nuggets of insight.

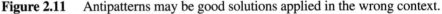

APPLYING THE VRAPS MODEL

The principles, criteria, patterns, and antipatterns complement one another. In each chapter describing a principle, we present three criteria for assessing the principle. For each criterion there is at least one corresponding pattern and one antipattern. Figure 2.12 illustrates how these elements work together.

The VRAPS Model does not exist in a vacuum; it is just one piece of the larger picture of successful software development. Figure 2.13 shows how our model for software architecture relates to other software development models and success factors for software development. Software architecture cannot be successful without effective leadership. Successfully applying the principles can engage management and help secure their support. The VRAPS Model does not specify a particular software development process, such as those proscribed by the Software Engineering Institute's (SEI) Capability Maturity

Model (CMM), but applying the principles should act as a driver for how those processes are carried out. For example, there may be a process for creating a build of an application, but the principle of rhythm might affect who is involved in that process and how frequently the process is conducted. Of

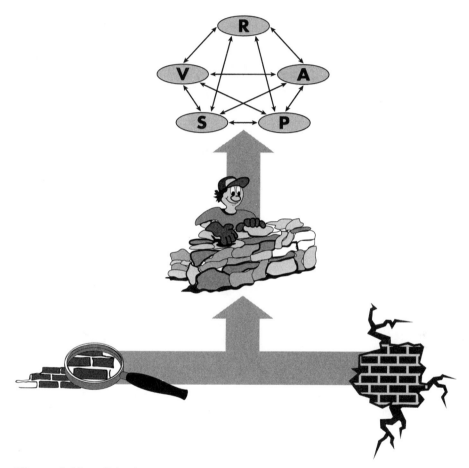

Figure 2.12   Criteria, patterns, and antipatterns together provide tools and guidance for taking action on the principles.

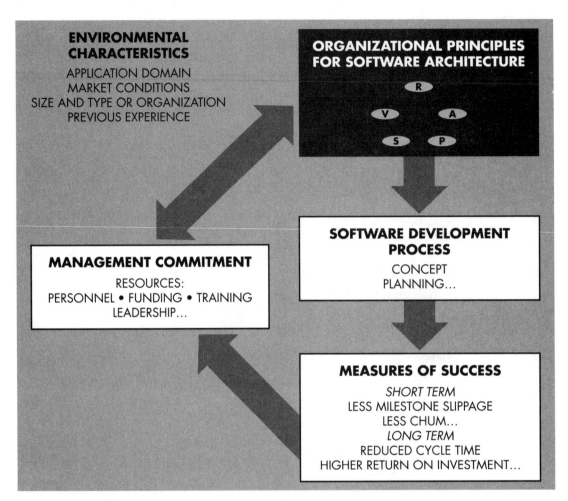

Figure 2.13   The principle-based VRAPS Model complements other software engineering work for successful software.

course, the environment in which the organization operates may also affect success and how the principles manifest themselves. The software development process should generate measurements of how successful the organization is, and these measurements may significantly influence management behavior and support.

VRAPS EVOLUTION

The VRAPS Model was first developed for a case study that we conducted at Nortel in 1995. The study sought to learn from Nortel's nearly 20 years of experience evolving massive, complex, and critical software architectures. The goal was to learn how to keep software architecture alive over a long period of time. We sought to identify and describe a small set of underlying organizational principles whose presence or absence resulted in long-term success or failure of the architecture. The Defense Advanced Research Projects Agency (DARPA) provided sponsorship for the study [Dikel95][Dikel97a].

After completing this initial case study, we expanded the model to support a benchmarking instrument for comparing the use and effect of the principles across organizations. We integrated concepts from organizational development theory. We also expanded the model to better incorporate the management of risks and opportunities, and we conducted a benchmark with four leading organizations. Participants' business units ranged from $30 million to $4 billion in revenue, and employed several hundred to over a thousand engineers. Their applications included business information systems, workflow management, telecommunications, and network management (See Chapter 9).

This benchmark approach was also used for the Allaire Corporation case study conducted for this book. As part of this work, we not only refined the principle definitions, but we also improved the criteria used to test each principle (See Chapter 8).

We used a number of elements of grounded theory for conducting our case studies. Grounded theory is an approach for identifying hypotheses for qualitative research. It is distinctive in that it involves recursively collecting, coding, and interpreting data [Locke96]. We differed from the traditional grounded theory approach in that we seeded our initial hypotheses with contributions from experts and existing work in the field. We analyzed existing literature and used the guidance of a panel of advisors to establish our candidate principles. In particular, Grady Booch of Rational, Ron Grace and Patricia Cornwell of Hewlett-Packard, Robert Charette of ITAHBI Corp., and Bob Savely and Jack Garman of NASA contributed significantly.

The VRAPS Model also reflects the work we have done in the area of best practices and patterns. In 1995 we conducted a benchmark of best practices in the area of software reuse for the Department of Defense (DoD) [Wilson96].

---

[4] This was an illustrative case study, that is, one that examines one or two instances and describes what happened and why [GAO90].

The benchmark included leading commercial firms as well as a number of accomplished government software development organizations. The participants included CMM level 2 or 3, ISO-9000 certified, and Malcolm-Baldrige award winners. We were especially concerned that readers of the benchmark recognize the context in which the practices were used. We recognized that if an organization mandated someone else's "best" practice in the wrong situation, it could do more harm than good. Measurement programs, for example, often assume quite a bit of infrastructure that may have taken years to put into place. They are sometimes introduced as a cure-all into chaotic software development situations. Faced with yet another improvement program, managers and practitioners often "achieve" the desired metric, through "creative" means. For example, to meet a schedule as measured by percent complete, one manager divided his program into about one hundred modules. Only five modules were larger than 100 lines of code. One of the five was over a million lines of code. This did more than create a false sense of security; it forced unnatural partitioning of code and a lot of unnecessary work.

In response to this concern, we used a template to describe each practice that made the context of each practice very visible. We structured the template so that readers could quickly learn enough about the context to make the decision whether the practice would be appropriate for their own organization.

It was a natural transition to move from this notion of best practice to patterns. Many of the characteristics of our best practice approach are reflected in patterns. Both have a strong emphasis on understanding the context in which the approach is appropriate. Both use a standard form so that the information describing approaches is consistent. Lastly, both are based upon the practitioner experiences.

As we were conducting these case studies and benchmarks, we were also conducting public workshops to examine principles for software reuse. These workshops brought together the threads of principles and practices. We were able to validate whether our principles resonated with practitioners. We also gathered practices from these practitioners. Finally, the workshops gave us an opportunity to explore the relationships between the principle and the practices. Workshops were conducted at the Workshop for Institutionalizing Software Reuse, Reuse98, and at meetings of the Reuse Steering Committee [Dikel97c][Dikel97d].

SUMMARY

This chapter describes the foundation for this book—VRAPS, our model for software architecture and organizations. The model is built around five principles—*Vision*, *Rhythm*, *Anticipation*, *Partnering*, and *Simplification*. Each of these principles can be acted upon, is based on experience, and helps make sense of our experience. Complementing these principles are criteria, patterns, and antipatterns. The criteria help assess how well the principle is being done. The patterns and antipatterns provide guidance on how to apply the principles.

PROJECTING AND UNIFYING VISION

Vision without action is a daydream. Action without vision is a nightmare.

—Japanese proverb

OVERVIEW

Since ancient times, leaders have used vision to govern action and shape experience. The architecture of buildings has long provided a means by which vision is translated into physical forms that shape our action and experience as well. Although software architecture may have no physical form, even when implemented, its effects on how well products, systems, and organizations perform are unmistakable. Vision shapes an organization's future, providing context and motivation for software architecture's successful use.

The relationship between architects and executives can have a profound impact on the vision of the architecture. For example, in many software start-ups, the founder creates both the corporate and architecture vision. As the company grows, the founder often maintains control of the architecture vision by assuming the role of Chief Technology Officer. The responsibility for realizing the architecture vision is passed to someone the founder knows well and trusts implicitly. In many cases, such as this one, a software architect enters the scene after the corporate vision is formed. It is essential that the architect work with the executive whose vision is shaping the organization and its future.

Surprisingly, many architects treat the architecture vision as their sole creation, and they alter it as they see fit. They work to sell this vision to stakeholders whose context is shaped by the corporate vision and are then surprised when disconnects occur. It is also surprising how often someone other than the executive who holds the product line vision decides whom to hire as architect. By not being involved in the architect's hiring, the executive is unable to assess the architect's ability and desire to understand and implement his or her vision. In larger organizations, layers of management separate the architect and the executive who maintains the architecture vision. This distance can add complications, especially when communication is poor.

There are many challenges to establishing and sharing an architecture vision. No matter how good a job an architect does, elements beyond his or her control—other members of the organization, as well as the organization itself—can and often do foul things up. There are other challenges. When product lines are supported with an architecture, the vision is pulled in many more directions. Further, if the shared vision of the architecture is breaking down, it may not be immediately apparent. Fortunately, these challenges can be overcome with effective leadership and a strong relationship between the executive and architect.

VISION DEFINITION

Vision is the mapping of future value to architectural constraints as measured by how well the architecture's structures and goals are clear, compelling, congruent, and flexible.

Peter Senge writes that "A vision is a picture of the future you seek to create, described in the present tense" [Senge94]. We have found that those who share this picture of the future must also see their contribution to getting there. The architect develops the vision by mapping tangible future value to constraints, by clarifying risks and by designing the architecture so that it can remain flexible. Stakeholders make the vision become reality by living within its constraints and mitigating against its risks.

Mapping Value to Architectural Constraints

"Unless developers can map constraints such as interfaces, development languages, and module boundaries to a specific customer value, they are likely to take shortcuts," according to Dean Thompson, of Agilent Technology, who served for several years as Senior Architect for Hewlett-Packard's Open View Program. The observation holds for other stakeholders as well. Coupling constraint and customer value must hold true at each level. Thompson's three-step process for achieving this goal is described later in the chapter.

Getting stakeholders to tie constraints to customer value in a compelling way involves art and, some say, a little magic. Use-case modeling is one approach for connecting the expected use of the architecture with tangible goals of the user that can be satisfied. Unfortunately, not focusing on the real goals of users is one of the common pitfalls of use-case modeling [Lilly00]. Reflecting the goals of the users is not enough if developers are presented with many disconnected scenarios with no explanation of how they relate to a clear and plain result. Identifying and conveying a substantive connection between seemingly unrelated use cases is an important part of constructing the vision.

Congruence and Flexibility

Congruence is the quality of agreeing or coinciding. McLenden and Weinberg further define congruence as "a concept that describes the human experience of alignment between … what is thought and felt (the internal) and what is said and how it is said (the external)" [McLenden96]. In this context, congruence is how well stakeholders' expectations fit with one another and with the current and future architecture.

To be flexible, one must be capable of responding or conforming to changing or new situations. *Flexibility* is how easily a stakeholder can create new and unanticipated solutions with the shared architecture without violating the architecture itself. Shared vision, says Senge, "provides a focus and energy for learning…" [Senge90]. An example of what we mean by flexibility and how it can be achieved is discussed in GENERATIVE VISION later in the Chapter. Unless the visions of each user and contributor remain agile, the software architecture will begin to deteriorate.

The term *congruence* does not mean that all stakeholders share an identical view of the architecture. It does mean they share a vision that is consistent across stakeholders' perspectives. Kruchten's "4+1 Architecture Views," which are incorporated into the Rational Unified Process (RUP), provide one approach to achieving this consistency. RUP models an architecture through a Logical View, an Implementation View, a Process View, a Deployment View, and a Use-

Case View. These perspectives of the architecture are different in that they represent the system for different purposes (e.g., the Logical View represents the end-user functionality of the system) [Kruchten98]. However, the views are congruent in that they represent a consistent understanding of the architecture.

VISION CHALLENGES

We have found that many factors influence whether the architecture vision is congruent and remains so. While some are under the control of the architect, many factors that are critical to the success of an architecture vision are beyond the influence and scope of an architect. Cooperation between the architects and executives is essential. This is especially true for product line architectures. The different perspectives that stakeholders have of the architecture also present challenges. Sometimes it can be hard to distinguish between differences in perspective and architecture breakdown.

Limits of Architect Influence

Many factors that shape architecture vision are beyond the control of the architect. Aspects of the firm's corporate culture, such as the effectiveness of informal network, and how honest and open communications in the organization are, can have a tremendous effect on how the vision is shared. The vision and direction of the products supported by the architecture can alter the architecture vision, especially as the products are positioned for new and changing markets. Figure 3.1 illustrates many of these factors that we identified at one software product firm.

Executive and Architect Cooperation

Executives have a hands-on role in creating and maintaining the architecture vision.

Executives have a hands-on role in creating and maintaining the architecture vision because they have a wider scope of influence in the organization, and because they have an important role in shaping the vision. Executives and architects must exercise leadership to resolve very complex tradeoffs. For example, a senior executive can see and create new opportunities for growth. However, an "optimistic" senior executive or an uninformed product support engineer can create severe stress on an architecture through interaction with customers or sponsors by making promises that cannot be fulfilled without breaking the architecture or depleting resources. Executives can also play an important role in shaping corporate culture and policies such that they will complement the efforts of the architect. Cooperation between architects and

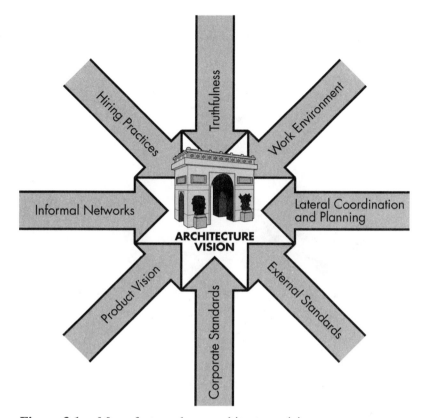

Figure 3.1   Many factors shape architecture vision.

executives can be a foundation on which a vision can be successfully projected; the lack of cooperation, however, can be especially painful.

Executives or managers need to keep their architecture team, product managers, and designers focused on delivering product, or they run the risk of creating a gold-plated architecture that no one uses—at least not more than once. On
the other hand, if there were a museum of doomed and dead architecture projects, it would have many pictures of leaders who took bold and enterprising
moves without listening to messengers that relayed the consequences (see
Figure 3.2). The museum would also house a large collection of un-architected,
impossible-to-maintain components that were boldly shipped before their time.

Figure 3.2   Boldly launching an architecture before its time. Source: National Air and Space Museum, Smithsonian Institution (SI Neg. No. 91-1830).

Product Lines Increase the Challenges to Architects and Executives

The number of organizational factors beyond the control of the architect grows as the number of products supported by the architecture grows, sometimes at an exponential rate. In fact, large product lines may not even be under the control of a single executive. For example, architects can do their best to keep sales executives informed about what features can and cannot be adapted and implemented. When more products are supported, it becomes more challenging to keep everyone up-to-date on what can be expected from the architecture. More products in the product line also means that there are more directions from which the vision is pulled, and that a smaller portion of those influences are under the direct control of the architect (see Figure 3.3).

The vision for the architecture can break down if the product line is driven too quickly into areas for which it was not designed. The architect who would normally be evangelizing the vision of how the architecture fits could be overwhelmed with addressing immediate crises. More engineers might be added than can be trained by existing practitioners, evangelized by the architect, or inculcated into the culture. These engineers learn to do their job but don't learn the vision or culture that governs and shapes the job. Without a

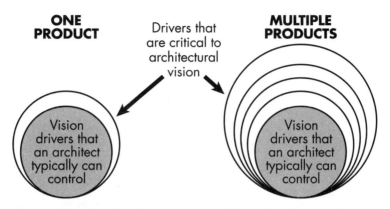

Figure 3.3   Product lines present additional challenges for architects and executives.

commitment to the vision, they may violate interfaces, bury assets that should be made more general, or skip layers without coordinating their actions. As a result, the clean lines between the components of an architecture can quickly blur, resulting in a kludgy solution.

Recognizing Breakdown

While it is expected that managers and developers would view an architecture differently by virtue of their different roles, this expectation could mask the signs of a deteriorating vision. The design may be clean and compelling on paper even though its use is messy. Managers still present tidy diagrams of this architecture to customers and explain how this architecture will enable the product team to respond quickly to any customer requirement (see Figure 3.4, Manager's View). Practitioners will, no doubt, see the architecture differently as coherence deteriorates (see Figure 3.5, Practitioner's View). This disconnect can lead to chaos as managers and customers become more convinced of how easy it is to add new capabilities and less sympathetic to the "whining" of the architect and developers. Instead of providing a common means for communication, the architecture acts to create and enforce an increasingly dysfunctional relationship. The two sides no longer share the vision and can no longer communicate with each other.

Manager's view...

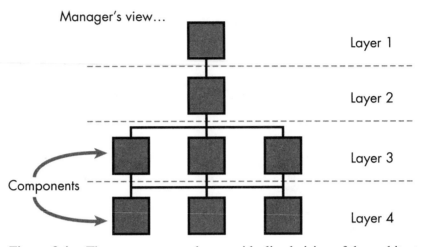

Figure 3.4   The managers may have an idealized vision of the architecture.

Practitioner's view...

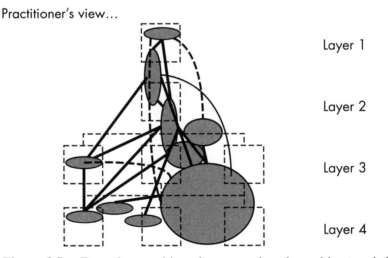

Figure 3.5   From the practitioner's perspective, the architecture is in shreds.

SHAPING A VISION

Architects are often charged with bringing reality into business vision and bringing business vision into reality. Architects may recommend technologies and how and when to use those technologies. As such, they help determine what part of the business vision can be implemented in the short term, and the order in which other parts of the vision can be phased in. Architects, of course, play an important role in shaping and communicating the vision of the architecture. However, who is playing the role of architect is not always obvious. Aside from potential obscurity, the task of architect is often a thankless one. Still, the role of architect in maintaining an effective vision is important. There are several approaches that can be used in carrying out this role.

Will the Real Architect Please Stand Up?

Not everyone who has the title of architect has a meaningful influence over— let alone, control of—the architecture. Similarly, not every architect holds or communicates the architecture vision. You may need to turn over a lot of rocks in an organization to find out who fills the "keeper of the architecture vision" role. In a startup, the company's founder may be the real architect. Sometimes a senior developer or a group of senior developers holds this power because of their unique understanding of how a component or set of components works. The people in the organization who secure a unique chunk of the architecture vision must be consulted when decisions involving the architecture are made.

When more than one person controls the architecture, both organizational protocol and culture must drive toward alignment or severe problems will occur. A senior engineer in a telecommunications company related the following story: "One of the most severe problems we have seen in our postmortems came from a team of 70 people that had *two* chief architects. These two architects did not share the same vision for the architecture or the product. You can imagine what resulted. Eventually the project was cancelled. The team produced nothing."

Vision and Leadership

Dean Thompson observes that an architect is more like a manager than a practitioner. "Being an architect," Thompson says, "is much more about understanding how to balance business, organizational dynamics, and technology than it is about technical gears." For example, he or she must look across the organization, identify pockets of concern and either modify the solution or describe it in terms that satisfy these concerns. The architect sometimes uses business terms, sometimes uses technology terms, always aligning the discussion with the organization's culture and history.

Thompson prescribes a three-step approach for projecting architecture vision, drawing on his observations of the eight-person team that developed Network Node Manager (NNM), a product line of network management tools.[1]

---

[1] Thompson observed the development of NNM, but was not a member of the original team.

1. *Articulate a compelling customer value clearly and concisely.* For example, the NNM development team constantly repeated the mantra, "Just add water." This represented a dramatic change in mapping network topology. Instead of "getting under the floorboards and composing PowerPoint charts," with NNM, the network engineer could get an up-to-date map of the network without leaving his or her workstation.

2. *Map the value to a small set of specific, solvable problems.* To achieve the goal of making it easy, the NNM development team would have to figure out how to determine the physical or logical network elements; how to monitor, alarm, and troubleshoot these elements; and how to project this information onto a graphical map format.

3. *Translate these problems into a minimal set of constraints.* To solve these problems, the NNM team had to forego what was "standard practice." They could no longer depend on input from a technician with a flashlight and a protocol analyzer. The NNM team worked under two constraints. First, they could not ask the user to do anything that required manual input. So, for example, when the team came to building a mapping capability, it became clear they would have to build automatic layout algorithms. Asking users for input was not an option. Second, the team limited themselves to the most common protocols—Simple Network Management Protocol (SNMP) and Internet Control Message Protocol (ICMP)—so that the customer would not have to build or buy anything extra. Not coincidentally, SNMP became ubiquitous.

"Unless developers can see a clear connection between a compelling customer value and a constraint," Thompson says, "they are likely to view the constraint as a burden." Architects must connect constraints to compelling problems at each level to ensure that the vision will be enacted. Architects who build solutions that stand to transform a market, as NNM did, must also communicate their vision to thought leaders for their technology or industry.

No Respect

Even the best architect sometimes feels like a prophet in his own hometown[2] when starting a new project. Even the stunning success of his or her last product doesn't ensure that colleagues will take time to understand the architect's guidance and direction. Sometimes the most stunning architectural solutions appear obvious. Developers who do not understand the depth of the problem addressed often minimize the architect's contribution. It is also hard for management to separate the worth of an architect's contribution from that of the

---

[2] "… no prophet is accepted in his hometown." [Luke 4:23]

development team. Both developers and managers tend to see external experts in a brighter light than those within their organization.

From the architect's point of view, this does not seem fair. Regardless of fairness, the architect must gain the trust and support of each new team. Approaching a new assignment in this way can help the architect avoid coming across as "detached from reality"—being too focused on perfection and failing to take schedule and staff power constraints into effect.

The architect must see farther into the future than developers, and therefore may know a lot more about what his many end-customers will want and need when products are finally delivered. While developers are talking to customers who are themselves engineers building products, a talented architect may be talking with his or her counterparts in the same organizations. Developers hear about today's requirements. The architect listens to peers' longer-term views as well as their concerns about not getting their own developers to see the perils of fielding the hot technology *du jour*.

In this situation, successful architects project a future with a clear mapping to the customer value so that users and their customers alike can relate to the vision. The architect must look outward into the worlds of product developers and end-customers and at the same time look inward into the worlds of the architecture and business groups, *and* motivate everyone else to do the same, in order to succeed. Obviously, this is easier said than done.

LATERAL INTEGRATION PROMOTES VISION

Lateral integration is a concept from organizational development that acts to ensure and stabilize vision. Lateral integration is the coordination of information, decisions, and resources across a common organizational level. It enables first-level managers in hardware design to understand, negotiate, and keep up with the expectations of their counterparts in software design and development, marketing, customer support, and manufacturing.

We have found that the presence of lateral integration increases an organization's capacity to communicate with customers and external suppliers. When lateral integration is not present, the number and severity of unpleasant surprises becomes unbearable for all concerned—and surprises occur at the worst times.

There is more than one way to improve lateral communication. The first is to effect deliberate alignment of vision through a change in organizational structure. Susan Albers Mohrman has developed innovative approaches to designing a team-based organization for knowledge workers. According to Mohrman, lateral integration as a management concept has its roots in the research of Lawrence and Lorsch, who in 1969 studied ways to coordinate across specialized teams [Lawrence69]. Mohrman's work is based on over ten years of grounded research. We recommend her work as an important part of the solution to implementing software product line architectures. The work is especially valuable to medium and large hierarchical organizations [Mohrman95].

The second way to use lateral integration to stabilize vision is for individual teams to accept turbulent and unpredictable change and to constantly adapt. One such method is called *Scrum*, a term taken from rugby. In a scrum, players from both teams bind themselves in a circle and compete for the ball, pushing each other in an attempt to gain control [Gartner99]. In our context, Scrum involves only one team, which uses a daily "huddle" to mesh both vision and action.

The overall Scrum process organizes work into short time periods, or SPRINTS, that produce a deliverable. Scrum has a systematic method to monitor progress. Daily SCRUM MEETINGS are used to check status. The SPRINTS are sandwiched between two defined processes, planning and closure [Beedle99].

Scrum involves rethinking requirements, design, approach, schedule, assignments, and more, every day. Everyone in the project participates in the SCRUM MEETING. During the meeting, each participant focuses on three questions: 1) items completed since the last SCRUM MEETING; 2) issues or blocks that need resolution; and 3) team assignments, drawn from the BACKLOG, that will be due at the next meeting. The BACKLOG is a prioritized list of open issues, features, and tasks. The SCRUM MASTER plays the role of team leader, tracker, and facilitator. The architect helps with vision and assignments [Beedle99].

Scrum has also been used with promising results for coordinating across teams in a small organization by involving selected members of other teams in the daily meeting [Olofson99].

PUTTING VISION INTO PRACTICE: CRITERIA, ANTIPATTERNS, AND PATTERNS

The principle of Vision is a point of reference that transcends technologies, tools, management techniques, and raw foolishness. The following criteria, antipatterns, and patterns can help you establish, project, and maintain a shared vision.

 CRITERIA

It is easier to grasp the principle of vision than it is to apply it to a specific situation. To put vision into practice, specifics are needed. Criteria translate the broad principle into specifics that can be used to determine whether and how well the principle is being practiced. They can also be used as a road map to guide implementation. When vision is in place:

1. The architect's vision aligns with what his or her sponsors, users, and end customers are trying to accomplish.
2. Practitioners trust and use the architecture.
3. Tacit knowledge about architecture and components is visible and accessible to users.

ANTIPATTERNS

ANTIGRAVITY MODULE is an antipattern in which the vision of the stake-holders is aligned by planning a component to satisfy all of the competing interests with minimal compromise and maximum optimism. The problem with such alignment is that the resulting component generally runs a lot better on a view graph projector than in real life.

TREND SURFER describes a situation in which the vision is not well established, so the direction of the architecture changes frequently in response to competitive and customer pressure. The vision is never stable enough to be effectively shared.

FOLLOWING ORDERS results when developers become too application-focused and do not create common solutions for problems shared by other architecture users.

PATTERNS

FRONT-END ALIGNMENT calls for the executive driving an architecture investment to take an active role in maintaining the vision and to protect the vision from short-term pressures.

ROTATION calls for people who work with architecture to be rotated to work in different areas of the architecture. This gives them both a direct understanding of more of the architecture and an opportunity to develop their informal networks.

GENERATIVE VISION reflects the recognition that the architect is not always the source of the architecture vision. The architect helps establish a vision that users can flesh out and bring to life.

Table 3.1 illustrates how the remainder of this chapter is organized.

TABLE 3.1   *Mapping Criteria to Antipatterns and Patterns*

CRITERION— HOW YOU MEASURE	ANTIPATTERN— WHAT NOT TO DO	PATTERN— WHAT YOU CAN DO
Architect's vision aligns with what his or her sponsors, users, and end customers are trying to accomplish	ANTIGRAVITY MODULE	FRONT-END ALIGNMENT
Practitioners trust and use the architecture	TRENDSURFER	GENERATIVE VISION
Tacit knowledge about architecture and components is visible and accessible to users	FOLLOWING ORDERS	ROTATION

Criterion 1: The architect's vision aligns with what his or her sponsors, users, and end customers are trying to accomplish

 Antigravity
Module

 Front-End
Alignment

"A product needs a positive, well-articulated 'sense of self' to survive."

—Roger Sessions [Sessions99]

Who must provide the leadership necessary to achieve a congruent, compelling, and flexible architecture vision? Product line manager? Architect? Product manager? Practitioner? CEO? Answer: *All of the above.* The architect cannot do it alone. To facilitate this cooperation, these roles must be in alignment. When the architect and the sponsors are at odds, it is a sign that the vision is faltering. The vision must also focus on solving tangible problems for the users of the architecture. If the value to customers cannot be clearly articulated, it is a sign that this focus is lacking.

Antipattern: ANTIGRAVITY MODULE

Aliases: UNIVERSAL TRANSLATOR, OPTIMISTIC PRODUCT TRACKING, PORTABLE HOLE

General Form.   You are the architect or manager of a new product line. The plans call for one or two components that look great on paper, but are going to be risky to implement. The business case, if the product line is successful, is tantalizing. The components may never have been built by anyone before, or the only currently available components are orders of magnitude too slow or resource-hungry. The engineers grumble that the project will require "laws of physics" to be broken to complete the project, and they dub the risky components as ANTIGRAVITY MODULES (see Figure 3.6). Still, a couple of engineers are chomping at the bit to face the challenge of building the components. They may even attempt to dismiss as uninformed other engineers who question the proposal. The project goes forward, and the risky components are scheduled to be completed last so that there will be more time to address their risks. The project moves forward, but as the planned completion date nears, the ANTIGRAVITY MODULES still have not been delivered. While the architecture runs adequately as presentation slides, the ANTIGRAVITY MODULES never work as well as they need to, and the planned product line is never fielded.

Forces. Executives face severe pressures to stretch the limits of optimism to keep development dollars flowing and to keep their organizations alive. Similarly, customers often demand estimates for unprecedented products, options, or features in a lot less time than it takes for developers to make a sound evaluation of required technology, cost, or schedule. Sometimes stakeholders will try to avoid or postpone decisions by asking for both of the possible alternative options to be supported. Even with plenty of time, it can be difficult to separate technologies that will be implemented and bulletproof in months from those that will take years. Executives have been known to promise features that are impossible to build within reasonable constraints.

Figure 3.6   The launch module is 99% built; all we need is the antigravity module.

To make matters worse, there is often no shortage of competitors who "can" meet the challenge, at least on paper. As a result, developers and their managers are called upon to work miracles.

Since many project tracking techniques allow unequal "chunks" to be labeled as equal, architects (and managers) sometimes schedule the most complex and risky tasks last. The more unrealistic the pressure, the greater the percentage of capabilities promised in the last "chunk" of tasks. Executives who are behind on other unrealistic commitments look at schedule end-points and miss underlying schedule factors, such as, percent of resource allocation. Then they add new commitments or pull key staff. This approach usually leads to unpleasant surprises.

Solution.   Analyze and articulate risk and provide the executive with a choice of either assuming the risk or renegotiating commitments. In particular, you should analyze how the proposed module maps to the constraints for the customer. Test the assumptions that underlie the proposed component so that they can be tested. Since making such pivotal decisions can lead to much heated debate, try to keep the discussions from becoming bitter. Whatever decision is made, the team will need to come back together to move forward.

Step back from the hypnotic excitement surrounding pending sales and ask for and accept honest answers.

If you are a customer, you can find out whether fielded applications exist that do what the unfinished components claim to do and determine how much they cost to build or buy. If you are the executive, you can step back from the hypnotic excitement surrounding pending sales and ask for and accept honest answers from engineers and developers.

Rationale.   This approach brings to mind the 1955 animation, *The Hole Idea*. In it, a dog named Robert carried around a "portable hole." Robert would take the hole out of his suitcase, apply it to the wall, crawl through, and peel it off the other side of the wall. No matter how sticky of a situation Robert found himself in, he could use the portable hole to escape [Costello96]. Making a portable hole a reality is a far cry from depicting one in a cartoon, yet organizations that embark on building an ANTIGRAVITY MODULE face that same gulf. The ANTIGRAVITY MODULE is compelling, and it does look great on paper, but putting the component into reality almost never happens.

Example.   In the early 1980s, the U.S. Army put out a Request for Proposal (RFP) for a command and control system written entirely in a new programming language called Ada. The RFP asked bidders to propose to write either a network or relational database, citing tradeoffs for each. The successful bidder replied that the customer could get both databases. The bidder's answer: A "software switch" that would toggle between the database approaches. The solution proved to be impossible to implement even with a world-class development team.

When This Antipattern is a Pattern. Sometimes extremely optimistic goals motivate people—when a company is just getting off the ground and people are really committed. The overall vision of the company would need to be in alignment with the proposed component, and the risk of the component would be something that the company is willing to bet on. An executive's vision can result in a positive effect; even though the architecture team may not be able to develop the feature as specified, it may have the potential to produce far beyond what they see as possible. The demand may result in rethinking staffing requirements and baseline technology and demanding a reward structure that compensates extreme innovation or effort.

Related Antipatterns and Patterns. In BIG RED BUTTON Don Olson describes an experience in which he jokingly said, "Yep, we're gonna be able to feed in those requirements, push the BIG RED BUTTON on the wall and out will come…." A few months later, he saw a manager's presentation describing the company's "state of the art" software engineering environment in which the only interface was a BIG RED BUTTON [Olson98]. Sometimes, truth really is stranger than fiction.

In the absence of a great dream, pettiness prevails.
—*Peter Senge (commenting on Robert Fritz),* The Fifth Discipline *[Senge90]*

Pattern: FRONT-END ALIGNMENT

Problem Statement. How do you know whether to press the architecture team to incorporate a feature that will take the architecture in a new direction?

Context. You are an executive who is faced with a decision. Your career depends on a product line of applications. Should you commit to a new feature on a schedule the architect has deemed impossible, or should you risk losing a major customer?

Several products share a common architecture. The common architecture has become more complex than expected. Customers have demanded features on each product that had not been initially anticipated, and in response, the architecture team is frantically exploring new technologies.

Forces. The vision of the architecture is based in part on assumptions about the direction and use of the architecture. The proposed feature challenges these assumptions. There may not be agreement on the underlying assumptions if the vision is not stable. Stakeholders can drive the architecture in directions that had not been initially planned. Change and evolution is an expected part of the life-cycle of a successful architecture, but there is also resistance to change. Not all proposed changes in direction can be acted upon, and not all of the proposed changes will yield long-term success. Architectures that have regular investments in their renewal and maintenance are more resilient to change.

Solution.   Assess the quality and stability of the architecture vision before striving for particularly aggressive goals. Move forward only if this alignment is in place.

Is the commitment you are about to make within or outside the product vision you have expressed? If the answer is "outside," you should probably not push the architect or product team. When the vision is unclear or churning, pressure to deliver "tomorrow" is likely to result in yet another buggy point-solution. Right now, the required "bold action" is to get with your customers as well as your architect and sales, product, support, and development managers and strengthen the product vision.

If the answer is, "Yes, the feature does fall within a stable product vision," check the alignment within the development organization. If the architect and developers are already working miracles on a daily basis, you may be facing Staff burn-out.

Result.   The organization is better able to accomplish the commitments it makes. It may also be a catalyst for recognizing and solving other problems with the vision. When organizations make good decisions about how to evolve the architecture and their vision for it, they are more likely to make decisions that work well in the long run. Avoiding choices that organizations regret and have to backpedal from later avoids potentially embarrassing and trust-eroding situations.

Consequences.   This practice can take time and resources, and often there is not enough of either before a commitment is needed. It is possible that an organization could miss out on opportunities, if the time spent in analysis is interpreted as indecision, or if the result of the assessment is unfavorable. Applying this pattern could become an excuse for ANALYSIS PARALYSIS to set in [BrownW98].

Rationale.   When the vision is in flux, it is much harder to get the architecture team sufficiently focused to achieve very aggressive goals. A unifying vision is needed for the team to work most efficiently. The good news is that analysis before a commitment is made can reveal whether the vision is stable and whether it is aligned with the direction of the commitment being considered. The bad news is that even if there are warning signs that the vision is not as it should be, there may still be very strong pressure to commit anyway. Hopefully, the assessment would provide enough information for a suitable middle ground to be found.

Example.   There are two cases at Allaire that illustrate both affirmative and negative FRONT-END ALIGNMENT decisions. In the first case, there was a group of ColdFusion customers who wanted a run-time version of the ColdFusion engine. With such a tool, they could deploy ColdFusion as part of applications that could be run locally on a computer without the need of a server. Allaire decided that while it would have been feasible to implement such a solution, the application development model implied by having a runtime version did not fit with their vision of ColdFusion as a large-scale Web application development framework. In another case, though, Allaire saw such a fit, and decided to move forward. Allaire released a Linux version of ColdFusion in 1999. A Linux version was a good fit because Linux appealed to grass-roots developers, much as the ColdFusion did. In addition, Linux had been gaining increasing attention in many enterprises. Allaire was reshaping their vision to appeal to this new market. In both cases, Allaire was able to use their vision of their architecture as a way of guiding the evolution of the product line.

Criterion 2: Practitioners trust and use the architecture

Trend
Surfer

Generative
Vision

"There is a danger in designing the future.... Things that are too fanciful date very quickly. The future needs a past."

—*Doug Chiang, Design Director for*
Star Wars, Episode I: The Phantom Menace [Parisi99]

Unless an architecture is used, no value can be gained from it. However, making an architecture vision believable enough for a developer to trust it requires more than just consistently delivering on promises. Developers need to relate what they know to the vision and feel positive about taking the next step. As developers make use of the architecture, they will pull it many different directions. Keeping the vision intact, while still satisfying the needs of users, is an important sign of a healthy architecture.

Consider J.J. Allaire's vision for the ColdFusion product line. The product vision proved contagious because J.J. Allaire matched it to the evolving vision of the Web. Allaire's products enabled people who understood the potential of the Web to build applications that changed their organizations. This vision applied to Allaire employees, partners, and customers. J.J. attracted people who had a common vision of how the Web could make fundamental changes in how people relate, and he articulated a vision of how to get there. Unlike architects that see a future that no one else can quite understand, Allaire's vision cascaded to allow everyone to test, adapt, and learn. Because the vision was shared and well aligned, Allaire was able to adapt their product line from grass-roots Web development to support corporate application development, and garner and maintain a strong base of usage in both categories.

TREND SURFING can erode an architecture's structure and cloud vision.

Antipattern: TREND SURFER

Alias: A MINUTE ON THE LIPS

General Form.   You are a senior manager who is the sponsor for a software architecture. There are mounting pressures from customers, competitors, and executives to add expensive capabilities mid-way through a release. Executives may even commit to delivering these features without consulting the architect. You can either add these features to the core, or lose a major customer. The resulting dramatic mid-stream shifts strain the architecture and create a support nightmare. As soon as one of these radical features gets delivered, the organization is locked into supporting the feature. Later releases become more complex because they usually have to provide backward compatibility.

The problem is complicated when the feature becomes part of the common architecture because all products must suffer with the feature's bloating effect. All too often the new feature is not fully implemented, which turns developers who are already late for the next release into mad bug-fixers.

Forces.   When there is no "core" or fundamental agreement across all parts of the organization (e.g., senior executive, sales, marketing, support, design) on how the product line should evolve, panic can begin to govern organizational behavior. There are many pressures to move an architecture in various directions. New technologies come to the market, competitors field new features, and customers create demands for new capabilities. Keeping pace with this changing environment is key to long-term success. However, changing direction to respond to these pressures is not free; time and resources are needed to respond to any of these pressures. Further, changing directions can disrupt the successful approaches that are already in place. Changes late in a release cycle are much more disruptive than a change early in the cycle.

Solution.   The vision needs to be understood and articulated. The need to change direction is part of a successful vision, so plan for it. Work closely with the architect so that consequences of a proposed change can be understood and tradeoffs can be made wisely. If the vision has been established, a FRONT-END ALIGNMENT can be used to evaluate any particular, proposed change. Insist on common agreement before a feature is added to a release. A regular mechanism is needed so that reaching such an agreement is a regular part of business. You should be willing to miss once in a while. If the high-level constraints have been satisfied by the architecture, you can allow more flexibility in how the details are approached. In the most extreme cases, resolving the problem of a TREND SURFER may require finding new stakeholders for whom expectations are more closely aligned.

Rationale.   TREND SURFER is often a symptom of a lack of vision. Without a vision to compare proposed changes, there is not a framework against which to evaluate possible changes. TREND SURFER can also surface when the vision is not shared. If different stakeholders have incongruous visions of the architecture, each group could continually push the architecture in directions that fit with their perspective, but are jarring to the other stakeholders. While the software business has more than its share of people who thrive on adrenaline, a TREND SURFER is often a person who is expressing an organizational imbalance.

Example.   A software development tools vendor was well into the development of the latest release of their product. The features for the release were well defined. A competitor came out with a product that included a key feature that they publicized heavily in trade shows and in their marketing. To respond quickly, the firm quickly adopted their competitor's approach to the feature. It proved to be a very bad decision. The approach proved to not be scalable and did not fit the existing architecture. When the firm wanted to remove the troublesome feature in a release, they met with resistance from customers who had adopted the feature.

In another example, the founder of a successful Internet start-up told us how he had avoided disastrous swings. The organization had grown to over 200 people including an externally recruited CEO and development manager and now involved a venture capital firm. This founder was able to remain successful by maintaining a clear focus himself, by insisting on consensus, by requiring detailed bi-weekly meetings to negotiate and coordinate all aspects of a new release, and by choosing both venture partners and executives who shared his vision.

When This Antipattern is a Pattern.   There is a balance here. Executives are driven to "read the market and give it what it is asking for." From this perspective, Internet time may not provide the luxury of waiting until the next release cycle for a critical new feature. The antipattern may be a pattern when an executive perceives and validates a shift away from the core features the architecture would support, once mature.

Pattern : GENERATIVE VISION

Alias: SOUND OF SILENCE

Problem Statement. How does an executive project a generative vision—a vision that gets everyone to innovate in keeping the architecture relevant to the products it supports?

Context. You are an executive, and you envision a shared architecture or platform as a key element of a product line strategy. You want to enable and encourage product groups to develop "killer solutions" while avoiding the thrashing that goes with chasing every new standard, adaptation, and trend.

A high level of trust has not yet been established between you and the architect, product managers, and developers. As a result, your instructions often contain details that constrain the ability of both architects and practitioners to implement an architecture-based approach.

Forces. Visionary executives sometimes see the end-goal so clearly that they try to specify everything. Executives sometimes fail to see the complexities in combining their vision with existing products. Architects, on the other hand, often see little value in the executive's vision. For them, architectural vision is a technical matter. Without a balanced contribution from each, the product line is not likely to succeed.

Expecting the architect to be "the 'Aha!' guy," someone who magically implements each of the executive's hot ideas, can lead both executive and architect into burn-out and failure.

An architect must respond in the short term to executive direction and rapidly changing customer need. Yet, it can take several releases before the contribution of an architect is fully realized. In the words of an accomplished architect, "Most of the architectural success I have seen was not the result of a few moments of sheer genius, but of many months of steady, quiet contributions by a long-term guiding hand."

Solution. Resist the temptation to create an architecture that does everything. Rather, establish a vision that enables the architect and the users to flesh out and bring features to life. You provide vision, goals, and principles, but leave the architecture and platform to the architect and implementation details to the appropriate team or level. To succeed, a product line architecture must

▶ Remain the best overall solution to a changing product mix—fit the market
▶ Adapt to and incorporate new technologies
▶ Solve problems that are not known at its conception

This is a task that few architects could accomplish alone. However, success can be achieved with the right top-level business vision from the executive and action to implement that vision from the architect. Just as the architect cannot create a success alone, neither can the executive.

Result.   The architect is able to understand the executive's vision and gain the executive's trust by making the architecture responsive to the vision. Each is more effective at his or her job because the roles for both are clearer, and because they will both be able to make better decisions. The vision that is established will better match the needs of users, and it will be more robust.

Consequences.   For an executive that built the original product line in the living room, allowing an architect that has not yet demonstrated competence over the long-term to figure out the best way to implement a solution may be unsettling. Risks may be severe if the architect has not bought into the executive's vision.

Rationale.   We have observed a strong correlation between product line success and a visionary who is in an executive role. The visionary provides the seed of an architecture vision and works hand-in-glove with successful architects.

Organizational researchers have explored this solution in the context of team-based organizations [Mohrman97] [Mohrman98]. We have observed that the concept holds for product line organizations. Management literature tells us that unless people in multiple roles and levels of an organization engage their talents to understand the changing problem as well as execute a solution, success is unlikely. A multi-year study conducted by the Center for Effective Organizations at the University of Southern California concluded that "Learning processes have to occur in all units at all levels of the system—one level or unit can't learn for another" [Mohrman97]. In this case—an executive's vision that gets bogged down in the details, or an architect that misunderstands who the visionary is—the direction can become blurred and progress falters.

Example.   A visionary executive was convinced that his company would make "bucketfuls of money" if they focused on the core issue of integration for a software product line. The product line would be in a very high-value position if it would integrate with other systems, like specific contact management software, Microsoft Exchange, security systems, and electronic payment. The architect had been working on this project for only a few months, and the visionary (who also furnished much of the capital) was uncertain how to proceed and what would work. He had endured several past failures with other architects. As a result, the visionary felt compelled to provide more detail, and he went on to fill whiteboard after whiteboard with detail. The executive drew and described a picture that, if realized, implied hundreds of lines of fixed interaction.

The architect pushed back. He knew, intuitively, that the vision if implemented as the executive described would take a huge amount of time and many thousand lines of code to build and maintain, and would be complex and brittle. The executive offered to do more research and draw additional wiring diagrams to make his vision explicit. "No thanks. Let me mull it over," the architect said. The architect tried to *forget* the "vision" and to rethink things.

The architect proposed a solution based on LDAP (Lightweight Directory Access Protocol). He built a prototype that provided a functionality that two other teams had been struggling weeks to accomplish on another project with an off-the-shelf component, and some glue code. The executive visionary was delighted. He beamed, "that's amazing."

The visionary and architect learned. The visionary learned to scope his vision to more functional or business requirements and to let the architect worry about implementation. The architect learned not to jump on the silliness of the executive's implementation ideas, and learned to listen to what the executive wanted to accomplish.

The evolution of the eXtensible Markup Language (XML) is also a good example of GENERATIVE VISION. The core XML 1.0 standard is very short, just over 30 pages. As its name implies, one of the design goals of XML was eXtensibility. New standards are created as complements to the core standard, so that the core can remain simple. XML was also created with the intent that organizations in various business domains can create their own markup languages pertinent to their domain. This approach allows the vision of XML to be shared across a wide range of stakeholders, even as those stakeholders flesh out that vision to use XML in a variety of application areas and domains.

Related Antipatterns and Patterns.   In SIZE THE SCHEDULE, Coplien describes the problem of sizing the schedule when the product is understood and the project size has been estimated [Coplien95]. The solutions, rewarding developers and keeping two sets of schedules, complement GENERATIVE VISION.

Following
Orders

Rotation

Criterion 3: Tacit knowledge about architecture and components is visible and accessible to users

Even when architectures are beautifully structured and documented with the most advanced tools, context and "lore" have a strong influence on whether users get value or simply get into trouble using the architecture. Conversely, very ugly architectures have enjoyed great success because a large group of people reveled in knowing and sharing the architecture's arcane complexities. When the sphere of use is limited to a small product team, tacit knowledge is conveyed person-to-person—for example, through mentoring or getting up and asking someone in the next cubicle.

When the sphere of use expands, this knowledge is often conveyed through informal networks (Chapter 6, Partnering). As important as they are, informal channels of communication can break down through the unintended consequences of executive action. When executives look only at formal structure, engineers who acquire and disseminate information to and from peer groups can be vulnerable to downsizing.

Antipattern: FOLLOWING ORDERS

General Form.   You are the manager of one of several teams of engineers. The team is practicing CODE OWNERSHIP, and the engineers are very focused on their immediate tasks and responsibilities [Coplien95]. However, that focus becomes a trap if they do not see themselves as stewards of a shared resource. The world of an engineer trapped in this antipattern becomes very narrow. Previously small problems become overwhelming. The trapped engineer considers co-workers' requests to modify the engineer's component or to explain how it works as intrusive and non-essential. When fellow developers ask for additional considerations, you ask, "Should I spend this extra effort, or should I just solve the problem at hand?" Too often, the answer is "Just solve the problem." This works very well—except when the solution needs to be modified. Then you start over, unwiring and re-designing. The work of the trapped engineer can become very complex, brittle, and subject to errors resulting from conditions that a single engineer could not anticipate.

Forces.   One of the biggest barriers to sharing tacit knowledge is the tendency to exclude everything and everyone except the most visible boss or immediate customer. Most reward and advancement mechanisms provide a great deal of weight to the satisfaction of an engineer's immediate supervisor. Creating and maintaining an architecture requires a willingness on the part of developers to think beyond the immediate problem, and to see how the solution will advance the organization's vision. Political and geographic divisions in an organization may discourage such sharing. The culture of an organization may act as either a barrier to or a catalyst for such cooperation.

Solution.   Create an expectation of sharing. There are many approaches for creating this expectation. The way engineers are trained and organized can play a role, as can the entire organization's policies for hiring and promotion.

Teach new hires, especially when they take over leadership positions. When new hires are placed as team leads, provide them with a serious exposure to the architecture and resources to help them understand how it works. Insist that work products such as design and code are reviewed by peers outside of the team. When problems surface, take action.

Engage developers and architects in planning. When developers see how everything fits together, they are more likely to build solutions that support the overall product vision and less likely to build disjointed solutions. Be sure to make it clear that the architect owns the architecture.

Promote internal and informal partnering. Reward developers for their sphere of influence and intake, and for the value of their work to those within and outside their team. Assign a GATEKEEPER to the team. A GATEKEEPER provides a different look at the problem [Coplien95]. Coplien observes that engineers are often introverted and therefore less likely to network. The solution is to identify an extroverted engineer to network with other teams and broker solutions internally and externally.

Be careful whom you hire and promote. Be aware of a candidate's interest and ability to build solutions that benefit co-workers as well as solve the problem at hand. Similarly, consider the contributions that engineers make to their peers when making promotion decisions. Screen candidates for integrity and honesty and have them interview with as many team members as possible. One successful technique involves giving absolute veto power to each interviewer. Questioning should be precise and in-depth and focus on the candidate's technical, and learning communication skills. This applies to both developers and managers. It is also wise to involve the best people in interviews. We have seen truth to the adage, "A players hire A players, B players hire C players, C players hire D players."

Rationale.   CODE OWNERSHIP does provide a model by which tacit knowledge about the architecture can be maintained and shared. However, if the ownership model becomes a pretext for territorialism, then it can create a barrier to sharing components. With a little creativity, the solution could be reused to help get teammates home a few hours earlier. Similarly, without consideration of other groups, a developer could create hundreds of unwanted surprises and sleepless nights for those who depend on the component he or she has modified. When developers take an interest in helping others, they often make their own "blind spots" smaller and build better, more robust solutions.

Example. A supplier of communications equipment had developed a product line that shared components built within and external to the business unit. Every component had an owner. Engineers across the 200-person organization could readily identify each component's owner and would involve the owner when changes to the component were required or made.

Competitors capitalized on delays in the start of a major new project, depleting the ranks of senior staff. When the project did start, the company had to place new hires as team-leads without providing the traditional apprenticeship and acculturation. The gaggle of fresh-out engineers did not buy in to the company's long-standing culture. The new hires began to take shortcuts, accomplishing their assignments but adding complex dependencies and often creating surprises for other component users. Within a few months, only a few people in the business unit could see how to make modifications to large chunks of the products.

One highly successful provider of Internet platforms insists that each candidate have at least five interviews. The company screens for "niceness," communication skills, bright intelligence, and creativity. They downplay knowledge of specific technology and play up basic technical skills and knowledge of how customers use technology. The company has an uncanny ability to field on-target features for customers that work for a surprisingly broad range of domains.

When is This Antipattern a Pattern. There are times when it is important to focus on the immediate issues and concerns at hand, even if it means making requests from other groups a lower priority. However, making such requests a lower priority should not be a license for dismissing them entirely and treating them as rude interruptions.

Pattern: ROTATION[3]

Alias: IN A STRANGE LAND

Problem Statement. How do you keep tacit "lore" accessible to users as specialized product and project teams are formed?

Context. Product line sales have grown to the point where a single, co-located team cannot support both architecture and implementation. The

---

[3] This pattern is based upon the ROTATION pattern submitted and reviewed at the 1997 Pattern Languages of Programming [Dikel97b].

number of developers has grown and people are reorganized into geographically distributed goal, project, or product-oriented teams.

Channels for lateral integration across teams have been designed and implemented, yet many questions do not readily fit the structure, and engineers often need answers much more quickly than these channels allow. For example, even though components have individual owners [Coplien95], engineers have difficulty finding out what the owners assumed about their component's environment or even who the owner is.

Forces. Unless an architecture is shared over time, it delivers little value. To achieve this common use over time, a lot of tacit information must be disseminated quickly. When a product or product line group expands from one group to many, the formal, intergroup channels of communication often prove ineffective. Engineers are often not comfortable getting solutions through official channels, nor are they always confident with the solutions they receive.

Detailed knowledge about components is hard to retain and disseminate. The component owner may feel roped in by becoming the "expert" for a given component. If such employees are dissatisfied, the likelihood of losing (or overpaying) them increases. When the only person who knows a component well leaves the organization, it is very expensive for the new component owner to acquire that knowledge from scratch.

While some engineers feel roped in by their specialized component knowledge, others get into a groove and do not like to change. These engineers may be perfectly happy in a shepherding role.

Still other component owners may hoard information about the component to maintain unique "employment" value. Since component owners often need to work with each other to get necessary revisions and additions from other components, key people are in a position to take advantage of their irreplaceable status. Organizations may make decisions to avoid offending key people, even if those decisions are not the best for the organization as a whole. For example, organizations may not take action when component owners try to maintain and expand their position and/or block the progress of anyone whom they feel threatened by, often at the expense of losing a large number of promising but more replaceable engineers.

Solution. Periodically rotate component ownership by means of APPRENTICESHIP [Coplien95]. It is critical that the organization and individual managers allow and encourage ex-owners to take time out of their schedules to support new owners. To the extent possible, rotations should be synchronized with release schedules, so that new owners aren't thrown directly into the fire, and so that former owners will have time to act as mentors.

Before rotating engineers, find out whether they are ready to rotate and, if so, where he or she would like to go next, as described in LET 'EM CHOOSE [Olson97]. The rotation should enable engineers to spiral upward, so that as people rotate they also move up into areas of more difficult technical expertise and/or greater responsibility. As a rule of thumb, rotate engineers about every 12 months, but this rate may vary due to the size and complexity of the components.

Result. Developers can more easily find out where to go to find esoteric knowledge about components. The likelihood that a team member has either owned the component or knows whom to ask is greatly increased. As a result, the number of surprises is reduced. This means the wrenching experience of finding out a week before delivery that your assumptions are wrong about a component you depend on are less likely to occur.

Staff is more content because they get to work in a variety of areas, and turnover is reduced [Couger88]. The organization has more depth, so if a component owner leaves the organization, there are other previous component owners who also have detailed knowledge of the component. This makes it easier and less expensive to replace the departed component owner. Since component owners will have worked in a variety of areas and apprenticed with a number of different people, they will develop stronger social and informal networks with other component owners.

Component owners will be better trained to assume positions of greater responsibility; as people rotate and move up in an organization, they will increase the portion of the system with which they have hands-on knowledge. They will then be more qualified to make decisions or identify efficiencies that affect larger portions of the system.

By rotating in spirals instead of flat rings, component owners who tend to resist change will have more incentive to move from their existing component to those with more challenge and responsibility. Component owners who are able to pick up new components quickly will not feel "roped-in" by becoming the "expert" in a given area, because there would be a clear path to greater challenges and responsibilities.

A ride around the track as a component owner increases an engineer's skills, ROTATION builds on organizational capabilities.

Consequences. A lot of caution should be used when considering the use of this pattern with large, complex architectures, particularly those subject to severe operational constraints. Critical "you don't want to do that" knowledge could be lost with disastrous consequences. There is also a danger of engineers taking a short-term view. Rather than learning the details of the architecture, an engineer might learn only enough to get the immediate job done and ignore consequences that would take effect after he or she left the project.

There is an overhead of training and retraining that results from this pattern. While the organization does not need to recreate detailed component knowledge from scratch, effort is required to routinely train new component owners as they are rotated to new assignments. There may be a schedule impact as well.

While component owners who seek to learn and grow will be more content and less likely to leave, some may feel threatened by starting all over again in a new area. As a result, they may leave or subvert the implementation of ROTATION. Some other approach may be needed to accommodate their interests.

The organization may not be able to grow quickly because it takes time to apprentice new component owners. Similarly, if the organization is shrinking, for example, through staff cuts, this pattern may break down.

There may be resentment generated from the addition of new people from outside the organization. For example, if new people are brought in and given ownership responsibilities in the middle of the rotation spiral, there may be resentment from long-time organization members who started at the spiral's bottom.

Rationale.   Component owners acquire a significant amount of tacit knowledge as they carry out their responsibilities. That knowledge could be lost if the developers were to leave the organization. Rotation mitigates against this risk in two ways. By periodically placing component owners in the role of mentor, they can share their tacit knowledge with the people they apprentice. The apprenticeship may provide a motivation to document this knowledge. Further, since multiple people in an organization would have had the ownership responsibility of any particular component, there is not just one person who has detailed knowledge of it, so the organization is less vulnerable to the loss of any one person.

Example.   A senior manager for a telecommunications company was faced with a less-than-cooperative internal supplier of a component critical to his product. Cross-border rivalry made communication even more difficult. To solve the problem, the manger transferred one of his most talented designers to the supplier's organization. As a result, his staff was able to get needed answers from the designer. The designer was often able to see how to get needed features into earlier releases.

Related Antipatterns and Patterns.   APPRENTICESHIP provides a path to turn new hires into experts by allowing them to work alongside an established engineer for six months to a year. By applying APPRENTICESHIP, subtle understandings are transferred along with intellectual skills [Coplien95].

CODE OWNERSHIP assigns a single point of responsibility for shared sections of code. Rotation assumes that code ownership is an ingrained practice within the organization [Coplien95].

DEVELOPING IN PAIRS pairs compatible designers to work together. The pair is more likely to pick up on signs one person might miss. Also, each partner will learn to back up the other. DEVELOPING IN PAIRS allows the code owner to transfer tacit knowledge while benefiting from his partner's work [Coplien95].

SUMMARY

Architecture vision is the mapping of future value to architectural constraints as measured by how well the architecture's structures and goals are clear, compelling, congruent, and flexible. The better the architecture vision, the better each stakeholder understands his or her role. Without a common architecture vision, communication breaks down, and with it the structure of the architecture. This chapter provides executives as well as architects and practitioners with a means to establish and share a vision.

Software architects are frequently not the source of architecture vision; often they enter the scene after the vision has been formed. In many start-ups, for example, the vision originates from the firm's founders. At other times, the person with the role of translating this vision may not have the formal title of software architect. Whoever has the role of architect, executive cooperation is essential. An effective vision is one that is congruent—consistent among stakeholders—and flexible—adaptable to new environments and challenges.

However, no matter how good a job an architect does, elements beyond his or her control—other members of the organization, as well as the organization itself—can and often do foul things up. Organizational culture and policies can shape how well stakeholders communicate. External factors such as customers and competitors can drive the vision as well. Executives can play an important role to ensure that these factors do not impede the architecture and to help ensure that the corporate and architecture vision are in alignment.

An architect can make an abstract architecture personal and compelling to each stakeholder by providing a map between the constraints of the architecture and the compelling value delivered to its customers. The architecture can also serve as a useful benchmark and reference point when the implementers are making hard decisions. By focusing, motivating, and coordinating the stakeholders' activities, each stakeholder can make better, more focused use of their energy, time, and money.

OTHER APPLICABLE PATTERNS AND ANTIPATTERNS

There are other patterns that can be used to put the principle of Vision into practice, as well as antipatterns to avoid along the way. Table 3.2 lists organizational patterns and antipatterns cataloged in the 2000 edition of *The Patterns Almanac* [Rising00]. Table 3.3 lists antipatterns from *Antipatterns: Refactoring Software, Architectures, and Projects in Crisis* [BrownW98].

TABLE 3.2   *Organizational Patterns and Antipatterns That Can Shape Vision [Rising00]*

AD-HOC CORRECTIONS [Weir98]	MANAGING AND MEETING CUSTOMER EXPECTATIONS [Whitenack95]
APPRENTICE [Coplien95]	MASTER-JOURNEYMAN [Weir98]
ARCHITECT ALSO IMPLEMENTS [Coplien95]	MERCENARY ANALYST [Coplien95]
ARCHITECT CONTROLS PRODUCT [Coplien95]	MULTIPLE COMPETING DESIGNS [Weir98]
ARRANGING THE FURNITURE [Taylor99]	ORGANIZATION FOLLOWS LOCATION [Coplien95]
BOOTSTRAPPING [Taylor99]	ORGANIZATION FOLLOWS MARKET [Coplien95]
CODE OWNERSHIP [Coplien95]	OWNER PER DELIVERABLE [Cockburn98]
CONWAY'S LAW [Coplien95]	PATRON [Coplien95]
CULT OF PERSONALITY [Olson98]	PHASING IT IN [Coplien95]
DAY CARE [Cockburn98]	PROBLEM-ORIENTED TEAM [Taylor99]
DECISION DOCUMENT [Weir98]	PRODUCT INITIATIVE [Cunningham96]
DESIGN BY TEAM [Harrison96]	RECOMMITMENT MEETING [Cunningham96]
DEVELOPMENT EPISODE [Cunningham96]	REFERENCE DATA [Cunningham96]
DOMAIN EXPERTISE IN ROLES [Coplien95]	REQUIREMENT WALK-THROUGH [Cunningham96]
EFFECTIVE HANDOVER [Taylor99]	SCENARIOS DEFINE PROBLEM [Coplien95]
ENGAGE CUSTOMERS [Coplien95]	SPONSOR OBJECTIVES [Whitenack95]
ENVISIONING [Whitenack95]	TEAM SPACE [Taylor99]
FORM FOLLOWS FUNCTION [Coplien95]	TECHNICAL MEMO [Cunningham96]
FUNCTION OWNERS/COMPONENT OWNERS [Cockburn98]	TRAIN HARD, FIGHT EASY [Olson98]
GURU DOES ALL [Olson98]	TRAIN THE TRAINER [Olson98]
IMPLIED REQUIREMENTS [Cuningham96]	UNITY OF PURPOSE [Harrison96]
LOCK 'EM UP TOGETHER [Harrison96]	WORK FLOWS INWARD [Coplien95]

TABLE 3.3   *Antipatterns That Can Derail Vision [BrownW98]*

AMBIGUOUS VIEWPOINT

ANALYSIS PARALYSIS

BLOWHARD JAMBOREE

CONTINUOUS OBSOLESCENCE

COVER YOUR ASSETS

DESIGN BY COMMITTEE

FIRE DRILL

GOLDEN HAMMER

JUMBLE

MUSHROOM MANAGEMENT

REINVENT THE WHEEL

SMOKE AND MIRRORS

STOVEPIPE ENTERPRISE

VIEWGRAPH ENGINEERING

RHYTHM: ASSURING BEAT, PROCESS, AND MOVEMENT

Rhythm is one of the principal translators between dream and reality. Rhythm might be described as, to the world of sound, what light is to the world of sight.
— *Edith Sitwell in* Taken Care Of *[Sitwell65]*

OVERVIEW

Grady Booch points out in *Object Solutions* that the iterative nature of object-oriented development makes rhythm a critical element for success. He writes that having a rhythm forces closure at periodic intervals, coordinates supporting activities, and helps organizations react better when problems arise [Booch96]. Rhythm is important to any development process, but especially for architecture-based development. Rhythm can battle complexity, keep competition off-balance, and maintain sanity and predictability for architecture and development teams.

The sharing of an architecture is like an improvisational jazz ensemble. Each player in an ensemble is autonomous, but each musician's performance is coordinated by cues exchanged with the other musicians as well as the tempo, key, and style of the performance. While the basic elements of the performance may be written down or planned, many elements are performed by the musicians relying on their instinct, training, and talent.

Just as a jazz combo must share a common tempo, phrasing, and progression to have a rhythm, an architecture team must share work products with predictable timing, content, and quality. Software architectures are developed and used in many different organizations. Since many of these groups are autonomous, it is not possible to fully coordinate all of them from the top down. Without rhythm, sharing an architecture can befuddle even the best-designed schemes for communicating across teams.

Rhythm provides a temporal framework that allows groups sharing an architecture to synchronize activities and expectations. With rhythm, stakeholders know when and on which activities to focus. Not only can organizations with rhythm coordinate planned activities, but they can also coordinate those tasks that do not show up on plans because they are performed by other organizations or are not visible enough to be included in the planning process. When rhythm is weak, dissonance between organizations emerges, paving the road to architecture breakdown.

RHYTHM DEFINITION

Rhythm is the recurring, predictable exchange of work products within an architecture group and across their customers and suppliers.

There are three elements of rhythm: tempo, content, and quality (see Figure 4.1). As in music, architecture rhythm is not just the repetition of a beat. Effective rhythm enables teams throughout the organization to coordinate explicit and complex activities without the corresponding load of communication and coordination. If tempo, content, or quality is lacking, these benefits will not be realized, and progress will not be made.

Figure 4.1
There are three elements of rhythm:
Tempo, content, and quality.

Tempo

Tempo is the frequency with which the same type of handoff occurs between one group and another—for example, between the architecture team and product development engineers. The more predictable the timing of each handoff becomes, the easier each transition is to manage. As illustrated by Figure 4.2, there may be many different tempos. Some organizations have different intervals for major releases, minor releases, and bug fixes. DAILY BUILD AND SMOKE TEST is one example of this notion of tempo [Cabrera99]. Microsoft has popularized this practice [Cusumano95][McCarthy95][McConnell96]. Regular release schedules are another example of tempo.

Content

It is not enough to maintain a beat of daily builds if the builds are not used.

Content is the delivery of value from one group to another. An example of the delivery of content is when a group develops a new or modified feature that another group uses to fill a need. Moving completed builds from development to testing is another example of the delivery of content. Content requires that the receiving group derives value from the delivery. For example, it is not enough to maintain a beat of daily builds if the builds are not used. Figure 4.3 illustrates an organization that maintains a regular tempo without delivering enough content with each beat. In this situation, stakeholders tune out the rhythm because so little progress is made with each beat. Iterative development, when working effectively, exemplifies content delivery as illustrated in Figure 4.4. Each iteration builds on the previous cycle. Figure 4.5 describes the situation in which value is added from each handoff, but because there is

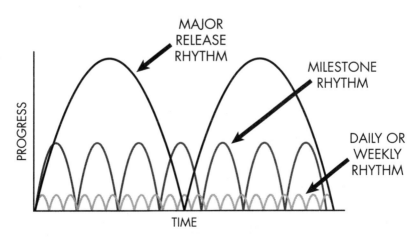

Figure 4.2   There may be rhythms of many different tempos at once.

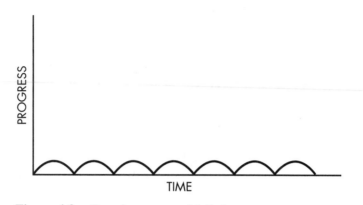

Figure 4.3   Regular tempo with little content.

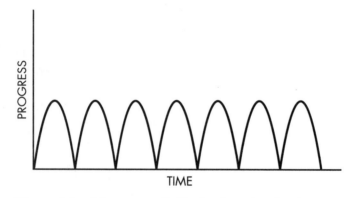

Figure 4.4   The tempo of effective iterative development.

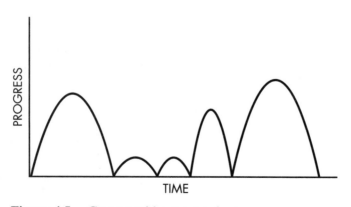

Figure 4.5   Content without a regular tempo.

no regular tempo, the timing of these handoffs is irregular. In this situation, rhythm is lacking because participants cannot anticipate when handoffs are going to occur.

Quality

Quality means that processes are followed to ensure that the architecture is free of deficiencies.[1] Organizations sometimes try to sustain their tempo by compromising on quality, for example, by skimping on testing, or by redefining what is required by a handoff. This situation is illustrated in Figure 4.6. Organizations may be able to accelerate their tempo by eliminating steps that do not add value, but if essential processes are truncated, rhythm will break down.

Consider the following example of the deterioration of quality. A development group was trying to achieve a goal of reaching an established milestone every three months. It became clear that the group was not going to reach a particular milestone, so they redefined the criteria for passing a milestone to maintain their schedule. They reclassified the severity of a number of outstanding defects. In this case, the process was abbreviated and the product was able to pass the milestone with lower quality. Additional effort was needed to improve the quality before the product reached the next milestone. Even though beat was maintained for the initial milestone, it just postponed the breakdown until a later milestone.

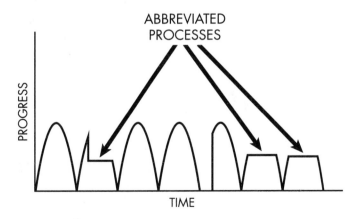

Figure 4.6   Incomplete rhythm: Truncated process to maintain a tempo

---

[1] This definition is based on the American Society for Quality's definition of the term quality. [ASQ00]

MOTIVATION

Why is rhythm so important to software architecture? Since software architectures are developed and used across many organizational boundaries, rhythm provides a stabilizing force that coordinates activities within and across teams and organizations. Like an improvisational jazz ensemble, architecture stakeholders need to be able to anticipate the activities of the other stakeholders. If stakeholders cannot plan activities and budget resources, then each transition requires a great deal of effort and time for communication and coordination among the involved parties. Maintaining a rhythm over multiple releases also strengthens the credibility of the architecture supplier.

Our interviews with Allaire Corporation demonstrated how this ability to anticipate enabled the organization to act quickly and efficiently. When Allaire experienced growth, managers knew when in their release cycle to hire testers, when to hire developers, and when to hire customer support personnel. Managers also knew what training to provide and when. Shortages or oversupply of a skill set were identified as a sure sign that rhythm was breaking down.

Rhythm Aids Transition Management

When rhythm is strong, stakeholders build strong skills that enable them to anticipate and execute transitions and handoffs. Organizations are then able to treat transitions as a recurring, regularly planned activity. When rhythm is not strong, transitions and handoffs often come as a surprise. Kathleen Eisenhardt and Shona Brown point out that "because major transitions are periods when companies are likely to stumble, we expected to find that managers would devote extra attention to them. The surprise is that they don't"[2] [Eisenhardt98].

Rhythm Drives Closure

Rhythm also helps an organization bring activities to closure. "Iterative and incremental releases," writes Booch, "serve as a forcing function that drives the development team to closure at regular intervals" [Booch96]. A study by Connie Gersick illustrates this notion. She observed project groups from six organizations. She found that even though the studied projects ranged from several days to several months, every group exhibited a distinctive approach to its task when it commenced and remained with that approach "until precisely halfway through the group's allotted duration." At the

---

[2] K. Eisenhardt, S. Brown, "Time Pacing: Competing in Markets that Won't Stand Still." *Harvard Business Review* (March–April, 1998).

Figure 4.7
Halfway to a deadline, teams typically adjust their approach and make dramatic progress

halfway point, she observed that the groups "dropped old patterns, reengaged with their outside supervisors, adopted new perspectives on their work, and made dramatic progress" [Gersick89] (see Figure 4.7). An organization with a good rhythm establishes regular intervals and halfway points to motivate this reassessment and progress.

USING RHYTHM TO TAKE CHARGE

Developers can use rhythm to take charge of their fates, even when their parent organization is bureaucratic. In one large, hierarchical information technology organization, a team built a component. Unlike most of the components owned by the parent organization, both the parent organization and customers in other chains-of-command used the team's component. The parent organization controlled the schedule. Component users could not count on timely delivery because release dates were tied to releases of the rest of the architecture, whose tempo was generally chaotic, as illustrated in Figure 4.8.

To resolve the situation, the component team began a regular release cycle, decoupling the release of the component from the release of the rest of the architecture. The component team was capable of delivering multiple releases for each release of the parent architecture. As a result, the component team was able to release more frequently because they cut the time required to deliver a release in half, as illustrated in Figure 4.9. Not only were customers outside the parent's chain-of-command pleased by the predictable schedules, but customers inside the parent organization found it easier to coordinate their releases. Testing became more predictable, quality

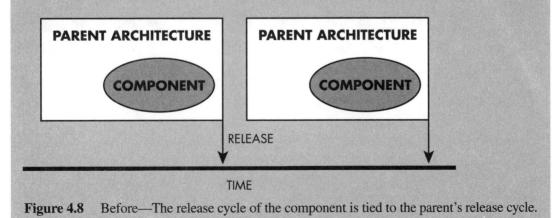

Figure 4.8 Before—The release cycle of the component is tied to the parent's release cycle.

improved, and customer satisfaction increased. In addition, the parent architecture release cycle became shorter and more regular.

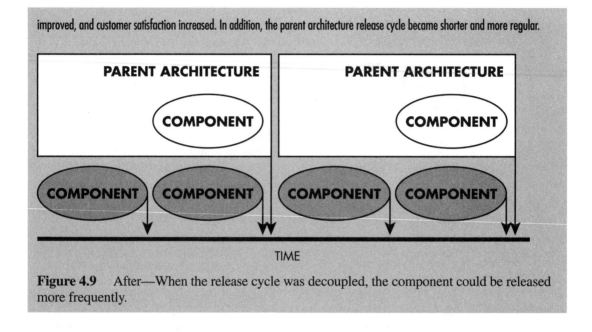

Figure 4.9   After—When the release cycle was decoupled, the component could be released more frequently.

PUTTING RHYTHM INTO PRACTICE:
CRITERIA, ANTIPATTERNS, AND PATTERNS

The previous sections describe how the principle of rhythm is important for coordinating the activities of architecture stakeholders. The consequences of failing to establish a rhythm can lead to dissatisfied customers, unexpected defects, and components that do not work well together.

CRITERIA

The following criteria, patterns, and antipatterns provide guidelines and techniques that organizations can use to determine how well they establish a predictable execution of process, movement, and beat within an architecture group and across its customers and suppliers.

When rhythm is working…

1. Managers periodically reevaluate, synchronize, and adapt the architecture.
2. Architecture users have a high level of confidence in the timing and content of architecture releases.
3. Explicit activities are coordinated via rhythm.

ANTIPATTERNS

KILLER FEATURE is what happens when an organization becomes so focused on getting one feature to market that the internal rhythm is disrupted. Even if the feature is delivered, the organization may be blind-sided by competition because of the single-minded focus on getting the feature to market. It is an example of what happens when the management does not regularly reevaluate and adapt the architecture.

SHORT CUT can happen when the organization tries to maintain a regular beat of releases by taking short cuts in the organization's process. This antipattern compromises the quality and content that users expect from the architecture.

BROKEN LOADS can happen when an organization has tried to implement regular builds, but the builds frequently fail to compile or pass automated tests. This represents a breakdown of coordination.

PATTERNS

RELEASE COMMITTEE describes an approach for coordinating the parties involved in releasing a new architecture. The pattern illustrates a way for managers to reevaluate, synchronize, and adapt an architecture during the final stretch of an architecture's release.

DROP PASS examines how organizations can maintain a beat by moving less critical features to later release cycles. By maintaining the rhythm, this pattern gives users more confidence on the timing of architecture releases.

SYNCHRONIZE RELEASES is a technique for extending the notion of rhythm beyond an organization's boundaries. This pattern provides a way to synchronize the activities of the architecture team and their users.

Table 4.1 illustrates how the remainder of this chapter is organized.

TABLE 4.1   *Mapping Criteria to Antipatterns and Patterns*

CRITERION— HOW YOU MEASURE	ANTIPATTERN— WHAT NOT TO DO	PATTERN— WHAT YOU CAN DO
1. Managers periodically reevaluate, synchronize, and adapt the architecture.	KILLER FEATURE	RELEASE COMMITTEE
2. Architecture users have a high level of confidence in the timing and content of architecture releases.	SHORT CUT	DROP PASS
3. Explicit activities are coordinated via rhythm.	BROKEN LOADS	SYNCHRONIZE RELEASES

Criterion 1: Managers periodically reevaluate, synchronize, and adapt the architecture.

Killer
Feature

Release
Committee

A good rhythm needs a regular beat. From the perspective of management, this means shifting from *event-pacing* to *time-pacing*. Rather than making decisions when there is a change in competition, technology, or customers, decisions are made on a regular, calendar-driven schedule [BrownS98]. For managers of architecture organizations, this means that they must reevaluate, synchronize, and adapt their plans for the architecture at regular intervals. Time-pacing is effective as a strategy "because it forces managers to look up from their business on a regular basis, survey the situation, adapt, if necessary, and get back to work" [BrownS98].[3] The beat of the rhythm can also provide a framework for the planning process. Instead of asking "How long will it take to implement a feature?" an organization with a good rhythm can ask "How much of the feature can we do in a single beat?" or "How many beats will it take us to fully implement the feature?"

Antipattern: KILLER FEATURE

   Alias: CLOSE TO EVEREST

   General Form.   You are an executive or architect and you are planning a new release that will be driven by a major, cutting edge feature. While drop-dead great features provide a serious competitive edge, focus on the impossible dream of one feature can literally kill a product or product line by

---

[3] S. Brown, K. Eisenhardt, "Competing on the Edge." Harvard Business School Press (1998).

destroying internal rhythm. You sincerely believe that if the team can just get this feature out, everything else, such as increased sales and marketshare, will fall into place. The team is driven to deliver this feature to the exclusion of others, often cutting corners on quality. Managers do not look up until the KILLER FEATURE is delivered or until they are blind-sided by their competitors or customers. When the release containing the feature is finally delivered, the team is exhausted. Worse, since everyone had been so focused on the feature, no one knows what to do next.

Forces.   Customers and potential customers are not shy about tying leading-edge features to their commitment of continued business. These statements can lead entrepreneurs to conclude that if they could provide one single feature, they would gain a prized customer's business. While some key customers make decisions solely based on the presence or absence of one feature, other potential customers may be discouraged if there is no definition of or commitment to a broad array of features, or if the future direction of the architecture is not articulated clearly. A successful architecture is never finished, but is continually evolving to keep pace with changing customer needs and environments.

Solution.   The key feature should be implemented as part of the team's rhythm, not in spite of it. A particular release may be focused around a particular theme, which may help the release to take advantage of opportunities in the marketplace. If the key feature is particularly complex, it may need to be implemented across several iterations. If it becomes difficult to maintain the rhythm while implementing the key feature, it is most likely a warning sign that the risk and complexity of the feature is greater than anticipated, and that replanning is necessary.

Rationale.   A KILLER FEATURE can be like mountain climbers scaling Mount Everest. The climbers see the summit, and it appears easy to attain, but in reality the distance is an illusion—a hard and treacherous journey to the peak remains, and the oxygen becomes thinner with each step. Similarly, the drive for a KILLER FEATURE may seem like a short diversion for the team, but may expose the organization to a number of risks. Organizations with an effective rhythm benefit from the tacit coordination of many activities and groups. When an organization trades this rhythm for a drive to implement a KILLER FEATURE, this coordination will suffer. Further, successful software architectures can remain in use for a very long time, and it is impossible to forecast all of the turns in the marketplace over that period of time. While it is true that a killer feature may increase revenue or marketshare, it is also true that another brand-new technology could be around the corner that will completely reshape the marketplace. Without regular cycles to reevaluate and adapt the architecture these changes in environment might be missed. The sponsors and senior management for a software architecture must periodically reevaluate and adapt the architecture to respond to these challenges.

Example.   A major vendor of a very successful accounting and constituent management software product line hired a CEO whose primary mission was to take the company public. The CEO recognized that going public as an Internet company would result in a much higher valuation. However, changing the research and development (R&D) to focus on a KILLER FEATURE, a Web front-end integrated with the legacy product line, would pose a massive disruption of the company's long-established rhythm and release cycle. The company would have to establish a new division, manage and evolve new skills, and establish new interfaces to integrate technologies that did not exist when the disparate legacy technology was developed. It was a massive challenge.

What did the CEO do? He punted. Instead of investing in R&D for the required technology and setting an impossible schedule for delivery, he shopped to acquire an Internet company and settled on a seven-figure transaction with a proven Web-application development firm. The CEO said, "Time-to-market is everything." The company brought to market a credible Internet offering and stayed on track for its IPO.

Another leading software and hardware vendor applies a number of strategies to avoid this antipattern. One group uses an approach in which they split the time in the release into four roughly equal parts for requirements, design, implementation, and delivery. If the features for a release cannot fit into the time allotted for requirements, they re-plan the release based on the logic that if the requirements couldn't be completed in the allotted window, then the other planned windows would not be sufficient either. Another group in the same company takes this management of features in each release a step further. They plan more releases, some of which are developed in parallel, and partition the features between the releases. Each release is implemented more quickly, so the important features get to market more quickly. Candidate and Upcoming features are always in the pipeline, so the direction is clear to both the team and the customers.

When is This Antipattern a Pattern?   Sometimes it makes sense to organize a release around a particular theme. This is particularly true when the feature enables users' products to move in a strategic direction. Some organizations use this theme as a way to prioritize which features are essential for a release and which are optional. In these cases, the essential features do receive more attention and resources, but they are still approached within the overall vision of the architecture.

Variation: LATE KILLER FEATURE.   The worst case of this antipattern is the LATE KILLER FEATURE. In this case, the feature surfaces very late in the development cycle. Just when things are settling down and a release seems imminent, it suddenly becomes necessary to add something new to address "market conditions." These late additions are uniformly regrettable. Since they were not part of the vision for the cycle they do not fit into the architecture and are implemented as kludges. Even though the new feature seems critical, the long-term impact on the architecture and on the customers is harmful. Correcting mistakes added at these late stages leaves hanging the customers who bought into them.

Related Antipatterns and Patterns.   This antipattern is similar to TUNNEL VISION (Chapter 5, Anticipation); in both cases, the organization is driven to a particular goal. Unlike TUNNEL VISION, where the direction is maintained in the face of contrary evidence, there may be no such evidence in KILLER FEATURE. The KILLER FEATURE antipattern may result even if the feature in question does indeed turn out to be very important to the marketplace.

Pattern: RELEASE COMMITTEE

Problem Statement.   How do you get teams with conflicting perspectives and agendas in sync to meet a planned release date?

Context.   A product organization with a dozen to several hundred people, including product support, marketing, architecture, testing, and design, is developing and supporting an architecture. These groups do not all report to the same manager. A configuration control board, or similar process, is in place and the organization has committed to a set of features for a particular release. The product involves several components that must be coordinated for customers to get the most value from it.

Forces.   Many different groups within an organization are involved when releasing a version of an architecture. Participating groups may include development, marketing, testing, quality assurance, configuration management, and subcontractors. Groups that report to different managers may have conflicting, and often hidden, priorities and agendas. It can be particularly difficult, for example, for a manager to state the obvious when a positive change could threaten the size or viability of his or her group. Even when everything is arranged perfectly, group dynamics produce unexpected results [Smith87]. Larger groups take more time to make decisions than smaller groups. When one group is clearly behind, other groups may try to play SCHEDULE CHICKEN and take advantage of the delay and avoid blame. That is, groups may believe they can get away with risking a delay if they think another group will be even further delayed [Olson98].

Solution.   Hold regular and formal meetings that include each critical stakeholder in the organization to guide the progress of the release. During the meetings, review changes in product features and priorities, so that product documentation, marketing promises, public relations, testing, and development are in agreement. Where appropriate, metrics should be used to measure the progress of the release. At these meetings, commitments and dependencies are shared, and decisions are made about how to proceed. Document and distribute the decisions that are made at the meetings. The members participating in the committee should be stable. There should be consistent membership at the meeting, and the participants also need to have enough authority to make decisions. The RELEASE COMMITTEE differs from a configuration control board in that it focuses on the execution of a release, whereas a configuration control board is typically concerned with the content of a release.

Result.   As a result of the pattern, surprises are avoided, as are unnecessary delays. When issues arise, they can be fairly and adequately represented, and then quickly resolved. Because all stakeholders are represented, there is a better understanding of the context in which decisions are made. The use of metrics can help focus the discussion and make it easier for the participants to come to a common understanding on the progress of a release. The committee improves the timing of releases by enhancing coordination of the groups involved. The committee's decision-making process also improves the content and quality of releases, and it helps ensure that consistent information about the release is given to customers.

Consequences.   The practice is time-consuming, especially if the meetings do not have clear agendas established and enforced. The REPRESENTATIVE RELEASE COMMITTEE variation addresses some of these concerns for large organizations. The meeting may provide a forum for some groups to air pet peeves and introduce other obstacles—including participants who are not essential for a successful release, but who can make the RELEASE COMMITTEE less efficient. Because the RELEASE COMMITTEE can exert a strong influence on the execution of a release plan, a CORNCOB (a curmudgeon of the unwelcome kind) may cause havoc as a member of the committee [BrownW98].

Rationale.   Releases of large, complex software products typically involve a variety of groups that report to different managers. This makes lateral integration difficult, which can lead to risks, poor decisions, and delays. A RELEASE COMMITTEE provides a structure in which stakeholder groups work together to deliver an architecture or other major software component. This coordination can improve the delivery of content between the groups responsible for delivery. By avoiding missteps, the committee can also help maintain the tempo of a release. Stable membership is needed so that issues resolved during one meeting will not resurface at later meetings. If participants do not have enough authority to make decisions, then decisions cannot be made at the meeting, or the decisions made will have no influence on the organization.

Example.   This practice is used by a number of companies including Allaire, the maker of the ColdFusion Web application development environment. Allaire kicks off a new release with the stakeholders at an off-site meeting. A release plan is created at this meeting, and it ensures that all of the departments are in agreement regarding the priorities of the release. Then, as the release progresses, the group meets every week. These weekly meetings make commitments and dependencies visible to all of the participants. Changes are recorded in a release plan.

Variation: REPRESENTATIVE RELEASE COMMITTEE.   If the organization is very large, it may not be feasible to have direct participation in the RELEASE COMMITTEE. A REPRESENTATIVE RELEASE COMMITTEE can be used instead. A telecommunications firm had a very large product that involved more than 20 distinct organizations. Release committee meetings to determine whether a checkpoint had been passed were bogged down when participants began to air pet peeves and push pet features and often surprised everyone by blocking releases with issues that had not been previously raised. They adopted a three- (and later four-) member REPRESENTATIVE RELEASE COMMITTEE. While each stakeholder was not a direct participant in the committee, each member of the committee explicitly represented a stakeholder. If a stakeholder had an issue that needed to be addressed by the committee, the stakeholder raised the issue through this committee representative. The group used metrics, such as the number of outstanding defects, to assess the progress of a release. After adopting the smaller release committee, issues were resolved more quickly and meetings were more focused and productive.

Related Patterns and Antipatterns.   The RELEASE COMMITTEE needs participants who have sufficient authority to approve changes. If one group is delayed, SCHEDULE CHICKEN may ensue [Olson98]. A CORNCOB may wreak havoc if placed on a RELEASE COMMITTEE [BrownW98]. Although they focus on the software development process, some of the patterns in Ward Cunningham's EPISODES pattern language could be adapted for use by a release committee. For example, TECHNICAL MEMO could be used to document the committee's decisions [Cunningham96].

Criterion 2: Architecture users have a high level of confidence in the timing and content of architecture releases

 Shortcut

 Drop Pass

When no overriding rhythm is set for an organization, particularly a large one, executives set the pace by reacting to internal or external forces by imposing panic deadlines on their staff. These panic actions are rarely coordinated with one another and create dysfunctional rhythms that wreak havoc on the timing and content of architecture releases, in the same way that a mixer with three beaters running in one bowl would quickly drain a bowl and splatter a room. If architecture users do not trust the timing and content of architecture releases, then the users may not plan to adopt new architecture releases, or they may choose another architecture altogether. Therefore, a lack of user confidence in the timing and content of architecture releases is a warning sign that a good rhythm has not been established.

Antipattern: SHORTCUT

General Form. You are the leader of an architecture team that has established a good rhythm. There are regular builds and releases. However, it is becoming difficult to maintain your tempo, schedules have slipped, and you are now facing intense pressure to get back on track. In an attempt to sustain the tempo, you have decided to skip a number of process steps (see Figure 4.10). Peer reviews might be omitted, or a late change might be introduced without going through the entire configuration management process. While the immediate tempo is retained by the move, it sows the seeds for later disruption. Defects that might have been detected in the skipped steps can surface later when they will be more expensive to correct.

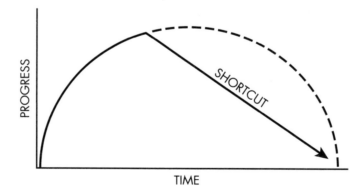

Figure 4.10 The SHORTCUT antipattern occurs when processes are skipped to maintain tempo.

Forces.   There is often intense schedule pressure in software development, and this is no less true for organizations trying to establish and maintain a rhythm. Customers, stakeholders, and managers can all bring significant pressure to complete a release. When deadlines loom, there is a tendency to make decisions with a short-term benefit in exchange for consequences that are longer-term. The benefits of such decisions are immediately visible, while the consequences are less tangible and may not be immediately apparent. Defects are typically less expensive to correct the sooner in the life-cycle they are detected.

Solution.   The appropriate way for processes to be enforced depends on the culture of the organization. In some organizations, periodic software audits may serve to ensure that the processes are followed. However, in many organizations, audits are not an effective way to change or enforce behavior. The actions of senior management can alter behavior more directly. Are there sufficient resources allocated to perform all the planned steps? Do managers create clear expectations so that processes are followed? Do they inquire if these expectations are met? Management actions can have a dramatic impact on whether the organization takes shortcuts to maintain the appearance of rhythm.

Rationale.   In these days of shorter and shorter product cycles, there is a great deal of pressure to take shortcuts. Ironically, organizations that try to establish a rhythm may be even more susceptible. A good rhythm is composed of tempo, content, and quality, but of these, tempo is by far the most visible. Action is needed to counter-balance the tendency to maintain tempo at the expense of content and quality. In the long run, such sacrifices undermine what makes rhythm valuable in the first place.

Example.   An architecture component developer for a large command and control system had well-established processes for creating and delivering new component releases. The component team was reorganized and received new managers. Just after this management change, the primary customer for the component requested some minor changes. In an attempt to please their customers, the new managers abbreviated the established delivery process, but in doing so several defects were introduced. Rather than pleasing the customer with their responsiveness, a defective component was delivered, followed by a delay as the component team redelivered the component using the established process.

When is This Antipattern a Pattern?   Sometimes it does make sense to trim steps out of a process or tailor a process for a particular situation if it does not add value in that context (Chapter 7, Simplification). SHORTCUT might also make sense if the project is in a do-or-die situation where long-term consequences are not as important because the company might not be around long enough to experience them. Skipping a step that both internal and external stakeholders are expecting should be approached with great caution and validated by a seasoned manager. In these situations, the organization needs enough discipline to record the shortcuts and mitigate the consequences once the immediate crisis has passed.

Variation: REDEFINE THE RULES.   Instead of explicitly skipping a process step, this antipattern sometimes emerges when groups REDEFINE THE RULES. For example, a beat might be defined as completing a major milestone every month, and one of the criteria for completing a milestone is having no outstanding high-impact defects. In this variation of the antipattern, a group redefines critical defects to lower-impact classifications in order to pass the milestone. It appears that the organization has maintained a regular beat but at the price of burying a potentially significant risk. Additional effort and discipline are needed to manage the risk because it has been hidden from the usual processes.

Related Antipatterns and Patterns.   SHORTCUT can result when there is too much emphasis on the timing of DAILY BUILD AND SMOKE TESTS but not enough emphasis on content of the builds or whether they are used [Cabrera99].

Pattern: DROP PASS

Problem Statement.   How do you maintain the tempo of architecture releases when components are delayed?

Context.   The architecture is released in regular intervals; for example, the architecture could have annual major releases and quarterly minor releases. Further, there are a number of independently developed components in the architecture. The release in question involves changes to a number of these components. The enhancements made to delayed components are not among the most essential features of the architecture release. Even though an effort has been made to get a component back on schedule, it appears that it will still be delayed.

Forces.   The developers using the architecture could be adversely affected if the component release date is delayed. If the delay is due to one component, the other component owners might be tempted to try to play SCHEDULE CHICKEN [Olson98]. Not all components are equally important to the developers using the architecture, but all customers may be affected if an architecture release is delayed. Many users of an architecture do not read the release notes in detail and may not see notices about delayed or dropped features. It is very hard for suppliers to fully understand the consequences of a delayed component.

Solution.   When it appears that revisions to a component will not be completed in time, alert stakeholders as soon as you think the feature might not be included and verify that it is not critical. Go ahead with the architecture release without changes to the delayed component. To avoid the problem of users who do not read or see announcements about the change in features, make sure to drop the feature from the preliminary releases, so they experience the changes in alpha or beta, and not in the production release. Incorporate the changes to that component in a later release of the architecture.

Result.   The tempo of the release is maintained. Activities planned after the release of the architecture can proceed as scheduled. The practice may also motivate component owners to finish their revisions on schedule. Developer trust grows because the architecture release occurs when promised. The developer also has more confidence that the next release will occur as planned.

Consequences.   The release will have less functionality than if the release was held up for the component. Developers with plans to use the new features in the delayed component will need to make alternate plans. If customers do not trust the architecture provider, the announcement of a DROP PASS may prompt them to find an alternate provider. Unless other stakeholders are involved in the decision to drop a feature, problems could surface. For example, the product could fail tests because the test cases were not updated to reflect the change, or marketing could provide incorrect information to customers.

Rationale.   Like a hockey player using a drop pass to give the puck to a teammate following from behind, this pattern moves a revised component to a following release. The pattern calls for an explicit tradeoff between the tempo and content of a release. Because there are many activities tied to the release of an architecture, delaying the release of the entire architecture could disrupt many organizations.

The pattern only works if the delayed component is not essential for the new architecture to be valuable to the developers who plan to use it. If the delayed component is critical, it may make more sense to delay the release instead. The onus is on the dependent parties here. They are the ones who can best judge the impact of postponing a component. The consumers have the obligation to push back on the suppliers if a component will be delayed too long.

Example.   Microsoft uses a common product architecture so that new features can be written once and shared across products. They also release their applications over a number of time-paced intervals. They can drop pass low-priority features to the next planned release to make sure that critical features are included in the current release [Eisenhardt98].

Related Patterns and Antipatterns.   A RELEASE COMMITTEE can be used to help mitigate the consequences of DROP PASS by ensuring that all the stakeholders are in agreement and aware of the changes. Many of the patterns from Linda Rising's Customer Interaction Patterns can be used to communicate the impact of a DROP PASS with customers [Rising99].

Criterion 3: Explicit activities are coordinated via rhythm

Broken Loads

Synchronize Releases

Software architectures have stakeholders in many different organizations. A shared architecture rhythm helps these autonomous groups to work together across organizational boundaries because it helps establish shared assumptions about when and how key events will occur. For example, if a product developer knows that there is a major architecture release annually and quarterly maintenance releases, the developer could time product releases to follow the expected architecture releases and take advantage of new architecture features.

Rhythm also coordinates activities across different groups in a firm. A daily or weekly build can coordinate activities across a development group. A human resources apartment can coordinate hiring to acquire developers early in a release cycle.

When rhythm is not a coordinating presence among stakeholders, decisions and transitions become more cumbersome. Human resources could hire staff the development group is not prepared to integrate into its team. Additional effort must be spent when rhythm is lacking to coordinate activities and to recover from transitions that occur at inopportune times. Developers might get slowed down because a shared component does not integrate cleanly.

Antipattern: BROKEN LOADS

   Alias: BROKEN BUILDS

   General Form.   You are the leader of a team that has established regular builds. However, even though the code is checked in, compiled, and tested regularly, it does not always do so cleanly. Broken compiles or failed test cases are not considered to be a big deal. The team may believe it will be possible to straighten out the inconsistencies later in the process, or perhaps the team is using an advanced configuration management system to continue working and still keep track of the code versions in conflict. However, when it comes time to get a release out the door, it takes much longer to get all the pieces to work together than was anticipated.

   Forces.   There are many benefits from regular builds; however, they require significant effort to implement, especially for very large applications. In large systems it may not be feasible to rerun all test cases after each build, and managing test case dependencies can be especially challenging. If a build breaks, it may be tempting to put off resolving the defect if there is other more interesting work to do. If the build breaks, the software is in an unknown state, and so larger problems may remain hidden. An advanced configuration management system can give the developers a false sense of security to manage multiple codebases when a build breaks. Such a system could allow developers to continue programming without stopping for the build to be repaired and without addressing the causes of the broken load.

Solution. Establish a commitment to regular builds. Management must clearly communicate to the developers that the regular builds are expected to be successful. The builds should include not only compiling the product, but also some form of automated testing. The process for regular builds may also be modified to prevent new work from moving forward until a broken build is corrected. Similarly, failed test cases that had been previously successful should be addressed immediately. Some organizations use social pressure on developers who break a load; that is, developers who break a load may be required to wear a proverbial dunce cap. Caution—this particular strategy has the potential to be counterproductive, depending on the culture of the organization.

Rationale. Builds must be used to be valuable. If they are not used as baselines, and if they are not used to keep the system in a known state, then they cannot help the organization maintain a rhythm. While a regular build process does introduce a regular tempo, if the build is always breaking, then the benefit of this tempo and the content delivered by the build is lost (see Figure 4.11). An effective regular build process can promote communication among developers and other stakeholders. For example, in organizations with such a build process, there is more cooperation among developers to ensure that their code works together so they can avoid breaking a load. When builds start breaking, it is a sign that this informal coordination among the component owners has deteriorated as well.

Figure 4.11
BROKEN LOADS are a sign that
RHYTHM is breaking down.

Example.   A group at a telecommunications firm had a process of completing weekly builds, but managers had not placed a priority on maintaining this schedule. When a build was not successful, development on new features continued as a "managed exception." An internal review identified this as a problem, and corrective action was taken. An engineer submitted new code that caused the build to break. The engineer had failed to coordinate the changes in his component with the other component owners before submitting the change. The engineer received a call in the middle of the night and received a visit from a vice-president first thing the next morning. The expectation was communicated to the entire team that both the schedule and the quality of the weekly builds needed to be maintained. After this new emphasis on rhythm was established, the team improved its ability to deliver on schedule.

The need to address Broken Loads is often balanced with the need to move forward. At one leading software firm, when a build breaks, a series of hot bugs are entered and dispatched to developers as quickly as possible. The developer must drop everything to fix the bug, and a fix is typically expected within minutes, or hours at worst. Many daily builds will generate no significant bugs, while others may generate five or ten (for a product with several million lines of code). The build lab waits for fixes to come in and then iterates the build. At a certain point in the day they will abandon the current day's build and start preparing for the next.

When is This Antipattern a Pattern?   Builds may occasionally break, and this may not be a big deal. But when this becomes a recurring event, then it is a problem that must to be resolved.

Variation: Continuous Builds.   Some groups have taken regular builds a step further by using Continuous Builds. Every time code is checked in, it must pass through an automated system which forces a complete rebuild and "sniff test" of all affected code before the check-in is committed. Teams that use continuous builds will have a daily build available for the developers as well.

This approach is similar to that of eXtreme Programming. In XP, no code goes more than a couple of hours without integration. When code is integrated, the latest release is used, and it is expected to pass all of the test cases [Beck00].

Related Antipatterns and Patterns.   This antipattern is an example of Daily Build and Smoke Test gone awry [Cabrera99].

Builds must be used to be valuable. Rhythm synchronizes content; content delivers value.

Pattern: SYNCHRONIZE RELEASES

Problem Statement.   How can you accelerate the release of products built on your architecture?

Context.   There have been a number of regular releases of your architecture, and there are a number of trusted developers who use the architecture to create products that add value to it. These developers are partners who receive early access to releases of the architecture so that they can provide feedback and accelerate development of their own products. The planned features for the release have already been determined.

Forces.   Increasingly, companies are partnering with other vendors to provide complete solutions for their customers. This means that when a new or revised architecture comes to market, other complementary products are also needed for the architecture to be successful. It takes time for these complementary products to come to market. Customers may hold off on adopting an architecture release or upgrade until these complementary products become available. If the complementary products are available more quickly, then architecture adoption can be accelerated.

Solution.   Work with your partners to determine the order in which the features of the architecture should be delivered for them to develop products using the architecture. To the extent possible, include these features in the early access releases of the architecture. If there are changes to the architecture that require substantial changes in complementary products, then these changes should be visible in the first preliminary releases. Communicate with the partners about when to expect which features. In exchange for adjusting the early releases in this manner, establish agreements with partners to quickly bring to market their products that include or require your architecture.

Result.   When this pattern is successfully applied, there is little or no delay between the release of the architecture and the release of value-added components built on the architecture. With more components available that work with the architecture, architecture adoption will be quicker and more widespread.

Consequences.   Not all developers will have the same needs, and so it may not be possible to coordinate the features incorporated in the releases in a way that satisfies everyone. The optimal release plan for the architecture team may differ from the optimal release plan for the partners. Some firms may be accused of "playing favorites" if they give early access to some firms but not others. Some partners may not be interested in making the commitment associated with synchronizing their releases; they may wish to wait until the architecture has gained market acceptance.

Rationale.   Synchronizing releases accelerates the availability of complementary products because the needs of the partners are incorporated into the release plans and communicated back to the partners. The tempo and content of the architecture releases can be coordinated with that of the partners using the architecture. Partners are better able to prioritize their own development processes. Because the needs of the partners are met, they can bring complementary products to market more quickly.

Example.   An operating systems development group noticed that it would usually take several months after the release of a new version of the operating system before compatible products and tools from third parties reached the market. The group partnered with the third-party developers to find out which features were needed for the early developer releases of the operating system. By allocating features across the developer releases in this fashion, the third-party developers were able to get more work done more quickly. Once the practice was adopted, new releases of the operating system were simultaneous with the release of compatible third-party products.

There are also examples of this pattern in other industries. A large household goods manufacturer adjusted the timing of its product launches to synchronize with the shelf-planning cycles of large retailers such as Wal-Mart and Target. The practice increased the shelf space for the manufacturer's products, and it helped the retailers stock the newest products [Eisenhardt98].

Related Patterns and Antipatterns.   Many of the patterns from Linda Rising's Customer Interaction Patterns can be used to work with partners to establish SYNCHRONIZED RELEASES. IT'S A RELATIONSHIP, NOT A SALE is particularly relevant [Rising99].

SUMMARY

Rhythm coordinates the activities of the architecture stakeholders, and it helps spur progress of the architecture team. There are three elements to rhythm—tempo, content, and quality. Tempo is the frequency with which the same type of handoff occurs between groups. Content is the delivery of value from one group to another. Quality is the set of activities needed to develop and maintain an architecture without deficiencies. When these three elements are present, an organization has a good rhythm.

Rhythm is important for architecture-based development because so many different organizations are involved in the development and use of an architecture. It is not possible to manage all of these groups from the top down, so rhythm is needed to coordinate these autonomous groups.

Rhythm has other benefits. First, it enables the architecture stakeholders to focus on transitions. Transitions are critical for success, but they frequently do not receive the attention they warrant. Rhythm also enables the architecture stakeholders to create an urgency that drives progress forward.

While there are many practices that support rhythm, such as regular builds popularized by Microsoft, there are a number of pitfalls. This chapter explored some of these pitfalls and described solutions to some of the problems encountered by organizations seeking to establish and maintain a rhythm.

OTHER APPLICABLE PATTERNS AND ANTIPATTERNS

There are other patterns that can be used to put the principle of Rhythm into practice, as well as antipatterns to avoid along the way. Table 4.2 lists organizational patterns and antipatterns cataloged in the 2000 edition of *The Patterns Almanac* [Rising00]. Table 4.3 lists antipatterns from *Antipatterns: Refactoring Software, Architectures, and Projects in Crisis* [BrownW98].

TABLE 4.2   *Organizational Patterns and Antipatterns That Can Shape Rhythm [Rising00]*

BACKLOG [Beedle99]	PHASING IT IN [Coplien95]
CASUAL DUTY [Olson98]	PRODUCTION POTENTIAL [Taylor99]
COMPLETION HEADROOM [Cunningham96]	PROGRAMMING EPISODE [Cunningham96]
COUPLING DECREASES LATENCY [Coplien95]	PULSE [Taylor99]
DECOUPLE STAGES [Coplien95]	SACRIFICE ONE PERSON [Cockburn98]
DELIVERABLES TO GO [Taylor99]	SCHEDULE CHICKEN [Olson98]
DIVIDE AND CONQUER [Coplien95]	SCRUM MEETINGS [Beedle99]
DON'T INTERRUPT AN INTERRUPT [Coplien95]	SOMEONE ALWAYS MAKES PROGRESS [Cockburn98]
EARLY AND REGULAR DELIVERY [Cockburn98]	SPRINT [Beedle99]
EFFECTIVE HANDOVER [Taylor99]	TAKE NO SMALL SLIPS [Coplien95]
GET INVOLVED EARLY [DeLano98]	TAKE TIME [DeLano98]
GOLD RUSH [Cockburn98]	TEAM PER TASK [Cockburn98]
HUB, SPOKE, AND RIM [Coplien95]	TIME TO TEST [DeLano98]

TABLE 4.2   *(Continued)*

INTERRUPTS UNJAM BLOCKING [Coplien95]	WORK GROUP [Cunningham96]
KEEP IT WORKING [Foote99]	WORK QUEUE [Cunningham96]
LONG POLE IN THE TENT [Olson98]	WORK QUEUE REPORT [Cunningham96]
MICROCOSM [Cockburn98]	WORK SPLIT [Cunningham96]
NAMED STABLE BASES [Coplien95]	

TABLE 4.3   *Antipatterns That Can Derail Rhythm [BrownW98]*

ARCHITECTURE BY IMPLICATION

FEAR OF SUCCESS

FIRE DRILL

IRRATIONAL MANAGEMENT

PROJECT MISMANAGEMENT

SMOKE AND MIRRORS

THE GRAND OLD DUKE OF YORK

THROW IT OVER THE WALL

WALKING THROUGH A MINEFIELD

WARM BODIES

ANTICIPATION: PREDICTING, VALIDATING, AND ADAPTING

Events never arrive as we fear they will, nor as we hope they will.
—*Comtesse Diane,* Les Glanes de la Vie *(1898) [Maggio96]*

OVERVIEW

Investments in software product line architecture are often justified by their long-term payoff [Jacobson97]. Since a software product line architecture is shared across more than one system or product, or family of products, it can reduce the complexity and cost of developing and maintaining not only code, but also documentation, training material, and product literature [Dikel97a]. To achieve these payoffs, the organization must make sure that the core architecture continues to serve the needs of multiple products, including those that have not been envisioned when the architecture is designed.

The need for anticipation does not stop when a product line architecture is introduced. As the products evolve and as new product teams adopt the architecture, critical, often conflicting, requirements will arise that must be filled very quickly. The better the architecture team is at anticipation, the more time and information it will have to consider how to address seemingly conflicting requirements, and the more likely it will be to fill these requirements without breaking the architecture or maintaining multiple versions.

This required longevity has several implications. Assumptions found true when the architecture was initially devised may no longer be valid years later even though the architecture is still in use. Because of this, the organization must be able to anticipate and evolve the architecture. The architecture must be able to adapt to new technologies, standards, markets, organizational structures, and competitors. The principle of anticipation addresses how an organization identifies architectural requirements that meet these challenges and validates whether customers want and need these features.

While getting predictions right is certainly important to anticipation, it is not the whole story. Figures 5.1 and 5.2 serve as a metaphor to illustrate this point. It is unlikely that the architects who designed the grain silos predicted

Figure 5.1
These grain silos in Akron, Ohio were built in 1932 [Brand94]. Source: Bruce S. Ford, City of Akron.

Figure 5.2
In 1980 the building was adapted to become a hotel [Brand94]. Source: Bruce S. Ford, City of Akron.

they would become a hotel a half-century later. Anticipation also requires adapting to change. In the case of these silos, the economy and real estate of Akron, Ohio changed dramatically. As the pictures illustrate, the architecture was adapted from grain silo to hotel to address these changes.

ANTICIPATION DEFINITION

Anticipation is the extent to which those who build and implement the architecture predict, validate, and adapt the architecture to changing technology, competition, and customer needs.

Prediction

The software architect can't always predict the future. However, since a successful architecture lives long into the future, the architect at least needs to make reasonable guesses about what will happen. The architect must consider how the architecture's customers could change, how the competitive landscape may shift, and what the operating environment will be like in the future. The architecture must also be able to adapt to new organizations, particularly in fields such as banking, where mergers and takeovers are a fact of life. Many plans are constructed on assumptions about what the future holds, but prediction means that these assumptions are explicitly stated as part of the architecture description. For example, the assumptions might include a future where speed of processors continues to follow Moore's Law, doubling every 18 months for the next 10 years [Moore65]. Of course, unless the architect has been imbued with supernatural powers of premonition, these predictions may not always be correct, which brings us to validation.

Validation

Validation is not limited to traditional software engineering testing and inspection techniques, but includes the testing of the assumptions that underlie the architecture. For example, do the customers actually want what is planned, and can the available technology do what the customers want? The reason that it is important to analyze these assumptions is that architects and their sponsors make many difficult decisions about the architecture, and very expensive mistakes may result unless assumptions are identified and checked before the architecture is fielded.

Adaptation

The long-term success of the software architecture depends on its adaptability to changes in the assumptions and the information gathered through prediction and validation. Adaptation is the adjustment of the architecture plans and the architecture itself to incorporate new features, compete in new markets, or survive in new environments. As such, adaptation requires organizational agility. These adjustments can include not just the architecture itself, but the plans, and even the overall architecture vision. Introducing a new architect may also result in significant change.

Anticipation in Action

Even Microsoft is not perfect at predicting the future, but through validation and adaptation they have used their many software architectures to maintain a strong market presence. In the early 1990s, the Internet was not a priority for Microsoft because they did not expect pervasive interactivity to interest people until secure high-bandwidth connections were available. By 1995, when they recognized that this prediction was incorrect, Internet usage had reached critical mass even though access speeds were still slow and encryption use remained limited. Microsoft changed course, and now virtually all of Microsoft's activities are focused in one way or the other on the Internet [Gates96]. Microsoft made their initial prediction but recognized that their assumptions about their customers and the operating environment were no longer valid. Rather than continue on their initial trajectory, they adapted their many product line architectures and plans to focus on the Internet.

Pulling Architectures in Many Directions

Anticipating the future can be difficult for the designer of any single product. Customer needs, tastes, competitors, and operating environments are all subject to rapid change. However, a product line architecture supports not just one, but many different applications, and each application may have different requirements, constraints, and futures. Some of the hardest decisions an architect must make come when different products or user communities pull the architecture in different, even opposite directions (see Figure 5.3).

Even if there is a standard Application Program Interface (API) for an architecture component, users can still pull it in many different directions. An API often suggests, but does not dictate a particular implementation, and it is important for component owners to make good choices to shape the evolution of the component over time. Consider the example of providers of components that implement the Java Servlet API. The Servlet API is specified by Sun Microsystems, but even with a common API there is room for providers to differentiate themselves. There are over 35 implementations of the Servlet

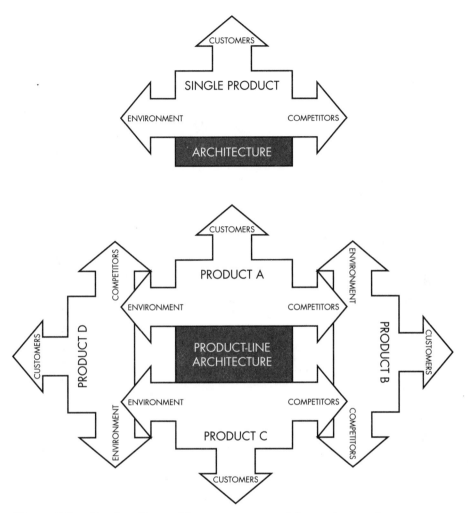

Figure 5.3 Product line architectures must anticipate changes from more sources than single-product architectures.

API. Some of these implementations are incorporated as part of application servers (e.g., BEA Weblogic Application Server or IBM Websphere Application Server). Other implementations are engines that are added to other Web servers. Allaire's JRun or Unify eWave's ServetExec are examples of this approach. There are open source implementations such as Apache's Tomcat and Jserv [Javasoft00].

Among the decisions these providers can make are which operating systems should be supported, what kind of encryption technology should be provided, and what kind of scalability is needed. So even though the products all support the Servlet API, they differ in terms of quality and unspecified features. Customers of these products have built a myriad of applications using these components, and these customer groups and their customers have different interests and priorities. For example, some may be more interested in ease of use; for others, tight integration with other products is key. Each possible direction requires hard choices about priorities. Even the decisions one vendor makes could influence the decisions of other vendors as they jockey for competitive advantage in the marketplace. How these providers manage these competing interests will determine their long-term success.

The Architecture Customers and Their Customers

Architects guide the direction of the architecture to satisfy many of these competing interests. They usually consider the concerns of the architecture's customers, but they often fail to understand the customers' concerns about the products built with the architecture (see Figure 5.4). For example, a company is considering adopting a risky new technology as part of their architecture. It is not surprising that the developers who are using the architecture are very interested in using this new approach. Developers are often leading-edge adopters of all sorts of technology. However, the customers of their products may have a very different tolerance for new technology. They have different concerns and constraints than the developers, and while the developers may be all for using the new technology, these customers may not. This notion is discussed more fully in BLEEDING EDGE and PILOT, but here the important point is that successful anticipation requires validation from both the architecture customers and their customers.

Aiming Too Far Into the Future

Another issue confronting architects is how far into the future they should plan. Difficulties arise at either end of the spectrum. If the architect is focused too far into the future, the architecture may be ahead of its time when completed. Similarly, when competing stakeholders or even architects cannot settle on issues, the planned architecture could expand to try to accommodate all possibilities. The available technology may not be sufficiently mature to implement the architecture adequately, or the market may not be vibrant enough to support its products. These architectures may take so long to implement that they may be obsolete by the time they are fielded because of changes in the environment. The architecture could also provide features that customers may not be ready to use. Settling on an achievable goal and scope is often the only solution.

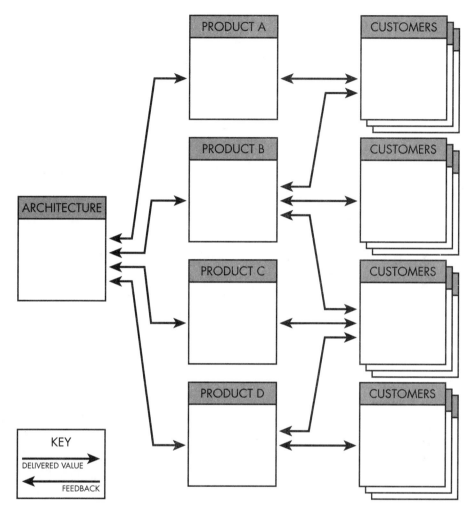

Figure 5.4   The architecture, the architecture customers, and their customers.

The Reuse Library Interoperability Group[1] (RIG), for example, was developing standards to enable software reuse libraries to exchange information about their collections. Early in the group's activities, two approaches emerged, a Universal Data Model (UDM) and the Basic Interoperability Data Model (BIDM). The UDM was a robust data model that could describe a variety of information that any two libraries would want to exchange about their collections, such as

---

[1] The Reuse Library Interoperability Group has been reconstituted as the Reuse Steering Committee, a standards working group of the IEEE.

security, intellectual property, and certification. The BIDM, on the other hand, sought to define the minimal essential information needed for two libraries to share their collections. The development of the UDM became bogged down whenever it was extended beyond the minimal information needed for an exchange. While there appeared to be some agreement on the basics of the model, moving beyond these basics opened a Pandora's box of issues, and the RIG found it difficult to achieve closure. Completing the UDM would have delayed its use by libraries that were already operational and in need of a standard.

When it became clear that it would take a very long time to complete the UDM, if it could ever be finished at all, work on the UDM was dropped. The BIDM, on the other hand, focused on the problems at hand, and proved to be much more successful. It was adopted as an IEEE standard and incorporated in a number of commercial products. The BIDM also served as the basis for the classification schemes of a number of large reuse libraries. Some of the features from the UDM were later incorporated as standard extensions to the BIDM [BIDM95]. The UDM was too focused on the future, and was not as successful.

The BIDM provided a solution to the immediate problems confronting reuse libraries, and it provided a framework by which additional concerns could be addressed through extensions. Two extensions built on the BIDM. The first provided Asset Certification Framework for defining the asset certification techniques of a reuse library [BIDM96]. The second describes an Intellectual Property Rights Framework for reuse library interoperability [BIDM99].

Aiming Too Close to the Present

However, architects can also get into trouble by not aiming far enough into the future. If architects are too focused on the immediate requirements of the current products they are supporting, they may miss the next big shift in the market. If the architecture can only satisfy the needs of a pilot project or two, the architect could become just a designer of a single product.

Quick cycles balance current and future requirements.

In the early 1990s, a product team was faced with a mission to deploy a suite of development tools on two separate platforms before competitors could gain a foothold. In response to these short-term challenges, they decided to split into two separate groups. Each group worked furiously and separately, even though both products shared a number of features. No sooner had the teams fielded their products than additional hardware platforms emerged as critical targets, each with more than one operating system. The team leader realized that his approach for supporting multiple platforms would not scale to support these new platforms. Not only did supporting many platforms in this manner prove too expensive, it started taking too long to field each release. It was only when the group built a common set of components to support the product line that they were able to reduce their costs and delivery time to acceptable levels [Wilson96].

Balancing the Needs of Today and the Future

So how can an organization incorporate new technologies into its architecture while still meeting the needs of its customers? The answer in part lies in building the architecture through quick cycles of development. These allow the architect to evaluate the performance of new technologies, and they allow customers to provide useful feedback on how well the architecture can be used to satisfy them. The practice also allows for more frequent, yet less painful (since they are smaller), corrections. This can prevent architectural drift and will keep the architecture in line with reality and with the current state of long-term trends.

Openness to customer feedback allows course corrections to be made when some of the decisions and assumptions that went into the architecture prove wrong. For example, when Apple acquired NeXT and announced plans to release Rhapsody, a new operating system based on the NeXT OS, many longtime Macintosh developers balked. While the announced plans would make it easy for existing NeXT applications to run on the new operating system, Macintosh applications would need major revisions to take advantage of the new operating system features such as protected memory and preemptive multitasking [Sherman97]. Key developers such as Adobe expressed their reservations about the strategy [Macweek97]. In response to this feedback, Apple announced a new strategy at the 1998 Apple Worldwide Developers Conference. Their new operating system strategy, Mac OS X, would be built around an API called Carbon. The new API closely matched the existing Macintosh API. The features that were changed were interfaces that could have caused the most difficulties supporting the new operating system. The new strategy required developers to do much less work to get their applications to run on Mac OS X and take advantage of the operating system's new features [Crabb98]. By responding quickly, Apple was able to test assumptions, such as developers' willingness to rewrite their existing applications, while there was still time to take corrective action. With stronger development support for the new strategy, Apple greatly improved their chance for success.

Quick cycles of testing and adapting are a common strategy for ensuring a balance of current and future requirements. But they do not guarantee success unless something can be learned from each cycle. A group was developing a new architecture using CORBA for an existing product line. The group applied an evolutionary development methodology that incorporated multiple cycles of development, testing, and integration. Despite this incremental approach, the project encountered performance problems and fell behind schedule. At the heart of the schedule and performance problems was an assumption, the architecture's use of CORBA, which was not tested or verified during the development cycles. For quick cycles to be effective at anticipating and reacting to the future, they must be focused on testing assumptions and revealing information. The organization must also be prepared to act on information revealed by the testing.

Striking a Balance

Even with these quick cycles, the architecture cannot be both completely flexible and also perfectly fit to all the applications that it supports. As Gerald Weinsberg was pointed out twenty-five years ago in *The Psychology of Computer Programming*, the better adapted a computer program is to its environment, the less adaptable it is to new environments [Weinberg98]. Within the world of open source, this tradeoff looks a little different. The Apache Web server is optimized to operate in an environment in which users are very knowledgeable and willing to reconfigure and recompile as needed. However, there are also distributors of Apache that target specific platforms, or operating systems. Their customers trade flexibility for ease of use. Through quick cycles of development that include prediction, validation, and adaptation, architects can strike a balance between delivering today's products while anticipating the needs of tomorrow's future.

PUTTING ANTICIPATION INTO PRACTICE: CRITERIA, ANTIPATTERNS, AND PATTERNS

The previous examples demonstrate that the principle of anticipation is both important and challenging. The consequences of failing to adapt to today's fast-changing markets can be severe, but finding the right balance between focusing on the present and the future is difficult.

CRITERIA

The following criteria, antipatterns, and patterns provide guidelines with which organizations can determine how well they anticipate, validate, and adapt their architecture for a long and productive future. When anticipation is working,

1. Architecture capability is regularly enhanced to respond to

    *   Anticipated risks and requirements of architecture customers and their customers,
    *   Market-driving standards and evolving technology, and
    *   Changes in strategic business directions.

2. Technical and business risks and opportunities are evaluated through quick cycles of review and development.

3. Features, budgets, plans, or schedules are adapted when it is recognized that critical estimates or assumptions are incorrect.

ANTIPATTERNS

MISSING PIECE describes the "Oh Shoot!" experience of finding that an obvious feature has been left out. Everyone has been so enmeshed in the release's powerful new features, they have overlooked capabilities that users cannot do without.

BLEEDING EDGE illustrates what can happen when architects get their users to buy into an immature technology without considering their users' customers.

TUNNEL VISION portrays what happens when plans for architecture development and implementation do not change as evidence mounts showing that their underlying assumptions and estimates are completely off the mark.

PATTERNS

PILOT builds on a proven technology transition technique to introduce and get the kinks out of a new architecture. The pattern illustrates how to select an initial product or application.

ARCHITECTURE REVIEW outlines how to organize and execute a focused, expert assessment of a developing architecture designed to uncover high-impact problems and opportunities, such as assumption conflicts, and existing solutions that could be reused.

OUTSOURCE illustrates how to adapt when your customers demand new standards or technologies that are not part of your current or planned core capabilities. OUTSOURCE provides guidance on when and how to select an existing third-party component, or partner with a supplier whose best interests are served by building a solution you can use.

The following sections provide a brief discussion of each criterion and then present a pattern and an antipattern, each examining the criterion from a different perspective. Table 5.1 illustrates how these sections are organized.

TABLE 5.1   *Mapping Criteria to Antipatterns and Patterns*

CRITERION— HOW YOU MEASURE	ANTIPATTERN— WHAT NOT TO DO	PATTERN— WHAT YOU CAN DO
1. Architecture capability is regularly enhanced to respond to • Anticipated risks and requirements of architecture customers and their customers, • Market-driving standards and evolving technology, and • Changes in strategic business directions.	MISSING PIECE	PILOT
2. Technical and business risks and opportunities are evaluated through quick cycles of review and development.	BLEEDING EDGE	ARCHITECTURE REVIEW
3. Features, budgets, plans, or schedules are adapted when it is recognized that critical estimates or assumptions are incorrect.	TUNNEL VISION	OUTSOURCE

Missing Piece

Pilot

Criterion 1: Architecture capability is regularly enhanced to respond to anticipated risks and requirements of architecture customers and their customers, market-driving standards and evolving technology, and changes in strategic business directions

Getting the architecture right is a critical first step. But once the step is complete, it is not quite time to pack up and go home. In creating your architecture, you (hopefully) documented and tested assumptions, of which there were many. As applications and products use the architecture, it will become clear how comprehensive and consistent with reality these assumptions are. Even if your technical predictions are absolutely right on, customers may decide they want your products to be compliant with an emerging standard or compatible with a product. Your company's business direction may change, or it may get acquired and product strategies may be realigned. If your assumptions, predictions, and design were all nailed, your users' products may take off in unexpected and incompatible directions. Unless the architecture is a total failure, your work is probably just beginning.

If you and your architecture team are shifted to a new project (see LOAN SHARK in this chapter) as soon as the architecture design is built, the architecture may not survive, at least as a shared entity. Continuing action is necessary. This criterion describes a set of activities and skills that indicate your organization has a long-term, focused, and significant effort in place and whether it is having an effect. This effort incorporates the results of ongoing risk and opportunity analysis and results in incremental changes to the architecture.

"Understanding your customer's customer is a mark of an industry leader."

—Robert Charette

Architecture Users and Their Customers. Robert Charette, a leading expert in software risk, suggested we test to see whether organizations consider the requirements and risks of their users' customers. "Understanding your customer's customer is a mark of an industry leader," he said.

Whether you like it or not, your users will probably tell you what they want now and in the future. If you listen carefully, you can also learn about their most daunting risks. If you ask questions, you can learn about their customer's requirements and risks. Learning about your users' customers can provide context for making sense of users' requests and even help you better anticipate your customers' future needs. You can, of course, learn about users and customers in other ways such as reading, attending conferences, and listening to the sales and marketing staff.

Antipattern: MISSING PIECE

General Form. You are the lead architect overseeing the development of a new architecture. Your architecture team and the developers planning to use the architecture are very excited because of the many powerful new capabilities it offers. In all the excitement about the new feature, the architecture team does not cover the basics well enough. While the architecture provides a lot of power and flexibility for users, it is missing a few key capabilities that users can't do without. As a result of the missing piece, the architecture will not be widely used when it is fielded. Like a fancy sports car that is missing a wheel, the impact of the missing requirements is enough to outweigh the value of any new capabilities (see Figure 5.5). In retrospect the missing pieces are obvious, but by the time they are recognized, architecture adoption may be delayed, or even cancelled. Many people, for instance, avoided or delayed adopting Java because its initial releases lacked features as basic as printing support and the use of more than one mouse button.

Forces. There is never enough time or enough resources to implement every possible feature, and so hard decisions must be made about what to

Figure 5.5   Even the best products will fail if they are missing just one basic feature needed by customers to get value from the product.

include and what not to include. Different architecture users may have very different needs that must be satisfied for the architecture to be useful to them, and there may not be agreement even within the user community on the essential features. An architecture that satisfies all of the minimum requirements of just one user community may deliver more value to users than an architecture that only partially satisfies many different user communities. Unless the architect has a good understanding of the architecture's users and their users, the architect may not correctly identify the key features, or even the key communities.

If the architecture is replacing legacy applications, it must offer improvements, while not leaving out anything important from the legacy system's features. Since every application includes features that were never used, imposing these "ghost requirements" on a new architecture can add time and cost to the process with little corresponding value. However, legacy applications are often poorly documented. As a result, it can be very difficult and expensive to determine which sections of code can be removed without serious unintended consequences. Architects and developers may give more attention to new features and technologies than to ensuring that critical existing functionality is preserved.

Solution.   Identify the key user communities and work with them to identify their most critical needs. Often this means the involvement of a subject matter expert who has detailed knowledge of these user communities. Ask, "What products are going to be built on the architecture?" and "Which products are most important?" While ideally this should be done before the architecture is fielded, this approach can also be used to guide changes in the direction of the architecture. While coverage is important, executives also need to be aware of the process so they do not inadvertently undermine delivery of these basic features when pushing for other high profile features and technology.

Rationale.   This antipattern results when architecture users are not given a whole solution [Moore91]. While the architects and developers may want to concentrate on new or flashy features, discipline helps ensure nothing falls through the cracks. If there are gaps in the architecture, some of these early adopters may try to fill in the gaps with their own components. However, mainstream users are not usually willing to patch these holes in the architecture. Inertia may cause them to continue to use their legacy software, or they might seek to adopt a different architecture altogether. For this reason it is crucial for the architect to identify key users and make sure the architecture meets their minimum requirements.

Example.   A Fortune 500 firm with a large information systems investment was replacing a number of legacy applications. They built the new systems by replicating the old system's functionality and adding a few new features. While they usually had pretty good coverage of the essential features from the legacy systems, on more than one occasion, there would be a few features from the legacy system that were left out. As a result, the client would have to support both the new and the legacy systems, causing an expensive maintenance nightmare.

The organization adopted a more rigorous approach for replacing the legacy systems that brought in a subject matter expert to help them understand the business purposes and processes of the components to be replaced, and to analyze the emerging processes and applications. They developed plans to ensure the right features were in the architecture, and to ensure a clean transition. After they adopted this new approach to upgrade a legacy system, the old system went away and they achieved the performance improvements and cost reductions they expected.

When is This Antipattern a Pattern?   While it is never a good idea to fail to deliver essential requirements, it is generally a good idea to deliver requirements incrementally. This means that initial releases will have pieces missing. They will not have the same level of performance and functionality as later releases. The architect should seek to have the features in each release that enable the architecture customers to make progress for that iteration. In particular, early releases should have enough capability for them to be useful to users [Cooper94] (see SYNCHRONIZE RELEASES in Chapter 4—Rhythm). The very first releases might include high-risk features: (1) to prove that they can be done before too much time and effort is invested; and (2) to get some real-world experience with them in the controlled environment of an early release. First releases might also include only features that require the greatest change on the part of the user. Regardless of how features are partitioned, the minimum essential features need to be in place by the time the architecture is operational.

Variation: MISSING SIDE PIECE.   The architecture team inadvertently leaves out part of the solution that is no less important to the customer but is outside of the core architecture.

Related Antipatterns and Patterns.   PILOT can be used to verify that the architecture meets the needs of the initial users. KNOW THY STAKEHOLDERS (Chapter 6—Partnering) helps an architect identify their key user communities and their interests. ARCHITECTURE REVIEW ensures that early architecture decisions don't miss gaps that would later be obvious. SYNCHRONIZE RELEASES (Chapter 4—Rhythm) aligns the presence and timing of release features with customer needs.

Pattern: PILOT

Problem Statement.   How do you determine which product should introduce a new architecture (see Figure 5.6)?

Context.   You are an executive who is planning to sponsor the development of a new product line architecture. The organizations that are going to build products using the architecture are not within your organization, and some of them are even in a different company.

Forces.   PILOT projects are a way of introducing a new technology while minimizing disruption to the organization [Delano97]. A pilot provides an architect the opportunity to identify and correct problems in the new architecture. Users are more likely to adopt a technology if they can see other users in similar circumstances. However, if users see others in similar circumstances

Figure 5.6   Choosing the right pilot project to lead the way for your architecture adopters can be a critical success factor.

having a bad experience with a new technology, they may be wary of adopting it. If the project is too trivial, it could be dismissed by other candidate users. If it is too challenging, other candidate users might be scared off. If the pilot and the architecture team work too closely together, others might perceive the architecture as only suitable for the pilot project [Kane97].

Solution.   Select a project to initially implement the architecture. The project should be sufficiently challenging so as not to be dismissed as a toy by other potential adopters or by naysayers. The project should have customers who are eager to adopt new technology and willing to accept potential inconveniences to gain access to it. While the architects should be prepared to provide some additional assistance to the pilot project, the architects should be careful not to do the developers' job for them. Depending on the number and variety of architecture users, it may make sense to have a few pilot projects.

Result.   When the pilot is fielded, the architect will gain valuable feedback on the architecture based on actual use. Defects will be identified and resolved before the architecture has received widespread fielding. This also means that the repair of defects is likely to be less constrained by backward compatibility issues. The successful pilot can be referenced when bringing other projects on board.

Consequences.   It is possible for the architects to receive a false sense of security from the pilot. While a good pilot project can tolerate inconveniences in exchange for early access to technology, subsequent projects may not be as forgiving [Moore91] [Norman98]. Waiting to introduce an architecture into a single product before introducing it to other products may delay widespread fielding of the architecture.

Rationale.   Even architectures that are optimally simple are still complex artifacts, and they operate in organizational environments that are challenging and dynamic. It makes sense then that a new architecture should be tested in operational conditions. Actual use builds confidence on the part of a potential adopter of the architecture. It also provides an opportunity for a company to experiment with new technologies without risking everything.

Example.   In the early 1990s, a company had a software product line that commanded a majority market share, but the company predicted that future customer requirements would demand more than the current products could deliver. They decided to build a new CORBA-based architecture to meet the expected challenge. The architecture was piloted on one of the smaller market segments of the product line, with the expectation that it would be migrated to the other segments over time.

The pilot project did not go as well as hoped. The available implementations of CORBA were slow and not as interoperable as planned. Customer needs proved to be different than anticipated. The experiences of the pilot project caused the other projects to resist adopting the new architecture. The organization decided to stop the CORBA initiative and take a new, less technologically aggressive approach to upgrade the product line. In this situation, a market leader was able to take a risk to push the envelope of new technology, while protecting its customer base. If the organization had forced conversion of the entire product line to CORBA, it probably would have had eroded customer support.

Related Antipatterns and Patterns.   MAINTAIN PLATFORM IDENTITY describes how to avoid the perception that the architecture is only appropriate for the PILOT [Kane97]. Olson's TRIAL PROJECT describes a similar practice, but from the perspective of building a team's skills [Olson98].

Criterion 2: Technical and business risks and opportunities are evaluated through a quick cycle of review and development

Bleeding
Edge

Architecture
Review

Prototyping features or components that pose the most technical risk are well-known risk management practices. These practices are much harder to do when a customer or manager demands that you show "progress." High-risk components take longer to get right, and experimenting with them may call attention to the fact that schedules and/or budgets are unrealistic. Similarly, you can save a lot of time, money, and embarrassment by testing assumptions about the need for and qualities of an expensive new feature before investing a lot of effort. If you don't evaluate high-risk items early on, they can quickly become hard-wired into the project plan.

Antipattern: BLEEDING EDGE

Alias: RUNNING ON EMPTY

General Form.   At your sponsors' request you employ a new technology in building the next generation of an architecture. You, the chief architect, your sponsors, and your team are very excited about the capabilities of the technology. Everyone hopes to use it to get an edge on your closest competitors. The product developers are equally excited to work with the new architecture. The developers encounter some rough spots but are able to work around these difficulties. While some difficulties were expected with the product users since the technology was new, the number of unhappy product customers surprises everyone. Rather than customers who are satisfied with new features, they are disappointed about poor performance and assorted bugs. You expect that future technology releases will address these issues, but concerns remain about whether customers will wait that long. You and your team have persuaded developers to buy into new architecture technology, only to discover that the product customers are not as enthusiastic.

Forces.   There are many pressures on architects to adopt new technology. New technologies often promise ways to elegantly resolve seemingly conflicting requirements. This is particularly enticing for an architect who wants to satisfy as many of the users' requirements as possible. Product developers are also eager to work with these new technologies. Marketing and media attention build "mindshare" for their use. Organizations are interested in developing new technology capabilities to keep pace with the competition and enter new markets. More often than not, though, new architecture technologies are much harder to implement than they seem. When they are first implemented, they are inevitably much slower than they need to be to satisfy product users. It often takes several releases for all of the anticipated benefits to be realized.

Users are often not as eager to adopt new technologies as the architects and developers. While some customers insist on a particular new technology, many do not care about the underlying technology; they just want something that helps them meet their objectives. Others who have been hurt badly by a prior shift or upgrade react strongly and viscerally to promises about immature technologies. Architects who see the product developers as their primary customers may not recognize the reluctance of these product customers to put up with some of the inconveniences of new technologies.

Solution.   There is a time and a place for new architecture technologies. Take care in choosing the right places to introduce them. When they are introduced, provide extra support for initial adopters. In choosing a new architecture solution, you must be willing to make the ragged ends fit into a real solution. You cannot assume that an unproven architecture solution will do everything promised. You should test solutions in the specific contexts of both the developers and the product users. Even then, you must provide extensive support for users adopting the new technology, be careful to set their expectations appropriately, and be on the look-out for signs they are having problems.

Of course, making an appropriate technology selection in the first place can make a big difference. You can make a better choice if you have an understanding of not just the developers, but the product users as well. Unfortunately, a poor choice is often not recognized until it is too late. When the problem is recognized, a realistic appraisal of the new technology is needed. If the technology matures quickly enough, it may be worthwhile to stick it out. If the technology is not maturing quickly enough, it may make sense to try a new approach. In any case, if you are going to go with a new technology, you may need to provide extra support, recognition, and encouragement to customers who pioneer its use.

Rationale.   Picking the right places for introducing architecture technology has a big payoff for all parties involved—the architect, sponsors, developers, and product customers. The problem is that developers are much more likely to agree to new technology than most product customers. For architects and sponsors, it means avoiding building a product-line architecture product customers do not want to adopt. For developers, it means that they are less likely to have to construct kluges from the architecture to create products with performance that will satisfy their users. For product customers, it means avoiding the challenges of adopting brand new technology in situations where the payoff does not warrant the effort. Both users and customers who have been hurt badly by a prior shift or upgrade will welcome this caution. In the short run, avoiding this antipattern may disappoint some, especially ardent advocates of a particular technology. However, in the long run, avoiding this antipattern helps direct the energies of these advocates to the product lines and customers most suited for new technological approaches.

Example.   In early 1996, as part of Apple's development of OpenDoc, their software subsidiary Claris announced that their next release of ClarisWorks would support OpenDoc [Swartz96]. At the time of the announcement they had already shipped four major releases of this nimble product, which was popular with home and educational users. ClarisWorks was one of the first announced products to support OpenDoc, and it would have changed the basic architecture of the program from a traditional desktop application to an OpenDoc container that could incorporate components from other vendors [Crotty96].

An OpenDoc version of ClarisWorks was never shipped, and in March 1997 the OpenDoc project at Apple was cancelled by Apple CEO Gil Amelio [Beale97]. As columnist David Pogue pointed out, "it [OpenDoc] was actually dead long before [this announcement]… OpenDoc's own extensions took up a lot of RAM, and OpenDoc-based programs weren't exactly a model of stability" [Pogue97]. It is questionable whether a RAM-intensive, OpenDoc-based version of ClarisWorks would have gone over well with users accustomed to a lightweight tool that ran on even relatively old computers.

While the success of Java and CORBA have demonstrated that there is a market for portable component technologies, the question in this story is whether a product targeted at mainstream users is the appropriate place to introduce this new architecture. There is a time and a place to introduce new architecture technologies, but these opportunities must be aligned not only with the developers who will build on the architecture, but with the risks and needs of their customers as well.

When is This Antipattern a Pattern? There may be customers for the architecture who are willing to make the tradeoffs associated with new technology. Typically, these early adopters are trying to gain a competitive advantage by introducing a new paradigm [Moore91]. Product lines in new market segments without an installed customer base often fall into this category. In these situations, leading-edge technology may be appropriate for the architecture if the risks are well understood and accepted by both the architects and their customers.

Related Antipatterns and Patterns. Home-grown architecture components can lead architects into a similar briar patch. A planned architecture may call for a particularly complex component with which the organization has little experience building. ANTIGRAVITY MODULE (Chapter 3—Vision) describes this situation in more detail, and PILOT discusses some of the perils of piloting new technology in a software product-line architecture. ARCHITECTURE REVIEW should help organizations avoid BLEEDING EDGE, as should any of the solutions in the Partnering chapter (Chapter 6).

Pattern: ARCHITECTURE REVIEW *[Wilson96][Bass98]*

Problem Statement. How does an executive or business unit manager ensure that early architecture decisions are correct?

Context. You are creating a shared architecture or an application that is going to make use of such an architecture. The project's requirements have been initially defined.

Forces. Architecture mistakes can be especially costly to repair, but if defects are caught early in the process, they are less expensive to fix. A solid software architecture is critical to the success of the project, but skilled software architects are rare. Organizations look for ways to make their architects make the biggest impact, and architecture reviews are seen as a way to do that. Communication between the suppliers and the customers of the architecture is also essential to making the right decisions. People may use the review to advance a personal or organizational agenda and wreak havoc. The customer's perspective can reveal gaps that are not obvious to developers.

Solution. Create an architectural review board to examine the architecture at key points in the development cycle. The first review should take place once the requirements have been initially baselined. The review board should include experienced architects, members of the architecture team, and possibly customers. The review team should not be too large—seven or eight people at most. In early reviews check assumptions, look to see if there are off-the-shelf solutions, and perform other sanity checks. Later reviews should validate assumptions and verify that the architecture can meet its requirements. Facilitate these reviews to ensure focus.

Result.   The primary benefit of this pattern is cost avoidance, because the reviews are able to identify defects earlier in the process, so corrections can be made. Reviews may also identify components that can take the place of new development activity. The reviews also increase customer confidence that the architecture will deliver promised capability, thereby increasing architecture usage.

Consequences.   The pattern requires a commitment from the organization to devote appropriate resources for the reviews to be credible. If the architecture suppliers or customers send junior representatives, or if qualified architects are not involved, then the reviews will not be effective. Care should also be taken to ensure that architectural reviews do not displace other reviews.

Rationale.   Many leading organizations have recognized the value of reviews to identify defects and improve software quality [Gilb93]. Architecture reviews are useful for many of the same reasons that other review processes and inspections have been shown to be effective. Traditional software inspections find defects earlier in the life cycle when they are less expensive to repair [Gilb93]. Similarly, the architecture review board is involved early in the life cycle, so if corrections are required, they are typically less expensive to implement. The review board also provides a forum for architecture customers and suppliers to communicate their expectations and needs.

Example.   There have been several published accounts of AT&T's use of architecture review boards across a wide variety of projects over more than a decade. AT&T collected data from over 120 projects that had applied this practice. They estimated that they invested about 70 staff days per project, but saved 1.5 staff years per project. In one case, after two years of development, a first release project entered system testing. When system testing determined that the performance was not at the projected level, the project team sought counsel from the Architecture Review Board. Within the first hour of the presentations to the review team, a "back of the envelope" calculation indicated that the project was expecting a level of performance an order of magnitude greater than any existing hardware could provide. It became clear that two years of effort on a large development project and significant delays in delivering the desired results could have been saved if the architecture review had been performed before the project went into full-scale development. The Software Engineering Institute has also documented architecture review practices at AT&T as well as Rational [Wilson96] [Bass98].

Related Antipatterns and Patterns. There is a substantial amount of literature written about different kinds of inspection review processes, although most have not been described as patterns [Gilb93].

Criterion 3: Features, budgets, plans, or schedules are adapted when it is recognized that critical estimates or assumptions are incorrect

Tunnel
Vision

Outsource

Recognizing when estimates or assumptions are incorrect doesn't help much if the knowledge doesn't result in action. Architectures should play a critical role in supporting one or more systems. If architectures are successful, users depend on releases and other services from the architecture team. Yet, it is not always easy for users to get clear information about the timing and content of these releases. Those who are on the line to deliver do not always get relief when new information about the reliability or complexity of a critical component surfaces.

Adjusting feature sets, budgets, plans, or schedules is not always easy for an architecture team, but the alternative is generally much worse. Alerting sponsors to problems may cost managers a good deal of embarrassment or result in cancellation. Alerting customers may cause them to seek another architecture from a supplier who is better prepared or better at optimistic speech. We have found, however, that a high degree of transparency works to the advantage of both architecture supplier and user. Failure to take action can have much more severe consequences. Users who don't read the tea leaves will be unpleasantly surprised shortly before the scheduled release date. If they are still in business, users will probably find an alternate supplier the next time. The architecture team is likely to lose its best people, and burn out many others. Core capability and tacit knowledge about the architecture may be lost, further delaying the delivery date.

Antipattern: TUNNEL VISION

Aliases: BLINDERS, TRAIN TRACKS

General Form. You are the manager in charge of launching a group of products. You and your product managers have agreed to sponsor a common architecture and have incorporated the architecture into your plans. You have made commitments to customers based on the planned releases and have

It may have been clear that the schedule was blatantly unrealistic from day one.

shared this urgency on several occasions. As work progresses, there are signs that the initial assumptions were not correct. It may even have been clear to some team members that the schedule was blatantly unrealistic from day one. Despite the evidence that the estimates and assumptions are off the mark, neither the architecture team nor the product team reports problems or show signs that they are changing their course (see Figure 5.7).

If this antipattern has been in place for any length of time, the architecture is never taken seriously. Developers assume they will have to make do while inventing ways to show compliance to the new architecture. If the antipattern has not been in place long, what was once perceived to be a viable solution by users loses credibility quickly. People in the organization may start differentiating between the stated schedule and the real schedule.

Forces.   Changes in direction may be perceived as threatening by the advocates of the initial concept. In highly stratified organizations, when engineers tell the truth, they are often sent back to study the problem or told that management would never accept their message. Engineers may not be given enough time to prepare a sound case for changing the direction, and their analysis is subsequently attacked because their case is not sound. This may enable the manager to bully an agreement out of engineers. Everyone becoming reluctant to change because they are more comfortable with the "devil they know."

No single person or organization is able to completely anticipate the future, yet product budgets sometimes assume that once the architecture is complete, the architects can move to a different project. As time goes on, more information becomes available with which you can make decisions about the architecture. However, the more time and money you invest in an architecture, the more diffi-

Figure 5.7
Architectures stuck in TUNNEL VISION do not deviate from their planned course.

cult it can be to make a decision to change direction. This is especially true if the organizational culture discourages employees from making waves.

Solutions.   The solution involves two parts. First, identify the assumptions underlying the architecture and actively seek to test those assumptions. ARCHITECTURE REVIEWS and PILOTS are opportunities to seek this kind of information.

Secondly, once an incorrect assumption or estimate is identified, you should be prepared to act on that information. This could mean adjusting a project's schedule or features or invoking a contingency plan, as well as alerting customers and renegotiating schedule and/or release content. You should also be watchful of organizational cultures that stifle the flow of information and initiative and hide evidence of incorrect assumptions. SCHEDULE CHICKEN is a symptom [Olson98]. In any case, you should make sure that sufficient resources are budgeted so that there is schedule and staff allocated when inevitable surprises occur.

Rationale.   This antipattern results when organizations stop adjusting the direction of the architecture, or even stop funding its evolution once the initial plan and requirements are established. Like a train running on a long set of tracks, the architecture development proceeds along the path that was initially set. Software engineers and managers schooled against the dangers of feature creep may interpret suggestions to change direction as an attempt to change the scope of the architecture. Similarly, senior managers may see the engineers as out of touch with the business reality of the architecture, and therefore, they do not give sufficient weight to their objections to direction, technical feasibility, or schedule. Since managers and architects often have a stake in the selected direction, changes in direction may also be perceived as threatening. Organizations can improve the chances of long-term success by supporting efforts to test and monitor development against initial assumptions, revaluating, and adapting the architecture when appropriate.

Example.   A telecommunications supplier was upgrading a product in an existing product line. The product called for major improvements in capability and required new development of programmable chips, circuit boards, and embedded software. A very short time was allotted to construct the plan and schedule. A customer for the product had already been promised a delivery date, which was invariant for the scheduling activity. Managers deduced that since the original product was on one board and the new product would also be on one board, the level of effort for developing the hardware and embedded software would be about the same as the original product. However, the new product was more complex than had been initially estimated—it was at least an

*Morale was
abysmal.*
order of magnitude more complex and implementing the solution required state-of-the-art chip technology. Since the initial estimates were prepared so quickly, and because the delivery date was invariant, there was no opportunity to test the assumptions. Not surprisingly, morale was abysmal. The project was very late and everyone was working a lot of overtime. The project's pain rippled throughout the organization because the project shared components with other products in the product line. When the product was finally delivered, it was substantially late, which made customers very unhappy.

When is This Antipattern a Pattern.   True visionaries may see how the market is going to evolve before measurable evidence is available to validate the vision. The visionary may offer evidence that is tangible but which conventional wisdom would lead one to ignore. Upon closer inspection, this evidence may have strong merit. The visionary may identify show-stopping performance bottlenecks that current technology will run into that his or her solution can be demonstrated to address. If sponsors understand and are willing to assume the risk, it may be necessary to stay the course for cutting-edge work.

Related Antipatterns and Patterns.   You can encounter the opposite problem as well. TREND SURFER (see Chapter 3, Vision) describes organizations that are too quick to change course.

Pattern: OUTSOURCE

Problem Statement.   How do you adapt when new standards or technologies emerge that are needed by your customers but are not part of your current or planned core capabilities?

Context.   You are a business unit manager whose organization already has an architecture that has proven to be effective and adaptable. To remain competitive, you need to add a set of capabilities to your architecture that do not fit well with your organization's current or planned core capabilities. Your organization is evaluating whether to build the component itself or acquire a component from a third party.

Forces.   If the organization has a strong focus, it can really excel in its targeted areas. If the organization relies on others for key components, there is less control over these components than if they were supplied in house. If organizations trust each other, they are more likely to have a successful outsourcing relationship than if there is not trust between them [Sabherwal99]. If there are other customers for a component, then it may be less expensive to have the component provided by a third party.

Solution.   Select a third-party component, if such a component is available. If there is no such component, then the organization should seek a partner to develop and support the component. Determine whether the potential partner sees the component you need in their main line of business: for example, whether they can sell it to lots of other customers and assess the amount of unique development the partner will need to deliver and support the component. Assess the potential partner as a supplier and as a business partner considering both capability and trustworthiness. As a rule of thumb, the more unique development they must do on your behalf, the higher the level of trust that is required. Similarly, the lower the trust, the greater your schedule and financial risk. If you find a high level of trust in the potential supplier, outsource the component development.

Result.   The component is the product of another supplier. Both organizations can focus on their core technology and expertise. The product can be delivered sooner than if you hired or developed the needed experience. Component users should experience higher quality and lower costs than if the component were built by a team internal to your organization.

Consequences.   There is a tradeoff for outsourcing a component. The users of the component now have less control than if the component were maintained internally. In addition, both the component user and supplier need to devote resources to maintaining the relationship so that the component continues to meet the needs of the user. There is a risk that the component supplier could change business focus, drop the product, or make a decision that breaks compatibility with your architecture. If you do not have a solid architecture in the first place you may not be able to effectively incorporate a third-party component. Even if you do have a solid architecture, there may not be a good fit if there is a conflict of assumptions between the component and the architecture.

Rationale.   At the heart of this pattern is the notion that organizations should focus their efforts on their core competencies. When the idea of core competencies was introduced, it did not explicitly address software [Prahalad90]. Other authors have extended the idea to focus on how to select the software and processes in which to invest [Grady97]. There are never enough resources to implement all of the desired capabilities in the architecture. The architect's organization has to choose the best places to invest development resources, but that might not be enough for the architecture's customers or their customers. To field a complete solution then, the architecture may need to incorporate components from external suppliers.

Example.   Allaire had built a strong following for its ColdFusion Web development framework. However, in order to enter new markets, the architecture needed to be enhanced to support high-volume, fault-tolerant Web sites. Allaire decided to incorporate a third party's load balancing software so that customers could deploy clusters of ColdFusion servers to support these demands. Allaire was able to incorporate the load balancing technology with higher quality and lower cost than if they had attempted to build it themselves [Allaire99]. However, incorporating the component was not without its consequences. A feature for managing Web-client state that was introduced in a previous version of ColdFusion was incompatible with the load balancing software.[2]

SUMMARY

The need for anticipation does not stop when a product-line architecture is rolled out, no matter how effective the design. If designed and rolled out with good results, product teams will depend on the shared architecture. The more successful an architecture team is in supporting its users, the greater the number and criticality of the demands placed upon it. The better the architecture team is at anticipation, the more time and information it will have to consider how to address seemingly conflicting requirements in a simple and elegant way. The team will be more likely to fill these requirements without breaking the architecture or maintaining multiple versions.

This chapter described several activities that work together to improve an architecture team's anticipation. Regularly seeking information about the future requirements and risks of users, as well as their users' customers, reduces the chances of being blind-sided by panic requirements. Tracking new standards and technologies improves the ability to respond to customers and management and identifies opportunities for innovative solutions. Monitoring the organization's priorities and business directions can help the team better decide which core capabilities to build and which to outsource.

Teams can reduce the chance of wasting significant resources and precious time by testing technical and business assumptions upon which large investments are planned by utilizing quick cycles of review and development. The team realizes the value of these information-gathering and risk-assessment activities by adapting promised feature sets, budgets, plans, or schedules when change is warranted.

---

[2] Allaire subsequently acquired the firm that supplied the load-balancing technology.

Other Applicable Patterns and Antipatterns

There are other patterns that can be used to put the principle of Anticipation into practice, as well as antipatterns to avoid along the way. Table 5.2 lists organizational patterns and antipatterns cataloged in the 2000 edition of *The Patterns Almanac* [Rising00]. Table 5.3 lists antipatterns from *Antipatterns: Refactoring Software, Architectures, and Projects in Crisis* [BrownW98].

TABLE 5.2   *Organizational Patterns and Antipatterns That Can Shape Anticipation [Rising00]*

Application Design is Bounded by Test Design [Coplien95]	Managing and Meeting Customer Expectations [Whitenack95]
Architect Controls Product [Coplien95]	Market Walk-Through [Cunningham96]
Backlog [Beedle99]	Microcosm [Cockburn98]
Clear the Fog [Cockburn98]	Organization Follows Market [Coplien95]
Comparable Work [Cunningham96]	Product Initiative [Cunningham96]
Completion Headroom [Cunningham96]	Prototype [Cockburn98]
Coupling Decreases Latency [Coplien95]	Prototype [Coplien95]
Creator-Reviewer [Weir98]	Prototypes [Whitenack95]
Design by Team [Harrison96]	Recommitment Meeting [Cunningham96]
Designers are Our Friends [DeLano98]	Requirement Walk-Through [Cunningham96]
Developing in Pairs [Coplien95]	Review the Architecture [Coplien95]
Domain Expertise in Roles [Coplien95]	Scrum Meetings [Beedle99]
Early and Regular Delivery [Cockburn98]	Show Personal Integrity [Rising99]
Engage QA [Coplien95]	Take Your Licks [Rising99]
Envisioning [Whitenack95]	Time to Test [DeLano98]
Get Involved Early [DeLano98]	Trial Project [Olson98]
Gold Rush [Cockburn98]	Validation by Teams [Harrison96]
Group Validation [Coplien95]	Work Flows Inward [Coplien95]
Implied Requirements [Cuningham96]	Work Queue [Cunningham96]
It's a Relationship, Not a Sale [Rising99]	Work Split [Cunningham96]

TABLE 5.3   *Antipatterns That Can Derail Anticipation [BrownW98]*

ANALYSIS PARALYSIS

ARCHITECTURE BY IMPLICATION

CONTINUOUS OBSOLESCENCE

DEAD END

DEATH BY PLANNING

DESIGN BY COMMITTEE

FEAR OF SUCCESS

GOLDEN HAMMER

IRRATIONAL MANAGEMENT

STOVEPIPE SYSTEM

VENDOR LOCK-IN

WOLF TICKET

PARTNERING: BUILDING COOPERATIVE ORGANIZATIONS

Doveryai no proveryai
— *Russian proverb, meaning "trust, but verify" [Eigon93]*

OVERVIEW

Architecture can allow organizations and the groups within them to spend more time doing what they do best, while acquiring the rest [Prahalad90]. That's the theory. However, without serious, sober, and regular attention to both formal and informal relationships the "abstraction called reality," as one colleague puts it, often gets in the way. Partnering provides a frame of reference for managing cooperative relationships, in architecture-based development.

Cooperative Relationships

For many reasons, the mastery of cooperative relationships is a critical factor in the success of software architecture.

▶ *There is a diverse network of organizations and roles that must interact.* Many partners, who are critical to delivering the value of an architecture, cannot be directly controlled by the architect or his line of management.

Often sponsors, architects, and application developers belong to different organizations.

▶ *Many key customers demand features that call for immature products and standards.* It seems like each Internet application stretches the edge of technology even further than the last. This requires application builders to combine a number of tools that are themselves maturing in new ways.

▶ *The number of layers in an application is growing.* The move to Internet applications is just one example of a shift from monolithic applications within a single department to layered applications. As such, applications are moving from 1 Tier (Mainframe) and 2 Tier (Client–Server) to "N" Tier (Distributed). It is often hard to measure the number of layers in Internet applications. They often use an off-the-shelf database, a remote certificate server, an application development platform such as ColdFusion or Java, third-party components, and Web browsers. It is not uncommon for one Web application to draw on several other Internet data sources. This shift increases the urgency for both suppliers and users to negotiate and maintain effective partnerships.

▶ *Current technology drives and enables partnering.* Technology is expanding in so many directions that no one organization can "do it all." Technology now supports building a solution that takes advantage of what each partner does best. The Web provides an example of this, but it is just the leading ripple of a large wave. Banner ads provide an example of how technology drives and encourages partnering. It is pretty easy to put up a Web site and then use a "banner partner" to take care of the dirty details of finding advertisers, keeping track of page views and clicks, sending out bills, and so forth. XML technologies and content syndication enable tighter, more demanding, and more interesting forms of partnering.

PARTNERING DEFINITION

Partnering is the extent to which architecture stakeholders maintain clear, cooperative roles and maximize the value they deliver and receive.

The competencies associated with partnering are keenly relevant to an organization seeking to gain advantage from software architecture. In the context of software architecture, partnering describes the process of managing relationships among those who are critical to the software architecture's success—the stakeholders. When partnering is done well, stakeholders both contribute and receive a high value in exchange for their participation. The goal is to deliver a defined set of products and services of the highest possible value.

Architecture Stakeholders

The Software Engineering Institute defines an [architecture] stakeholder as "people and organizations [that] are interested in the construction of a software system" [Bass98]. The definition is significant because it focuses attention on the stakeholder's point of view and requires the architect to present multiple views of the architecture consistent with each stakeholder's interest.

However, people and organizations are not automatically interested in architecture, even if they ought to be. In most cases, the person or organization whose role it is to bring the system into existence determines who *should* have an interest and shows them how and why they should be interested.

This is a subtle distinction, but it is critical to anyone whose career depends upon the success of an architecture. An architect or architecture team must understand whose interest and participation is essential, what they must do, and what it will take to get their sustained participation and commitment. Without this information, "satisfying stakeholders' requirements" can be like catching an anchor.

For our purposes, an architecture stakeholder is a person or organization whose actions and ongoing trust are essential to establishing and sustaining the value of an architecture over time. We realize that architectures don't succeed on their own. Stakeholders generally include sponsors, application developers, and application customers. There may be other critical participants such as technology suppliers. The pattern KNOW THY STAKEHOLDERS describes an approach for identifying and prioritizing these stakeholders.

Consider the case of Allaire's ColdFusion architecture for building Internet applications. Figure 6.1 illustrates the participants necessary for ColdFusion to be successful. The firm's founders, the venture capital firms, and later the stockholders provide the capital to develop the architecture. Application developers use ColdFusion to build Web applications. The publishers provide books that help applications developers learn how to use ColdFusion. If any of these participants are dissatisfied and decide to not cooperate the architecture could unravel. For example, if managers of information system departments don't support the architecture, it would be much more difficult for ColdFusion to receive widespread adoption in larger organizations.

Figure 6.1   Allaire's ColdFusion stakeholders include a broad range of participants.

The roles of the various stakeholders may change as the architecture moves through its life cycle, from when the architecture vision is being established and initially realized, to the time when the architecture is fielded and supports multiple applications. In fact, even the composition of the stakeholders may differ at varying stages of the life cycle. When Allaire's ColdFusion was still in its early releases, the stakeholders were primarily developers choosing tools for their own use. Now that ColdFusion is used for business-critical applications, the stakeholder community is weighted less toward grassroots developers and more towards enterprise development.

Clear, Cooperative Roles

The stakeholders need to cooperate to make the architecture successful. Cooperation does not mean that the stakeholders will always be in agreement but that there is a shared set of expectations. When architects and component suppliers realize they don't have a common understanding of what features will be in the architecture, there must be an agreed-upon mechanism to resolve

There should be a clear communication of rewards and penalties for achieving or missing expectations.

the conflict. As part of this shared expectation there should be a clear communication of rewards and penalties for achieving or missing those expectations. The goal is to avoid surprises and provide stakeholders with at least the minimal, essential features as promised, while ensuring that future changes do not preclude them from using the architecture.

Maximizing Value

Successful partnering for architecture owners requires more than just meeting the terms of contracts and keeping promises. Partners must take action to identify and deliver the expected value—a solution to the problem for the agreed-upon terms. For example, a federal agency hired a company to develop a model of a customer's business processes and information systems as part of an improvement effort. The project included plans for building upgraded and new information systems based on the model. A separate contractor was hired to do the systems development. While the primary purpose of the modeling effort was to support systems development, modelers did not consider the needs of information systems developers. As a result, the model created was not very useful to those developers. While the modeling team met the terms of their contract, they did not deliver the expected value.

INDUSTRIAL ROOTS

The concepts of contracts, network organizations, value chains, and trust provide the foundation for the principle of partnering (see Figure 6.2). These con-

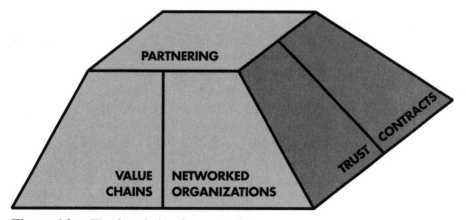

Figure 6.2 The foundation for partnering.

cepts contribute to mastering relationships, but they are neither new nor unique to software. However, these concepts have a direct impact on the development and use of software architecture.

Contract Management

Partnering grew from lessons learned in the world of acquisition. Business use of the term in the 1960s characterized the acquisition of small technology-rich companies and grew to include purchasing, distribution, as well as collaborative marketing and research [Clayton86] [Dowat89] [Cane85] [Kotler86]. According to a 1993 article in *Contract Management Magazine* entitled "Keeping Contracts out of the Courtroom," partnering means "building teamwork and commitment between parties to a contract" [Stasek93]. As the title suggests, without partnering, contracts, and the acquisition regulations governing them contained excruciating detail. Every time a supplier would find a loophole, new detail would be added. This approach left little time for either customers or suppliers to think about what was really needed in the first place. Relationships got so bad on both sides that the only remedy was the courtroom.

Partnering is built around a contract and the cooperative relationships between people and groups on both sides of the contract. Contracts need not be formal. Sometimes they grow out of an unspoken reciprocity and stay in force as long as each partner maintains its side of the exchange.

Networked Organizations

The effective use of software architecture enables organizations to deliver end-user solutions that incorporate components and products from external partners. Complex solutions generally require solution providers to coordinate closely with partners and form organizations to address these complex problems. Unlike a vertically integrated organization that owns all the activities necessary to produce a product, the networked organization contracts out many or most of these activities. According to Jay Galbraith, "a network of independent companies, each one doing what it does best, acts as if it were virtually a single corporation." The network integrator, says Galbraith, "is a firm that coordinates the decisions and actions of the companies that make up the network."[1] The communication and joint decision-making processes used to manage the relationships between companies in the network have many

---

[1] S.A. Mohrman, J.A. Galbraith, E.E. Lawler III, et al., *Tomorrow's Organization: Crafting Winning Capabilities in a Dynamic World,* Copyright © 1998 Jossey-Bass, Inc. Reprinted by permission of Jossey-Bass, Inc., a subsidiary of John Wiley and Sons, Inc.

similarities to the lateral processes that take place between organizational units within the firm [Mohrman98].

Companies seeking to expand their use of software architectures can learn a lot from industry experience with networked organizations. The focus on partnering has grown as companies recognize the competitive advantage of building these virtual or networked organizations. The better the solution provider is at managing customer and supplier relationships, the more competitive its solutions will be. Michael Dell pioneered the use of the networked organization model to manufacture computers. Ten years ago, while frontrunners IBM, HP, and Digital produced disk drives, graphics chips, and circuit boards from scratch, Dell focused on the activities that produced the highest value and purchased the rest. As a result, Dell was able to grow to a $13 billion company in 13 years, exceeding its competitors in PC manufacturing [Magretta98].

The Internet appears to have accelerated the trend toward networked organizations, increasing the importance of both software architecture and partnering. Propelled by the potential benefits of business-to-business electronic commerce, Internet developers have established alliances with other suppliers to provide technologies and services to complement their unique capabilities. Software architecture provides the structure that makes these alliances possible. Partnering enables an increasingly broad spectrum of organizations to share products, resources, information, and software.

Value Chain

Closely linked to the concepts of networked organizations is the concept of value chain. Value chain was first introduced in 1985 by Michael Porter to expose the underpinnings of sustainable competitive advantage. Value chain, according to Porter, is a "framework for thinking strategically about the activities involved in any business and assessing their relative cost and role in differentiation" in the marketplace [Porter98]. This concept is described in more detail in KNOW THY STAKEHOLDER.

There are many different value chains in each industry and in each customer segment within each industry. Successful network integrators are constantly focused on maximizing value through these value chains. For example, Dell cut out the dealer channel to sell directly to customers while providing support that was strong enough to overcome the hold of local dealers [Magretta98].

Many industries have seen changes in their value chains as a result of their use of the Web. The software industry has changed as well. Users now expect information to be accessible and not locked in the back office. As a result, legacy back-office product vendors face the challenge of migrating their applications to the Web. A number of these vendors have partnered with firms offering Web-enabled architectures to meet this challenge, altering their value chains in the process.

Consider the example of a financial back-office software vendor that sought to Web-enable its products. After several expensive false starts with its own developers, the vendor decided to look outside for help. The company chose a partner with experience in moving financial back-office operations to the Web. Together, they developed a DTD (Document Type Declaration), a shared set of semantics, and a strategy for exchanging legacy data using XML. The integrator stored legacy data in a database and used Allaire's ColdFusion to provide Web access to the data. The integrator became a link in the vendor's value chain, as illustrated in Figures 6.3 and 6.4. However, the product vendor had little interest in the implementation technology used by the integrator, although such technology was crucial to the integrator. The integrator's value chain was different from the vendor's, as illustrated in Figure 6.5. For the integrator to remain on the product vendor's value chain, the integrator must continue to deliver on promises and choose wisely for the future. Similarly, for a vendor like Allaire to remain on the integrator's value chain, Allaire must do the same.

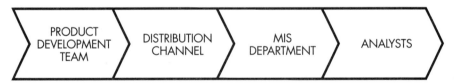

Figure 6.3   The value chain for the financial software vendor.

Figure 6.4   The value chain for the financial software vendor after Web-enabling their products.

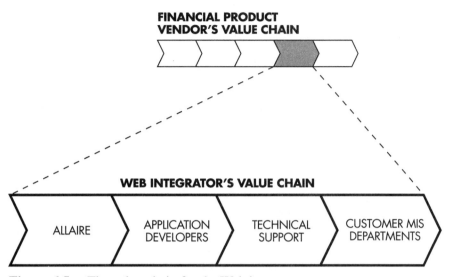

FINANCIAL PRODUCT
VENDOR'S VALUE CHAIN

WEB INTEGRATOR'S VALUE CHAIN

| ALLAIRE | APPLICATION DEVELOPERS | TECHNICAL SUPPORT | CUSTOMER MIS DEPARTMENTS |

Figure 6.5   The value chain for the Web integrator.

The value chain concept and lessons learned through industry provides solid guidance. While the concept dates back to 1985, its use within the world of product engineering is more recent. In the early 1990s, Geoffrey Moore adapted the value chain concept to help engineers design products that were more likely to be acquired, accepted, and used the first time. Working with several leading technology companies, Moore combined value chain with his concept of delivering a "whole product," tailoring both ideas to the customer's position on the technology adoption curve. We developed a prototype game for one of these companies to bring these concepts to life for product engineers and managers through fantasy role-play (see side bar, p. 149).

When it comes to any learning process, trust is one of the most critical ingredients.

—W.S. "Ozzie" Osborne
General Manager IBM Speech Systems [Muoio99]

Trust

One essential lesson to be learned from partnering relationships across both manufacturing and service industries is that trust is key. According to Susan Mohrman, "The integrator that has the trust and confidence of its network members greatly reduces its negotiating costs, as measured in the time and effort of its managers" [Mohrman98].[2] Trust opens the integrator to better information, more flexible contract terms and conditions, and fewer constraining conditions and covenants. When trust erodes, one or both parties pull the contract out of the drawer to figure out how to get the other party to do their part. If the relationship remains in place, the next contract is likely to be more complex.

Just as partnering can greatly simplify contracts, clear, commonly understood contracts lay the groundwork for building productive partnering relationships.

It may sound like the partnering model and contracting model are opposites. They are, in fact, complementary. Just as partnering can greatly simplify contracts, clear, commonly understood contracts lay the groundwork for building productive partnering relationships. Partners who establish relationships without establishing clear understandings about what each partner will do (and what will happen if they don't) put their partnering relationships—and their enterprises—at risk. Smith Wood, a successful Web entrepreneur and founder of seven companies, often quotes Robert Frost's "Good fences make good neighbors." Wood's companies are known for the diligence with which they form contracts and mature partnerships.

Software development requires a variety of people to work together. In the most successful groups, the participants are able to build trusting relationships. That is, the participants believe that those upon whom they depend will meet their expectations [Shaw97]. This said, developers tend to focus on their products rather than their customers. A number of patterns reflect the substantial success achieved by companies that encourage developers to earn and develop loyalty from their internal and external customers, such as IT'S A RELATIONSHIP, NOT A SALE; BUILD TRUST; and ENGAGE CUSTOMERS [Rising99] [Coplien95].

Product line architecture development also requires a variety of people to work together, but such development is more likely to cross organizational boundaries. Typically, trust diminishes as organizational distance increases [Shaw97]. As shown in Figure 6.6, more trust exists among people in the same work group than between people in different business units or different companies. Architects and their sponsors face the challenge of needing to establish trust with other stakeholders even as organizational boundaries create barriers.

Trust is much easier to lose than to gain.

One of the challenges of building trust is that it is much easier to lose than to gain. An incident in which expectations are not met may diminish trust for a long time. Mistrust in organizations using product-line architectures can take several forms. Developers who do not trust that the architecture will

---

[2] S.A. Mohrman, J.A. Galbraith, E.E. Lawler III, et. al, *Tomorrow's Organization: Crafting Winning Capabilities in a Dynamic World,* Copyright © 1998 Jossey-Bass, Inc. Reprinted by permission of Jossey-Bass, Inc., a subsidiary of John Wiley and Sons, Inc.

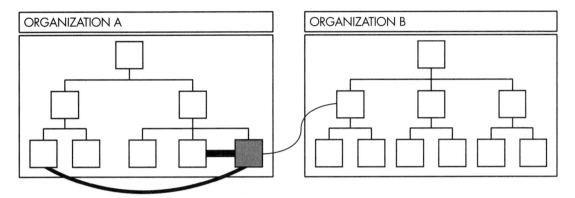

ORGANIZATION A   ORGANIZATION B

Figure 6.6   Trust diminishes as organizational distance increases

deliver planned features as expected may decide not to continue using the shared architecture. If they have access to source code, they may simply CLONE (see Ch. 7, Simplification) a portion of the existing architecture to add the desired feature, rather than wait for the architects to provide that feature. The developers get the feature they need. They may soon find themselves maintaining the entire portion of code they cloned. The architecture team may soon discover that their PHONE DOESN'T RING.

PUTTING PARTNERING INTO PRACTICE: CRITERIA, ANTIPATTERNS, AND PATTERNS

The remaining sections of the chapter are designed to help you understand and apply Partnering. The structure is as follows: First, you will find three criteria that gauge the extent to which the principle is working or not working. Second, for each criterion, you will find an antipattern, which shows how *not* to fulfill the criterion. Third, you will find a pattern that illustrates a solution to the antipattern and provides one way to fulfill the criterion.

CRITERIA

Partnering is simple to grasp, but not so simple to put into practice. This is especially true when many groups must cooperate at the same level within or external to an organization. Both formally defined networks and the informal networks hidden beneath determine the success of a software architecture. The following criteria provide a means for determining how well stakeholders cooperate to maximize the value of both architecture and the products and services built upon it. When partnering is working,

1. The architect continually seeks to understand who the most critical stakeholders are, how they contribute value, and what they want.
2. Clear, compelling agreements exist between stakeholders.
3. Both policies and informal rules of social conduct enforce cooperation.

The following antipatterns and patterns shed light on what actions should be taken to improve the situation. These are summarized below and articulated later in the chapter.

ANTIPATTERNS

PHONE DOESN'T RING shows what happens when the architect hears what his users want but misses the part about what he or she has to do to make it valuable to those users.

LIP SYNCHING shows what happens when an architecture team avoids taking the necessary action to arrive at a clear contract with their high-visibility users. When these users lose interest, discussions often continue. However, the discussions lose substance and generally waste everyone's time.

PERSONAL TIME describes what can happen when an engineer's proposal to modify a component to make it useful to other groups is met with a mixed message: "You can do it, but on your own time."

PATTERNS

KNOW THY STAKEHOLDERS illustrates using value chain to identify, actively listen to, and gain the commitment of key stakeholders.

RECIPROCITY describes behavior that is essential to building relationships strong enough to support the common, successful use of a software architecture.

NO SURPRISES is based on the premise that partners should avoid surprising each other, and the pattern helps build an environment in which partnering can thrive.

PROMOTE THE NETWORK describes an approach to granting promotions based not just on an individual's technical skills and experience but also his or her ability to make effective and ethical use of informal networks. The following sections provide a brief discussion of each criterion and then present an antipattern and a pattern, each examining the criterion from a different perspective. Table 6.1 illustrates how these sections are organized.

TABLE 6.1   *Mapping Criteria to Antipatterns and Patterns*

CRITERION— HOW YOU MEASURE	ANTIPATTERN— WHAT NOT TO DO	PATTERN— WHAT YOU CAN DO
The architect continually seeks to understand who the most critical stakeholders are, how they contribute value, and what they want.	PHONE DOESN'T RING	KNOW THY STAKEHOLDERS
Clear, compelling agreements exist between stakeholders.	LIP-SYNCHING	RECIPROCITY
Both policies and informal rules of social conduct enforce cooperation.	PERSONAL TIME	NO SURPRISES and PROMOTE THE NETWORK

Criterion 1: The architect continually seeks to understand who the most critical stakeholders are, how they contribute value, and what they want

 Phone Doesn't Ring

 Know Thy Stakeholders

The head of an architecture team has just returned from yet another presentation, this one to secure the next few months of overhead funding. Each member of her team has more than a full-time job getting out the first architecture release, a second full-time job preparing for demos, and a third full-time job supporting last year's architecture. Each member of her team began with a strong determination to make the architecture succeed.

Satisfying stakeholder needs is easy to articulate but, as the above story illustrates, much harder to put into practice. Picking a focused set of first customers, finding out what it will take to keep them involved, and delivering these items will improve chances for success.

Antipattern: PHONE DOESN'T RING

General Form.   You head a team that was charged with building a software platform that is envisioned to take over common functions for several existing and new applications. After gaining stakeholder "buy-in," you charged ahead with conviction. In line with several books you had read, you mapped out what the architecture will do for each of the stakeholders and presented and reviewed your findings with them. You used the most advanced modeling tools to present highly detailed, consistent, yet tailored views. However, you haven't yet gotten to the specifics of what it will take to deliver the value your stakeholders require.

Your team is hard at work responding to a ton of comments from the VP of Technology. They have been so busy that no one has noticed that phone calls from the developers who are to build on the architecture are almost non-existent.

If you had not been so busy, you would have expected a constant stream of communication from these developers—questions about usage, requests for additional features, and a complaint or two. Instead, you are up to your ears preparing to brief the CEO. When you finally "come up for air," you find out that the many documents produced by your team are unusable by developers. Each of the product teams you targeted has gone ahead and upgraded their own products, abandoning the clean interface they had agreed to provide. It is too late.

Forces.   It is easier to get users to buy in to a concept, such as using a technology improvement like a common architecture, than it is to secure their long-term involvement. In many companies, managers are encouraged to participate in improvement efforts and often sign up for more than they can sustain. People involved in improvement efforts such as architecture initiatives are often under intense pressure to demonstrate specific evidence of "buy-in." Once demonstrated, incremental funding is secured. However, the architect or team leader is often immediately faced with securing the next increment.

Architects are sometimes brought in from other business units, and it is assumed that they have the same culture, protocols, and processes. Stakeholders may answer detailed questions about what features they would like to see; however, unless the architect asks, he may miss essential details necessary to deliver value to a stakeholder. To get to the next step, a much more serious stakeholder is necessary. If essential details are left out, such as how to build architecture adoption into short-term plans and budgets, even serious stakeholders can be left behind or lose interest.

If the architect communicates the slightest degree of self-importance, the developers may feel that they are supposed to take the architect's pronouncements as gospel.

Sometimes the very word "architect" is to blame for an organization's inability to implement an architecture. The word carries a lot of weight, it implies a lot of authority, and it also implies a degree of finality in the results. If the architect communicates the slightest degree of self-importance, the developers may feel that they are supposed to take the architect's pronouncements as gospel. The most successful architects do not often label themselves as such; instead, they gain power by influence and demonstrated patterns of good judgment.

Solutions.   As with many antipatterns, the hardest part of this antipattern may be recognizing the situation as it is happening. If you find yourself thinking, "We can fill in the details later," make sure you and your team understand at least some specific and compelling examples of how developers will benefit from your platform. If you and your team don't know, take action to find out. KNOW THY STAKEHOLDER provides one approach to learning what it will take to keep a stakeholder engaged in a partnering relationship. Customer Interaction Patterns convey specific, simple, straightforward protocols, attitudes that can help you develop partnering relationships that work. IT'S A RELATIONSHIP, NOT A SALE and KNOW THE CUSTOMER apply directly [Rising99].

The architect can ensure that stakeholders get the value they expect by going through a whole product exercise, as described by Geoffrey Moore [Moore91]. This exercise will cause the architect to identify every element necessary to deliver the expected value. For example, the architect may learn that he needs to provide a database binding or more detailed release schedules.

In addition to methods and techniques, take time to simply listen to the stakeholders, and for heaven's sake, return calls promptly. Then adjust the design to indicate that their input has been respected. This does not always mean that the design must change. You may simply provide a rationale that acknowledges several ways of solving the problem and explains why the solutions suggested by the stakeholder were inappropriate. You may find that your title is part of the problem. An architect must act with humility and avoid words and actions that convey an attitude that says, "I'm the designer; you are merely the users."

When stakeholders are not communicating with the architect, one of several things may have happened. It could be that the architect has done such a good job of capturing and implementing requirements, building easy-to-understand user interfaces and rules, and conveying the architecture vision that no one needs to call. This is very unlikely. It is a lot more likely that stakeholders have lost faith in the architecture. Users have started to make changes to the architecture themselves instead of requesting changes from the architect. Product managers are seriously looking for alternatives [Kane97].

Example.   In a telecommunications firm, a seasoned project manager took over the architecture effort. He knew something was wrong when he observed that the phones weren't ringing. After talking with several managers targeted as adopters, he learned that the architects had not provided enough detail for adopters to incorporate use of the architecture into their short- and long-term plans. The manager conveyed this insight to his surprised architects.

The architects resolved the situation by getting more involved with their customers, articulating a vision of the architecture and showing in some detail how it would fit into developers' designs and plans in both the short and long term. The architects participated in meetings with their customers, often asking, "How can I help?" By doing this, they raised the visibility of the architecture in a nonthreatening way and were able to make the architecture relevant to the stakeholders. After this intervention, the architecture became more tangible as product groups began to account for the architecture in their plans. The architects were able to rebuild a relationship with their customers, who now call a lot more. When customers call to ask for things, the architects are able to help them immediately or at least point to a list of planned features.

When Is This Antipattern a Pattern?   If you have served as an engineer and manager of the organizations your platform is targeted to serve, the likelihood is high you will understand a fair amount about how these organizations really work. In this case, focusing directly on architecture features to the exclusion of questions about value may be more efficient. A word of caution: Your depth of understanding may make you feel impatient with your team. Unless they share your vision, your project is still at risk.

Related Antipatterns and Patterns.   PHONE DOESN'T RING describes how not to KNOW THY STAKEHOLDERS. PHONE DOESN'T RING can also lead to a breakdown in anticipation. As such, it can easily lead to MISSING PIECE (see Chapter 5, Anticipation). IT'S A RELATIONSHIP, NOT A SALE; KNOW THE CUSTOMER; BUILD TRUST; and SHOW PERSONAL INTEGRITY provide guidance on how to keep a meaningful flow of information even when things get hectic [Rising99]. KNOW THY STAKEHOLDERS helps you prioritize among many customer requests.

Pattern: KNOW THY STAKEHOLDERS

Problem Statement.   How do you identify essential partners and learn what it will take to secure their commitment to the architecture?

Context.   An executive charges an architect with incorporating an architecture into a set of new and legacy products. Success depends on influencing component suppliers, users, and other partners who are not under the direct control of the executive.

Understanding and responding to stakeholder concerns can be overwhelming.

Forces.   The task of understanding and responding to stakeholder concerns can be overwhelming and is often done under intense funding and schedule pressure. While common wisdom assumes that stakeholders have an interest in an architecture or the system it supports, not all people and organizations that are essential to architecture success want to be stakeholders. Candidate stakeholders have different perspectives and interests that must be translated into concepts the architect can work with. Some candidates are more important than others, and it is not always obvious which candidates are really essential.

Potential partners from whom commitments are easily gained may not be essential to architecture success. Some potential adopters are clustered around common customer segments, interests, or technologies. Stretching an architecture to address the needs of dissimilar adopters may satisfy no one. Intense schedule or funding pressure can result in targeting adopters that will most easily commit rather than those with the most shared interests (see Figure 6.7). Although it might require more short-term effort, choosing adopters whose needs align with each other will more likely produce greater value for the partners and for the sponsor (see Figure 6.8).

When architects are pressured to demonstrate customer buy-in too quickly, they can choose adopters that don't fit with architecture strengths or with each other, as illustrated in Figure 6.8.

Architects are also under pressure to justify their continued funding. Architecture investments are justified by long-term payoffs and measured by

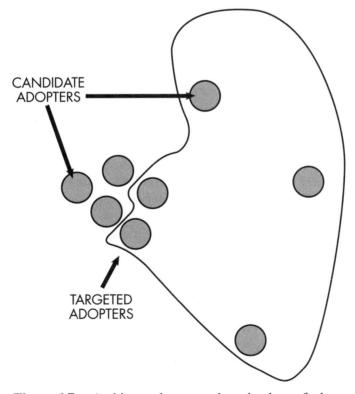

Figure 6.7 Architects choose a sub-optimal set of adopters when pressured to show buy-in.

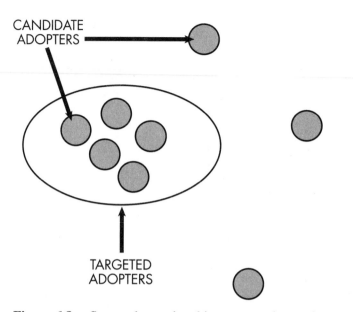

CANDIDATE
ADOPTERS

TARGETED
ADOPTERS

Figure 6.8   Some adopters' architecture needs are clustered.

*Forge and vali-
date each link of
the value chain:
negotiate with
each link; and
establish clear
contracts.*

short-term indicators. Signs such as buy-in from potential adopters may be inaccurate because the commitment needed to show buy-in for the concept is not as expensive as the commitment to actually use the architecture.

To make things worse, stakeholders may be invisible. Engineers are often reluctant to think about people in purchasing or financial roles who are involved in the approval process. Not all stakeholders fit into the standard categories of stakeholders such as marketers, sponsors, suppliers, channels, and customers. For example, standards bodies often influence decision makers.

Solution.   Align the vision of architecture success with the activities that best fit what partners are able and motivated to do. Articulate the envisioned value delivered by the architecture, such as how the architecture helps existing products achieve a consistent user interface or continue market dominance. The architecture might also be envisioned to open a new market for new products. After the vision has been initially articulated, identify the potential partners and how their capabilities and interests align with this vision.

The following questions can aid a systematic analysis of and interaction with potential partners:

▶ Who must be involved over time for the architecture to succeed? There are a number of commonly occurring roles in architecture development and implementation. For the architecture to be successful, someone will:

- Pay for the development
- Build individual components
- Develop products using the architecture
- Recommend their use
- Buy products built on the architecture

▶ Are there less obvious partners that need to be involved? If those who recommend purchase of products in a targeted industry care a lot about standards, a standards organization may be a key link in the value chain.

▶ What will these partners need to do to make the architecture successful?

▶ What will it take to keep them engaged?

Implementation involves fleshing out and validating the value chain, negotiating with each link, and establishing a clear contract with stakeholders. As you go through this exercise, the vision becomes refined and shared among the stakeholders. Base plans and priorities on what has been learned. Use the value chain to guide implementation, remembering that the value chain needs to be maintained as the partners and their interests change over time. (See the sidebar, "Introducing Value Chains to Engineers," for an illustration of how this process can work.)

Result.   Architecture initiative stays connected to those who are most important to its success. The number of stakeholders is reduced. Goals are clearer and easier to track. It is less likely that critical information about architecture value will be lost as it is in PHONE DOESN'T RING and MISSING PIECE (See Chapter 5, Anticipation). Methods and tools to gather and present stakeholder interests can work more effectively.

Consequences.   It takes time to do value chain analysis, and for these exercises to be successful, technical people must be involved. While the concepts of value chain are not hard, they may not be interesting to technical people and may be dismissed as useless. There is always a chance that value chain will not yield the correct result or be misused. This can result in a false confidence that can cause an architect to ignore real stakeholders even when they loudly proclaim their expectations—a very bad result.

Making a first cut at which potential stakeholders to seek and give priority to is one of many steps. You must then test your findings by taking steps to form or strengthen partnering relationships. No matter how important a stakeholder is, the value you can offer must yield a serious commitment and follow-through. If, for example, they do not actively and substantively participate in regular meetings about the architecture, and if you do deem them critical, you may need to rethink your offering.

Rationale.   By narrowing the pool of potential stakeholders, the pattern makes the task of understanding their interests and needs less daunting. Because the value of each potential partner is more clearly understood, the architect is better able to select and satisfy adopters. Because the commitments of the architect and partners are more closely aligned, articulated, and enforced, their commitments are more meaningful. Because the value is more clearly understood, the architect can build a more truthful and compelling case for funding the architecture. This pattern also provides a systematic approach for identifying stakeholders and their needs, making it less likely that an important stakeholder or stakeholder interest will be missed.

Example.   The success of Linux has caused many companies to turn to an open-source model as an approach for software development. Not only are the intellectual property restrictions different for open-source development than for traditional software development, but the value chains are different. Companies that want to turn to open-source must determine what motivates developers to participate in such projects. The Mozilla project, which is developing an open-source version of the Netscape browser, has reportedly had difficulty attracting developers beyond those funded by Netscape [Oakes99]. If this critical link of the value chain is not persuaded to participate, then the promised benefits of open-source development will not be realized.

Apple also ventured into open-source development when the company released MacOSX into open-source. However, when Apple did so, the company drew the ire of advocates in the open-source community [Kahney99a]. Critics such as Bruce Perens, co-founder of The Open Source Initiative, criticized the Apple Public Source License (APSL) because it "allows Apple to terminate our rights to use any or all APSL-covered code, at its sole discretion, in the event of an unproven claim of infringement, no matter how specious" [Perens99]. Apple adjusted its licensing practices to address the concerns of open-source developers and critics [Kahney99b]. Apple has since released several other products into open-source including their QuickTime Server and their OpenPlay network gaming toolkit. They have also attracted over 20,000 developers who have registered to download the source code for these projects [Apple99].

Eric Raymond's seminal essay "The Cathedral and the Bazaar" suggests lessons that can help organizations construct successful value chains for open source development. An open-source project is more likely to attract developers and meaningful revisions if the software can help solve a problem that interests developers, and if it is released into open-source with a good design

[Raymond99]. Frank Hecker's paper, "Setting Up Shop: The Business of Open-Source Software," provides an analysis of the issues involved with successfully constructing open-source value chains. In the paper, Hecker fleshes out the value proposition for businesses considering open source. Hecker presents the tradeoffs involved with various business models detailing a range of open-source strategies for licensing, developing, and marketing. For each business model and strategy, Hecker describes the value each party contributes and the benefits and risks they acquire [Hecker00].

Related Antipatterns and Patterns.   KNOW THY STAKEHOLDER provides the detailed information necessary to implement Jim Coplien's ORGANIZATION FOLLOWS MARKET [Coplien95].

MISSING PIECE and PHONE DOESN'T RING provide examples for which this pattern presents a solution.

INTRODUCING VALUE CHAINS TO ENGINEERS

Figure 6.9
Do you know who your
real stakeholders are?

Even though value chains were initially devised as an approach for making strategic decisions, Geoffrey Moore saw that value chain concepts could be combined with the idea of "whole product" to make project teams more effective. The concept behind a whole product is that a product is most valuable when other supporting products and services exist so that users can do something they really value. When the Macintosh was first adopted, the laser printer was an important part of the whole product that made desktop publishing possible [Moore91].

Moore worked with a leading supplier of high-technology products to introduce these concepts. Despite the power of combining the ideas of value chains and whole products, the company had difficulty introducing the concepts to their engineers, and approached us for ideas. We suggested using fantasy role play as a way of introducing the concepts. We created an exercise in which participants play the role of fantasy adventurers who must negotiate scenarios to successfully save a kingdom from the onslaught of demons (see Figure 6.9). To successfully complete the scenarios, the participants must recognize the compelling interests of the other characters. By introducing the elements of value chains and whole products in a fantasy setting, participants gained a model by which they could understand the same concepts in their workday environments.

The company built the exercise as a front end of a workshop which became very popular. There are several interesting observations that can be drawn from the company's experience. It validates the fact that the ideas of value chains can be extended beyond their initial application of strategic planning. It also reminds us that when we are introducing new models of thinking into our organizations, we need to work creatively to enable people to understand and believe the models.

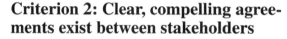

Criterion 2: Clear, compelling agreements exist between stakeholders

Lip-Synching

Reciprocity

Partnering works best when relationships are both clearly defined and personal. Without both ingredients, architectures of any size become unstable. An architecture often depends on getting priority action such as a feature modification, services, or information from a partner who is not in the same chain of command. This cooperation is easy in the best of times, but it is not so easy when all partners are working overtime and are still behind on meeting commitments within their own chains of command. The problem is, when partners miss their commitments, trust in the network quickly fades, as does use of the architecture.

Clear agreements set unambiguous and common understanding of what each partner expects. However, unless partners trust each other, no degree of specificity is sufficient. Positive relationships and trustworthy behavior cement trust that partners will get the value they expect from the contract. Corporate commitments must be backed by individuals on all sides who SHOW PERSONAL INTEGRITY [Rising99].

Antipattern: LIP-SYNCHING

General Form.   Meetings with your "anchor" customer for a new architecture have lost substance and focus. This is becoming clear to others who agreed to adopt your architecture based on your anchor customer's commitment. Architecture meetings continue, primarily due to senior executive support, but most of the senior managers now send subordinates.

You convinced your business unit manager to sponsor your architecture initiative and to back up the financial support by strongly encouraging several of the top product groups to participate. You negotiated an aggressive—perhaps too aggressive—schedule for implementation. One of your key commitments was to engage an "anchor customer," a product group whose participation would encourage other groups to follow. After furious activity, several product team leaders stepped out stating their interest in adopting the architecture. Not wanting to blow the opportunity, you postponed talking about sticky issues such as what the architecture could realistically do and when. As a result, you gain the commitment of a highly visible product team.

Your preliminary specification received only superficial comments. Concerned that your most important customer won't use the architecture as agreed, you coaxed and encouraged. Nothing happened. Not knowing what to do, you tried even harder and delivered a second release, specially tailored to this customer. Still, nothing happened, or worse, the customer now felt obliged to respond and made a request that forced your team to re-re-redo a feature or even a delivery process. Before you knew it, your team was spending a disturbing amount of time responding to these requests. This left less time to meet the initial schedule and to respond to other customers. Your team found itself bending over backwards to meet requirements that seemed less and less sincere.

Even though the architecture team was furiously busy, nothing meaningful was produced.

As a result, even though the architecture team was furiously busy, nothing meaningful was produced. By the time you realized the futility of pursuing the apparently perfect customer, all your other customers were ready to walk, if they hadn't already done so.

Forces.   Architecture initiatives often start off with a big bang, enjoying the sponsorship of a senior executive. Successful managers will often sign on to new initiatives because they believe in the potential benefits and are often targeted as anchor participants. Executives and other potential adopters look to these managers to determine whether to fund or participate. As a result, some managers responsible for architecture initiatives sometimes gloss over issues that would preclude an anchor's long-term involvement to gain their initial participation. The architecture team is pressured to overstate what they can deliver and when. Architecture team leaders or their managers may select an initial set of customers based on their enthusiasm instead of their fit with one another and with the primary strength of the new architecture. Everyone is interested in demonstrating success. Managers that agree to adopt the architecture get credit for participating in new technology initiatives; architects get credit for finding adopters.

However, unless agreements are clear, anchor customers are likely to divert resources initially assigned to the architecture initiative to more immediate, albeit unexpected, problems. When this happens, the relationship can spin out of control. The architecture supplier can go far beyond what was agreed to keep an anchor customer engaged.

Unless sticky issues are discussed, it is almost impossible to reach a meaningful agreement among stakeholders or even sort out who is and is not a stakeholder. It takes honest, painful and sometimes heated discussion to determine who will really benefit from the architecture project, gain their commitment to use the architecture, and tie down component providers and users with clear penalties and rewards.

When sticky issues aren't discussed, principals lose faith that the architecture can really deliver. Without the conviction that their participation will yield serious results, most managers will send representatives with less relevant knowledge or authority. Seeing this, other principals begin to do the same. Soon, meetings are reduced to meaningless discussions.

Solution.   Make especially sure to gain a clear understanding about both benefits and obligations from anchor stakeholders. Document this understanding, and refer back to the written document when interactions cease to be positive and productive. While this practice is always important, it is critical with those whose participation holds a strong influence on others. When things appear to be spinning out of control, going back to the contract can pull the architecture team out of this whirlpool.

This solution is as relevant to meetings as it is your initial agreements. In general, it makes sense to do as much homework and one-to-one preparation as possible before each meeting. It also makes sense to be as clear as possible about the scope and limitations of the architecture. This is especially true for a kick-off meeting, where the course of activities for half the group's life span is set within the first few minutes [Gersick88]. Part of the preparation should involve determining where potential adopters are on the technology adoption curve. If they are early adopters, little packaging may be necessary. Early adopters are willing to do what they have to do to make products work if they believe the product will help them gain a significant competitive advantage. Unlike mainstream users, early adopters will build or customize interfaces, work around defects and even rely on a small company as the single source of support. To win over mainstream users, the architect should expect to provide adopters with complete solutions that are accepted by their peers and compatible with other off-the-shelf products [Moore91].

Seasoned judgement is called for to know when and how to be specific. In some cultures, experienced managers won't even go to the first meeting unless they are very clear about how an initiative will benefit them and what they are expected to do. Most cultures encourage off-line discussions to resolve exactly these issues and avoid embarrassing surprises.

Rationale.   When partnerships begin to expend more than a little time and resources, participants should establish a clear and mutual understanding of why they are there and what they are expected to do. While this statement is broadly applicable, architecture initiatives face a greater risk that agreements will be neither clear nor workable. To implement an architecture, groups work together across organizational boundaries, borders, and chains of command, each with a different protocol and culture. This increases the risk that "hand-shake" or even written agreements will not be commonly understood. Both formal and informal communications that aim at common understanding reduce this risk. This risk is also mitigated when parties have social relationships as well as professional ones. Companies with iron-clad hierarchical structures are prone to set up architecture initiatives without really defining a clear role, expectation, or reporting chain for the architecture team. Lacking a clear role, expectation, or reporting chain, architecture initiatives can manifest "slow-motion" architecture teams that work 9 to 5 while everyone else works around the clock. As LIP-SYNCHING describes, even when the architecture team leader acts with resolve to build a strong customer base, lack of a clear, common understanding can result in frantic efforts to satisfy a customer who has never really decided to take the architecture seriously.

Example.   The following examples and figures illustrate how a lack of clear, compelling agreements can lead to an architecture breakdown.

Consider the case of two teams within the same business unit. Both teams built telecommunications products that shared a number of common features. We'll call the teams' products Rigel and Vega. The Rigel and Vega teams had an arrangement whereby each team maintained one shared component for both product teams to use (see Figure 6.10). However, the Rigel team encountered a number of difficulties. They had some particularly challenging customer demands and experienced some staff turnover. They were unable to deliver several agreed-upon modifications to the component rigelBean, which

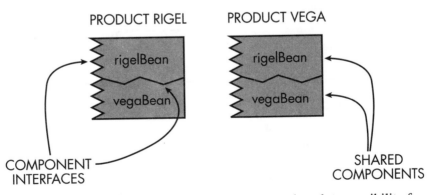

Figure 6.10   The Rigel and Vega product teams shared responsibility for a pair of common components.

they maintained and shared with the Vega team. The Vega team had its own deadlines to fight and decided to clone the rigelBean component to meet their deadline. At this point, the Vega team was in a hurry trying to make up for lost time, and for the sake of expediency, modified the interface between the rigelBean and their vegaBean component, this "clone and own" approach is illustrated in Figure 6.11. The Rigel team, facing the prospect of modifying the rigelBean to work with the new version of the vegaBean, instead decided to clone the vegaBean themselves in order to maintain the interface (Figure 6.12). As a result of the stresses of challenging times, the trust that enabled the

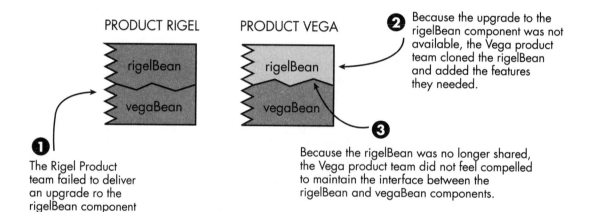

Figure 6.11   The Vega team cloned the Rigel team's rigelBean component.

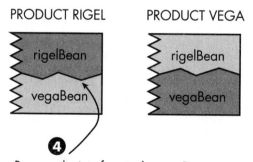

Because the interface to the vegaBean component was no longer the same, the Rigel product team cloned the vegaBean component to ensure they would have a component that worked with the rigelBean component.

Figure 6.12
The Rigel and Vega product teams no longer shared common components.

two product teams to share common components broke down. Without trust, each team took over the responsibility of building both components.

When is This Antipattern a Pattern?   Not all pomp and circumstance is bad. Meetings that don't have a prayer of accomplishing their stated goal can lead to better intergroup relationships, stronger partnering and even clearer contracts. IT'S A RELATIONSHIP, NOT A SALE and GO EARLY, STAY LATE speak to these tendencies [Rising99]. In some cultures, a business meeting will start with an entire day of pleasantries.

Related Antipatterns and Patterns.   Like LIP-SYNCHING, IRRATIONAL MANAGEMENT describes consequences brought on by managers who take their eyes off the objective [BrownW98]. A DOORMAT, or team leader who cedes all management decisions to managers outside the team, can easily end up with an initiative that has no serious customers [Olson98].

Every contact with the customer is a chance to BUILD TRUST.
> —*David Saar, Senior Product Planning Manager,*
> *AG Communications [Rising99]*

Pattern: RECIPROCITY

Problem Statement.   What can you do to ensure that partners who work within separate chains of command will be responsive when you need their help?

Context.   Code ownership is in practice, and you are an owner of commonly used code that is specified by the architecture [Coplier95]. You are also responsible for a larger module or subsystem that includes common code from other owners. These partners do not all work for the same managers, and a couple are in another organization altogether.

Forces.   Developers have a limited amount of time and attention. When people are busy, they focus on their immediate tasks. If someone has helped out an engineer or manager in the past, that engineer or manager may feel obligated to return the favor in the future.

Code owners are often asked to respond to requests that do not aid owners in accomplishing their immediate tasks. Yet common use of their code will diminish without strong and consistent support. Code owners may provide this support in their spare time (see PERSONAL TIME). However, their support may diminish when time pressures mount. Organizations that do not allow owners to charge time to support internal customers run a high risk that at least one code owner will not be able to respond and that trust will begin to break down.

If common use diminishes, developers will reinvent and maintain the code in their own way and the architecture will become more complex.

Solution.   Adopt a policy of reciprocity. Reciprocity calls for a fair and proactive exchange of value among partners. When relationships are defined among groups that share an architecture, both formal and informal contracts should be reviewed to ensure this fair exchange. Budgets should include time for code owners to respond to requests from other groups. Measures should gauge how well groups support other teams, not just how well they accomplish their own missions [Mohrman97].

Once the organizational structure and budget are defined, both individuals and groups can practice reciprocity. As an architect, you should take time to go out into the field. This will send a strong signal to partners. If partners must "come to the mountain," then there is definitely a lack of reciprocity. As an individual, go out of your way to be helpful when others request assistance. As a manager, encourage your staff to be helpful when there are external requests for assistance. Watch for signs that your group is taking advantage of other groups without providing value in return. As a manager, you can also take turns hosting face-to-face events.

Result.   Reciprocity increases long-term sharing of software code as well as the tacit knowledge necessary to use the code successfully. It increases individual and group cooperation across organizational boundaries and makes this cooperation more energetic and enjoyable. When a colleague or peer team is provided with a really good solution, it opens a positive flow of both emotion and information. When information flow is reciprocal, both parties enjoy the experience, forming a positive feedback loop. This positive feedback loop also applies to teams and groups. Contracts can inspire more confidence with less complexity and burden.

Consequences.   Even if you practice RECIPROCITY you still need to get your primary job done. Further, some individuals and organizations may take advantage of such generosity.

Rationale.   When engineers and managers are busy, they become very selective about what requests they will respond to in order to focus on their immediate tasking. They may be more responsive to a request if the engineer or manager has built a good relationship with that person and has helped them out in the past. The manager must set the example of how to provide great support to partners.

When engineers and groups demonstrate their commitment to give at least as much as they get, trust is built over time. On a personal level, this trust makes it rewarding to respond to requests and to alert partners about new information and unexpected events. The higher the trust, the less it is necessary to spell out penalties, terms, and conditions in a contract. Paradoxically, when trust is high and agreements are less explicit, partners have a clearer expectation of what they will receive and when.

Chrysler has a motto: "My enemy is my suppliers' costs, not my suppliers' margins" [Mohrman98]. [3]

Example.   Certainly, the idea of reciprocity is neither new nor unique to software architecture. Reciprocity has roots in both the New and Old Testaments and is also discussed in the Hindu Vedas. Today, reciprocity contributes to business results. In the area of business partnering, Chrysler has increased market share and profits through the use of win–win partnering with suppliers. Historically, Chrysler pressured its suppliers to reduce prices regardless of their costs, using contracts of less than two years to keep their suppliers off balance. Chrysler shifted to helping suppliers reduce costs, ensuring that they share in profits and giving them purchasing commitments throughout the life of a model. In response, suppliers have made substantial investments in plant, equipment, systems, and people dedicated exclusively to serving Chrysler's needs [Dyer96]. Now, "Chrysler adds only about 30 percent of the total value of the cars it makes and subcontracts for the remaining 70 percent" [Mohrman98]. [3]

Partners are often compelled to share information and components with stakeholders whom they cannot directly control.

Reciprocity is particularly important to software architecture because partners are so often compelled to share information and components with fellow architecture stakeholders whom they cannot directly control. One architect we interviewed told us that her project had been brought to a halt because it depended upon a major component produced by a separate business unit. The supplying business unit was in crisis mode and engineers had no time to return calls, let alone make changes to software. The architect convinced her fellow engineers to find ways to help their counterparts in the troubled business unit. This opened a flow of communication that was previously shut off. While the engineer's project was unable to get the business unit to make the changes, they were able to gain enough information to correct defects and make the changes themselves.

In another company, the designated Web architect was called in to help with a series of proposals to move products that were based on proprietary

---

[3] S.A. Mohrman, J.A. Galbraith, E.E. Lawler III, et al., *Tomorrow's Organization: Crafting Winning Capabilities in a Dynamic World,* Copyright © 1998 Jossey-Bass, Inc. Reprinted by permission of Jossey-Bass, Inc., a subsidiary of John Wiley and Sons, Inc.

communications infrastructure to the Web. After helping one such project make better early decisions, he asked for a copy of the resulting proposal, which contained a first cut at a new architecture. When the next proposal came along, the architect was able to provide a more finished example. Using this approach, the architect was able to build support for funding an architecture group.

Related Antipatterns and Patterns.   As described above, CODE OWNERSHIP provides the context for reciprocity and architecture [Coplien95]. NO SURPRISES describes how partners interact when RECIPROCITY is practiced consistently—the better the partnership, the greater each partner's ability to see each other's risks. ACTIVE LISTENING, BE AWARE OF BOUNDARIES, BUILD TRUST, MIND YOUR MANNERS, PERFUNCTORY MEETINGS, and IT'S A RELATIONSHIP, NOT A SALE, inform both engineers and management about how individual developers can interface with customers [Rising99].

Criterion 3: Both policies and informal rules of social conduct enforce cooperation

Personal Time

No Surprises

Partnering can have both formal and informal components, and for partnering truly to take hold, both policies and informal rules of social conduct should encourage cooperation. Managing the informal rules of social conduct can be especially challenging because organizational charts and contracts between organizations do not reflect the informal network of relationships of people within and between organizations. These relationships can be built from a variety of common bonds, including common schools, prior employers, professional experience, and religious or social activities. As illustrated in Figure 6.13, informal networks do not exist as alternatives to an official organizational structure, but are overlaid and interact within it [Fukuyama97].

Informal networks can play an important role in product line architecture development. In a case study at Nortel, informal networks were found to play an important role in the development of a product line of telecommunications devices. The architecture was controlled through a rigorous yet informal procedure. Decisions that had significant impact on the architecture were made in informal gatherings. These gatherings depended upon a group of people who were recognized by their peers as real architects, though their titles rarely said "architect." Rules of social conduct worked to encourage engineering discipline. For example, developers who carelessly caused the weekly compile to break were shunned by their peers [Dikel95].

If the stakeholders are not cognizant of the role played by the informal network, the architecture can be inadvertently yet seriously harmed. When the inevitable reorganization occurs, key players can be downsized out of the

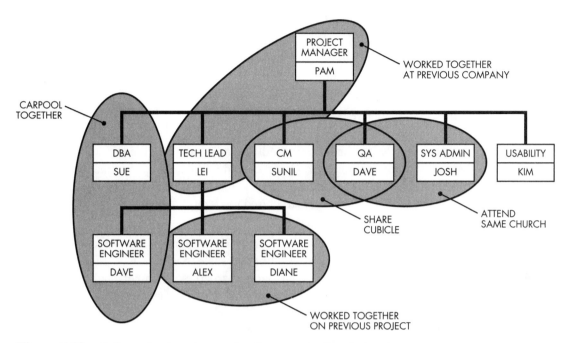

Figure 6.13   Informal networks overlay the organizational structure.

organization. As a result, practitioners can find themselves without access to very important answers that used to be a phone call away.

Antipattern: PERSONAL TIME

General Form.   You manage a development team. One of your engineers suggests that a unit of software your team is building could be shared if some modifications were made. In response to the engineer's proposal, you reply that he is welcome to proceed as long as it is on his own time. Without realizing it, you have opened your team, your company, and yourself to several serious risks.

The engineer may succeed in meeting other teams' needs along with your own. This sounds like a pretty good deal. Your team would earn favors you could collect during your next crunch. Your company would get extra product without extra expense.

The problem is that by asking the engineer to work on personal time, you have lost your ability to control his process and result. The engineer may or may not use the organization's standards for documentation, if he produces any at all. Steps such as peer review, even testing, may be truncated or completely ignored. If the product gets built into other teams' work products, the engineer's phone may begin fielding frantic calls from peers who adopted the module. Adding features to his module that support the concerns of outside interests as well as your own can eat all his time and that of several additional engineers. If he tries to help his peers, your team suffers. If he focuses on his day job, you may get panic calls from your peers or from senior management demanding support. If the engineer tries to do both, he may burn out.

Faced with these increased demands, the engineer may resign and demand compensation for code developed without company time or resources. Meanwhile, the teams that adopted the module could be faced with maintaining code that is neither well-structured nor well-documented.

Forces.   Work done on personal time does not show up on any budget, making it difficult to manage or establish accountability. Work done in this manner is also often limited in scope and scale to what can be done by a single engineer. Engineers who are encouraged to do work on personal time may be motivated to seek employment elsewhere. The message may be delivered by a manager who loads engineers, most of whom are salaried, with 60 hours a week worth of work—no holidays or vacations—and "allows" them to work on other projects if they get their primary work done.

Engineers who develop common solutions gain personal recognition and greater access to answers. They also open channels of communication for the groups to which they belong. There are often formal ways to fund solutions that benefit an engineer's group as well as others. It may be possible for organizations to reward work done on personal time through bonuses and other rewards.

Solution.   Plan to pay for the engineer's time spent on shared components whether they are developed on personal time or not. Paying early can save effort and a lot of stress. Whether you fund the efforts or whether you don't, think through how you will handle the possibility that the component will become critical to one or more outside projects. Discipline and common sense must be applied when considering the tradeoffs. Consider factors such as corporate culture, sensibility of your management, and the degree of schedule pressure as well as the specifics of the situation. Funding may be available, and sharing components may be encouraged or even expected. Many organizations budget staff hours for the development and maintenance of solutions that are shared outside of a group or project. This will ensure against the engineer taking shortcuts on personal time on your project's code. It will also ensure the supportability of what your team provides to other teams or projects.

You may consider an open "share the code" approach—joint development of a shared component where other teams contribute to both development and peer review. If you can manage the risk, you may also consider allowing the engineer to experiment. Grass-roots initiatives can yield a high payoff for both an organization and its staff. However, if you don't fund the engineer's initial efforts and you see signs the component is becoming adopted, take action to get the component documented and up to project standards. In any case, engineers should not be led on or encouraged to spend their own time if indeed the suggestion does not fit with the direction of the organization.

Rationale. Organizations face a balancing act when it comes to encouraging their staff to take initiative. On one hand, personal initiative is behind many of the improvements that organizations are able to implement. Many times this is an appropriate answer, but in some cases it can cause both the organization and engineer to assume substantial risks unwittingly. While the manager may feel that getting such work for free is a good deal, it is difficult to supervise work that is done on an employee's own time and enforce processes that ensure quality. The practice can spawn staff resentment, especially if the work sanctioned to be done on personal time is not actually used.

It is difficult to supervise work that is done on an employee's own time and enforce processes that ensure quality.

On the other hand, organizations have an interest in making decisions that some staff members may not agree with. How an organization makes decisions about its own investments while encouraging individual initiative can be tricky. The situation is further complicated when the problem being solved is one that crosses projects or organizational boundaries. Even if someone develops a solution to a problem on personal time, the organization may not have the mechanisms in place to maintain the shared solution.

Example. The following demonstrates how using personal time can avoid this antipattern. SRA International Inc., a systems integration and consulting firm, sought to address some of the challenges faced by their growth. There were some small-scale corporate efforts to exchange technical information among engineers and other experts in different pockets of the company. A group of advocates decided to expand on these efforts by creating an internal conference in which they held a series of seminars. Executives were invited to play roles in these events. This grass-roots event was very successful and spawned several other internal conferences in different technology areas. Rather than continue the effort exclusively on the personal time of the advocates, they secured sponsorship from the executives for additional, more elaborate events. Personal time still played a role in the advocates' efforts, but with corporate sponsorship, activities with a more direct impact on the company's activities could be organized, and the executive leadership also established a stake in shaping the direction of the events [Halverson99].

When is This Antipattern a Pattern?   It does not always make sense for a unit of software to be reused. It may not fit in the long-term plans of the organization, or the organization may not be prepared to support the component adequately once it is built. In these cases it may make sense for the organization to refuse to commit the resources necessary to make a component sharable, but the organization should also not encourage the work to be done on personal time.

Advocates for new technology and processes may use their personal time in order to establish an initial capability. When a new programming language is introduced, the first experience in an organization is usually that of engineers working on their own time. However, as technologies and processes become recognized as critical to the success of the organization, the relative role of personal time should diminish as the organization commits resources to the new technology or process. The efforts done on personal time should also be recognized through varied reward mechanisms, such as appointment to a leading role in the project.

Related Antipatterns and Patterns.   The pattern DEDICATED CHAMPION is a precursor to this situation [Delano97].

Pattern: NO SURPRISES

Problem Statement.   How can you adjust schedule or feature commitments without losing the confidence of groups that depend on your components?

Context.   You own a software component that is going to be used by a number of peer organizations and you have encountered some difficulties. A change to the plan is required. Something will have to give, and you are faced with deciding what it will be. Should the schedule be delayed? Should features be dropped? If features must be dropped, which will least impact your partners? Should performance requirements be relaxed? You also need to decide when and how you should communicate the slip to your partners.

Forces.   Component users who do not find out until the last minute about changes to a component can be put into a difficult position as they scramble to respond to the change. If component users are able to find out about changes sooner, they may be able to respond to the changes with less difficulty. If component users lose faith in a component supplier because of frequent surprises, they may decide to select an alternate supplier. Organizations that have an aversion to bad news may end up surprising their users by suppressing information about schedule slips, dropped features, or performance degradation.

Often, the channels and forums created for sharing bad news are not the best places to share this information. In a hierarchical organization, bad news may get sanitized as it moves up and down chains of command. Communicating changes through hierarchical channels almost guarantees surprises at every level. By the time the news gets to users, it may be neither clear nor timely. Users' comments that come back through the chain may be both distorted and energized. Meetings can provide opportunities for early warning, but unless alerts are provided off-line, presentations may not line up, demonstrating a lack of communication, and presenters may be embarrassed.

Solution.   Call attention to changes early and negotiate solutions. Make sure that those who depend upon components are informed and consulted before deciding where to compromise. While these actions directly affect software architecture, have much broader application.

This pattern is far more effective when executives and managers lay the groundwork by:

► Welcoming rather than punishing early notice of bad news
► Encouraging managers and engineers to inform their customers and partners of changes before meetings or demonstrations and showing low tolerance for behavior that results in unnecessary surprises
► Rewarding managers and engineers whose word is trusted by peers and customers

When the organization makes changes to their announced plans, the groups who are affected should be consulted as early as possible. This can be applied informally by a single engineer managing the engineer's commitments with other engineers. Management can also apply this approach by establishing expectations for their staff members.

Management must, however, be very clear about sensitivities, and engineers must be coached on issues like not giving away proprietary data or making snap judgements. Guidance for coaching engineers is provided in BE AWARE OF BOUNDARIES [Rising99].

Result.   NO SURPRISES enables users and partners to be more involved in changes to plans that affect them. This does not necessarily mean that all decisions will be their preferred choice, but they'll be in a position to learn of the change early enough to make necessary adjustments. If component owners do not surprise their users, then they will be able to build trust and increase adoption of the component.

Consequences.   In most cases, telling customers and partners about problems without forethought is a bad idea. You must spend enough time to present as clear a picture as possible of the problem and alternate solutions. Eventually, the level of trust will build to the point where problems can be revealed with only a few suggestions of what could be done.

It is not unusual to find organizations that are averse to bad news because their customers have threatened to terminate contracts if more slips occur. In situations such as these, component owners are strongly encouraged not to surface bad news. Instead, they are encouraged to LET'S PLAY TEAM [Olson98], pretending to be making progress long enough for everyone to get a positive evaluation, a promotion, or to move to another company.

Surfacing a risk in such a situation may chance a negative result for the component owner or for the larger organization—at least in the short term.

Rationale. If users of a component are surprised by late changes to the schedule, features, or performance of a component, they will lose trust in the component and the organization providing the component. If trust is lacking, the component won't be adopted. Lack of trust can also result in CLONING. Unless users trust that a supplier will make timely changes in response to their requests, the user might clone the portion in question and make the change rather than wait for the supplier. If, on the other hand, the news is relayed early, there may be time to negotiate a minimal solution that meets the partner's immediate need.

Example. A senior manager of a large telecommunications hardware and software development project made "no surprises" a cornerstone of his management style. He had an all-day monthly meeting with his first-level managers in which each of the engineering teams made a short presentation on their current status. When engineers described schedule slips, interface changes, and the like, the manager would ask other affected teams if they were aware of the changes. He made it clear that it was his expectation that no one should be surprised at the staff meeting; the affected parties should be consulted beforehand. The effect of communicating this expectation was to change the behavior of the engineering teams, who would take measures to ensure they were in contact with groups that depended on their work when they made changes that affected other engineering teams. As part of a comprehensive risk management approach, the practice helped identify issues that could be explored before decisions about them were made. Further, engineers and managers got help, not a reprimand, when an issue was raised.

Related Antipatterns and Patterns. The KNOW THY STAKEHOLDERS pattern may be helpful in identifying the parties who might be affected by a change. ACTIVE LISTENING, BE AWARE OF BOUNDARIES, BUILD TRUST, MIND YOUR MANNERS, PERFUNCTORY MEETINGS, and IT'S A RELATIONSHIP, NOT A

SALE, inform both engineers and management about how individual developers can interface with customers [Rising99].

Pattern: PROMOTE THE NETWORK

Problem Statement. What criteria do you use to select engineers for job promotion?

Context. You are a manager in an organization that is building a software product that shares an architecture with a number of different organizations. A senior position has opened in your group and you need to select someone in your group to promote to fill the opening.

Forces. Software development is a social activity; however, many engineers have introverted personality types [Coplien95]. In one telecommunications manufacturer, the engineering community took the Myers-Briggs test and nearly all were classified as introverts. Engineers communicate with others to get the information needed to carry out their work. Most senior technical roles require broad, rapid access to tacit information—some of which is written and hard to find; other information isn't written at all.

Engineers with large informal networks have access to better information.

Engineers with large informal networks of contacts have access to better information than engineers without such networks. Engineers require an investment of time and effort to cultivate an informal network.

Solution. Consider the effectiveness of an engineer's informal network when making promotion decisions. When considering effectiveness, look for specific examples. Has the engineer gotten answers to problems—ones that puzzled his colleagues and held up progress—by finding and tapping the right person outside of your group? If the organization has explicit criteria for making promotion decisions, then the criteria can be similarly modified. Managers should avoid undermining those informal networks. A manager who discourages engineers from devoting attention to their network may find that there are no networks to promote.

Result. Engineers with extensive informal networks are more likely to succeed once promoted. They have a broader base of experience to draw upon as they face new challenges in their new position. They are better able to troubleshoot problems and to find out where to get help. They are better able to negotiate changes with owners of other components if they have established contacts with that organization.

Consequences. Overemphasis on an engineer's personal network may distract extroverted engineers from the work at hand. Instead of leveraging their development efforts, you may end up with an overflow of solutions that don't fit, extraneous information, and just plain gossip. The engineer can become branded as a dilettante, knowing a lot of surface information but never getting his arms around the technology he is supposed to know cold.

Rationale.   Work in any software development organization does not occur in isolation. Engineers consult other engineers when troubleshooting problems; they discuss the latest technologies, and they share war stories of past successes and failures. Engineers who have a broad network of contacts with other engineers can be more effective when confronting a technical challenge. In groups that share components across organizational boundaries, this network of contacts can be even more important. An engineer who encounters a problem when using a component might be able to resolve the problem if he or she knew another engineer who worked with that component, or other users of the component. Just as an engineer's technology skills affect success and are considered when making promotion decisions, his or her informal network of contacts should be similarly considered. Networks become increasingly important as the engineer moves to more senior positions. Networks are often essential not only to finding information, but also to identifying resources and negotiating win–win agreements with other groups.

Informal networks are often essential not only to finding information, but also to identifying resources and negotiating agreements with other groups.

Example.   In a 1995 Nortel case study, the authors observed that an employee's "sphere of influence" was explicitly used as a criterion for promotion. Managers reported, "those with effective networks were better able to negotiate changes, and there was less management involvement and less cloning" [Dikel97a].

Related Antipatterns and Patterns.   The idea behind this pattern may be applied to more situations than described in this context. Engineers who practice RECIPROCITY and NO SURPRISES may be able to develop more effective networks. ROTATION (see Chapter 3, Vision) also has the effect of extending an engineer's informal network. GATEKEEPER describes how managers can utilize engineers with extroverted personality types to channel communication flow into and out of work teams [Coplien95].

SUMMARY

Partnering provides a frame of reference for managing cooperative relationships in architecture-based development. This cooperation is especially important because many different organizations and roles interact, but cannot be directly controlled by the architect or his line of management. Fortunately, there is a great deal of work that has been done that can address this challenge.

The principle of partnering is built on the concepts of contracts, network organizations, value chains, and trust.

Partnering is the extent to which architecture stakeholders maintain clear, cooperative roles and maximize the value they deliver and receive. An architecture stakeholder is a person or organization whose actions and ongoing trust are essential to establishing and sustaining the value of an architecture over time. The challenge is in identifying and gaining commitment from the stakeholders because they may not know that they are stakeholders, or they may not care to be one. Stakeholders also need to cooperate to make the architecture successful; that is, there needs to be a shared set of expectations. Successful partnering requires more than just meeting the terms of contracts and keeping promises; it also requires that the architecture deliver customer benefits at a reasonable cost.

Successful partnering yields many benefits for architecture-based development. More developers are able to use and achieve success with the architecture. It reduces the risk to all of the stakeholders by improving the flow of information among the stakeholders. Lastly, while it is easy to cooperate in good times, partnering helps groups cooperate even in challenging times.

There are many strategies that can be used to establish partnering. This chapter described several tactics that help organizations address partnering in both the formal organizational structures and the informal networks that exist within and between organizations.

OTHER APPLICABLE PATTERNS AND ANTIPATTERNS

There are other patterns that can be used to put the principle of Partnering into practice, as well as antipatterns to avoid along the way. Table 6.2 lists organizational patterns and antipatterns cataloged in the 2000 edition of *The Patterns Almanac* [Rising00]. Table 6.3 lists antipatterns from *Antipatterns: Refactoring Software, Architectures, and Projects in Crisis* [BrownW98].

TABLE 6.2   *Organizational Patterns and Antipatterns That Can Shape Partnering [Rising00]*

AD-HOC CORRECTIONS [Weir98]	HOLISTIC DIVERSITY [Cockburn98]
APPLICATION DESIGN IS BOUNDED BY TEST DESIGN [Coplien95]	HUB, SPOKE, AND RIM [Coplien95]
ARCHITECT CONTROLS PRODUCT [Coplien95]	INFORMAL LABOR PLAN [Cuningham96]

TABLE 6.2   *(continued)*

BE AWARE OF BOUNDARIES [Rising99]	IT'S A RELATIONSHIP, NOT A SALE [Rising99]
BE RESPONSIVE [Rising99]	KNOW THE CUSTOMER [Rising99]
BUFFALO MOUNTAIN [Coplien95]	LET'S PLAY TEAM [Olson98]
BUILD TRUST [Rising99]	LISTEN, LISTEN, LISTEN [Rising99]
CODE OWNERSHIP [Coplien95]	MANAGING AND MEETING CUSTOMER EXPECTATIONS [Whitenack95]
COMPENSATE SUCCESS [Coplien95]	MASTER-JOURNEYMAN [Weir98]
CUSTOMER MEETINGS: GO EARLY, STAY LATE [Rising99]	MIND YOUR MANNERS [Rising99]
CUSTOMER RAPPORT [Whitenack95]	MOVE RESPONSIBILITIES [Coplien95]
DECISION DOCUMENT [Weir98]	ORGANIZATION FOLLOWS LOCATION [Coplien95]
DELIVERABLES TO GO [Taylor99]	ORGANIZATION FOLLOWS MARKET [Coplien95]
DESIGNERS ARE OUR FRIENDS [DeLano98]	PRODUCT INITIATIVE [Cunningham96]
DEVELOPER CONTROLS PROCESS [Coplien95]	SCENARIOS DEFINE PROBLEM [Coplien95]
DEVELOPING IN PAIRS [Coplien95]	SHAPING CIRCULATION REALMS [Coplien95]
DIVIDE AND CONQUER [Coplien95]	SHOW PERSONAL INTEGRITY [Rising99]
ENGAGE CUSTOMERS [Coplien95]	SPONSOR OBJECTIVES [Whitenack95]
ENGAGE QA [Coplien95]	TAKE YOUR LICKS [Rising99]
ENVISIONING [Whitenack95]	TEAM SPACE [Taylor99]
GATEKEEPER [Coplien95]	TIME TO TEST [DeLano98]
GET INVOLVED EARLY [DeLano98]	WORK FLOWS INWARD [Coplien95]

TABLE 6.3   *Antipatterns That Can Derail Partnering [BrownW98]*

CORNCOB

E-MAIL IS DANGEROUS

INTELLECTUAL VIOLENCE

MUSHROOM MANAGEMENT

SMOKE AND MIRRORS

STOVEPIPE ENTERPRISES

THE FEUD

SIMPLIFICATION: CLARIFYING AND MINIMIZING

When the going gets tough, the tough get simple.
—Anthony Drew Blice, Col. USMC Ret. [Blice98]

OVERVIEW

Grady Booch identified "a ruthless focus on the development of a system that provides a well-understood collection of essential minimal characteristics" as one of the habits of a successful object-oriented project [Booch96]. This is true for software architecture as well as for object-oriented development. Nevertheless, finding the minimal essential characteristics—features that provide "just enough" functionality and flexibility to meet the needs of users—is one of the hardest tasks of the architect. Simplifying an architecture requires concerted effort, as does making sure those essential characteristics remain top priority for each member of the architecture team until the release is shipped.

But What is Essential?

Architects and executives must work to keep architectures and the organizations that build them balanced. A focus on customer and business value provides the architect with a compass and gyroscope. Pinpointing the essential value is rarely easy and becomes increasingly difficult as new customers and products come on line and take the architecture beyond its original dimensions. Vision defines this essential value and establishes constraints needed for its attainment. Simplification translates the vision into product.

When the business value is tied to building and maintaining a large customer base, it makes business sense to keep customer-specific features out of the core of the architecture. At the same time, the architect and his or her team must ensure that the core architecture continues to deliver something of compelling value to each customer. Rather than putting customer-specific features in the core, the architect makes sure that the architecture will support straightforward implementation of the features. The architect has to be able to recognize the common elements buried within multiple, disparate requests. For example, the architect for a business-to-business Internet firm frequently found himself negotiating features that did not need to be in the core out of the architecture. He did this in the face of Fortune 500 customers with large budgets. To address one customer's demand that the architecture implement a platform-specific Distributed Component Object Model (DCOM) interface, the architect described how the architecture supports integration engineering using Extensible Markup Language (XML) that enables external connection of DCOM to the architecture's data layer. This approach, backed up by a set of quick prototypes, enabled the firm's product line to meet more customers' needs and support a variety of implementation platforms. In the longer term, the architect's firm learned that burdening the core architecture with a grab bag of random features slows development and compromises the architecture.

Simplifying organizational structure can simplify architecture; just like removing weeds can improve the chances of actually getting food out of your garden.

Business process engineers often focus on value to simplify an organization's structure. This is good because it helps focus individual operating units on core competencies. If all goes well, effective interrelationships are identified. These interrelationships can also help simplify architectures produced by each operating unit by describing how the architectures should interact. Simplifying organizational structure *can* simplify architecture; just like removing weeds can improve the chances of actually getting food out of your garden. However, it depends on how you approach simplification. In both gardening and business process reengineering, the hack-and-slash method rarely produces predictable and positive results. Software architecture, too, requires great understanding and care for simplification to be effective (see Figure 7.1).

Figure 7.1   Focusing on the minimal essential feature of an architecture is the challenge of simplification.

SIMPLIFICATION DEFINITION

Simplification is the intelligent clarification and minimization of both architecture and the organizational environment in which it functions.

> *To the extent that an organization is not completely flexible in communication structure, that organization will stamp out an image of itself in every design it produces.*
>
> *—Melvin Conway [Conway68]*

Our definition of simplification recognizes the connection between software architecture and the organizations responsible for developing, maintaining, and operating the architecture. This relationship is examined in a discussion of Conway's Law. Organizational structures are simplified when the architect has the opportunity to clarify and minimize the architecture itself.

Conway's Law

Before embarking on a crusade to simplify the organization, it makes sense to observe the interaction between system and organization. In 1968, Melvin Conway wrote an article for *Datamation* observing that the structure of a system mirrors the structure of the organization that designed it [Conway68]. Conway said, "The very act of organizing a design team means that certain design decisions have already been made, explicitly or otherwise." Once structured, however, the organization shapes communication paths and protocols through which groups (hopefully) negotiate interfaces between and among each other. Thus, both formal and informal structures and communication paths influence system design. Conway's article formed the basis of what is now known as Conway's Law. James Coplien summarized this idea in a pattern called CONWAY'S LAW, which is also known by the aliases ORGANIZATION FOLLOWS ARCHITECTURE and ARCHITECTURE FOLLOWS ORGANIZATION. The forces in this pattern are reciprocal [Coplien95]. It is not hard to find examples in which architecture and organization reinforce each other's ability to deliver value or find examples of the opposite, where they completely destroy one another.

For those who puzzle over the question "Which comes first, organization or architecture?," the answer is, it really depends. When a large project begins with a clean slate, the resulting work breakdown structure is likely to follow the initial architectural concept. Once the organization is formed, it will constrain changes to the architecture. However, the insight that ARCHITECTURE FOLLOWS ORGANIZATION goes much deeper than work breakdown structure and organizational hierarchy. Architecture also is affected by and affects less visible aspects of the organization such as culture, informal networks, and collective beliefs. Some product teams fight to keep the core simple and enjoy strong organizational support. Others attempt to simplify and are pulled apart like a wishbone by the conflicting, often hidden agendas of multiple sponsors.

While some managers ask, "What can we build with the organizational structure that we have?," others have overcome this inertia by first figuring out what they want to build and then tuning the organization to fit. One large computer company we reviewed had no qualms about shifting tens or even hundreds of people around. They do this quickly, and there is a minimum of grumbling. People say, "We were working that way anyway." The reorganization is simply a reflection of reality.

A new insight emerges from this discussion. The more architecture enables its customers to solve problems simply, the less prone it will be to derailment by organizational issues. Similarly, the simpler an organization makes solving a given set of problems, the more immune it is to making an architecture unnecessarily complex and the more likely it is to choose or build an architecture that is simple. Allaire's ColdFusion has aided architecture and technical change even within highly compartmentalized organizations. J.J. Allaire infected his entire company with the mantra, "Make it simple and simple to use."

Why, we wondered, would IT managers in highly compartmentalized organizations who had silently shredded other modernization strategies support ColdFusion projects? We learned that in several cases ColdFusion enabled these generally conservative managers to respond quickly to table-pounding executives frustrated with backlogs. ColdFusion and Allaire Spectra—Allaire's packaged application for content, commerce, and personalization—provided a whole solution to a previously complex task. As such, ColdFusion was often able to amplify rather than conflict with IT interests.

Clarification

Whether you notice or not, organization shapes architecture and thinking about architecture. You should pay attention to organizational structure when you determine how to simplify architecture. If you don't, you may find the changes you make to be temporary. If ownership of two components lies within two groups and you arbitrarily simplify the design so that only one component remains, each group may find very good reasons why their team is uniquely capable of building the one component. Very quickly, each has a variation of the "simplified" design. The result is *more* complexity. And the rationale is now partially hidden, since most developers don't like to document rice bowl[1] or turf issues. The functional behavior of an organization is worth an equally careful look. Hidden agendas, protocols, cultures, and feuds over resources can blindside an unsuspecting architect.

> *Probably the greatest single common factor behind many poorly designed systems now in existence has been the availability of a design organization in need of work.* —Melvin Conway [Conway68]

What makes Conway's observation worse, as Fred Brooks points out, is that a lot of poor software is developed because the implementers (and their managers) wanted to "get busy" before the design was complete [Brooks82].

Before you can *simplify* architecture, you must *clarify* both organization and architecture. In a large bureaucracy (and in many not-so-large bureaucracies), people's belief maps are as strong as steel and quite often, incongruent beliefs rule. Similarly, architecture developers are often unable to describe how things really work due to lack of time, lack of a shared perspective, or reluctance to fully disclose the less flattering details of what they do know for fear that their users will bolt. The problem is, what makes simplification hard is often hidden from some or all players. The solution: clarify both organization and architecture.

---

[1] Rice bowl issues are described as guarantees of employment and minimum living standards, typically in Chinese domestic policy [Passell97].

Clarifying the Organization

Clarification of the organization means getting an honest reading of the organizational structures and forces where you plan to plant your architecture. While keeping architecture simple is never easy, it can become intractable within an organization that is at cross-purposes with itself. There are many methods for learning about these forces, both formal and informal. For example, ask stakeholders what they want, listen closely and watch their actions to determine who and what "ideas" are in charge; observe how much money stakeholders are willing to spend; and construct a step-by-step approach to mine the organization's beliefs and attitudes. Simply using a spiral development cycle can uncover much about an organization. However, some forces may not become visible until you cross an unforeseen threshold, or intrude on some part of an organization's holy ground—for example, a particular technology. While it is important to ask stakeholders what they want, the architect should keep in mind that in the end he or she must deliver what they need—which may be something different.

The work of Mark Simos provides a good illustration of how taking organizational considerations into account can simplify the sharing of an architecture. Simos developed an approach for domain modeling called Organizational Domain Modeling (ODM). Domain modeling is an approach for identifying common abstractions, called a domain, for a group of shared systems. The model not only describes common terminology, but it also captures a common body of knowledge about the domain. One of the major strengths of ODM is that it guides explicit domain scoping that integrates organizational and strategic factors with architecture and component engineering [Simos95].

Not getting the scope right is one of the most lethal pitfalls in developing an architecture. This is particularly true for the brave souls who work on enterprise architectures, who are no strangers to the feeling of trying to boil the ocean with a Bunsen burner. Understanding the organization provides a key to finding the right scope for an architecture. Without a clearly defined scope, it is very difficult to understand requirements and the context in which shared elements of the system or systems are to operate. As part of the scoping, ODM has steps for identifying the stakeholders, characterizing their interests, and even understanding their history of developing and sharing reused components [Simos95].

Simos adapted ODM for an internal Hewlett-Packard (HP) technology initiative, which has introduced it to a number of business units [Simos96]. HP managers reported significant benefits from this approach. One group was able to go from producing one product a year to six products a year. Another group was able to leverage an existing product line to move into a new product area. In contrast, HP managers also observed that other solid technical solutions did not receive widespread adoption because they were unable to map their solutions to the interests of the stakeholders [Cornwell96]. While some believe that ARCHITECTURE FOLLOWS ORGANIZATION is a *fait accompli,* ODM shows how organizational forces should be considered and incorporated into architecture planning.

Clarifying the Architecture

The architecture must be clear to both the architecture team and its customers. Before architecture can be simplified, the architect must know precisely what the architecture is supposed to do, how it is supposed to accomplish these tasks, and how these tasks are currently accomplished. Sometimes tasks that seem very straightforward turn out to be very complex to implement. If these complexities are not clearly understood, architectures can be built that are totally unsuited to the task. Such an architecture makes implementation more—rather than less—complex.

It is not enough for the architecture team to clarify the architecture for their own use. The easier it is for users to grasp how, as well as when and where, to use the architecture, the more likely they will be to use it effectively. Using the language or the metaphors of users can help (see MIGRATION PATH). In its early days, Allaire recognized that the largest and most committed builders of Web sites were bright and talented but were not trained programmers. Allaire developed a skills-migration path for these users, making their platform accessible by extending HTML with additional tags. (See Chapter 8, Allaire Case Study.)

The team and its representatives must also be transparent in communicating the good, the bad, and the ugly to its customers. Clarifying the architecture means providing details the users want or need to know. It does not mean leading users through gory details they do not want or need to know. This is not always easy, because current users have many tantalizing alternatives (some of which are actually viable). Nevertheless, transparency about time and functionality enables users to anticipate what they must build and what will be provided for them. As such, transparency builds trust. Lack of transparency leads to second-guessing and eventual loss of serious architecture use.

Minimization

As the definition states, engineers and managers work to minimize the architecture, focusing on a customer and business result. Minimization is not new.

About six hundred and fifty years ago, William of Ockham popularized what became his namesake, Ockham's Razor, which is often translated, "Entities are not to be multiplied beyond necessity" [Britannica00]. Ockham promoted the common use and minimization of assumptions needed to explain and predict occurrences. It would be uneconomical to hold that blue goblins make blue things fall and red goblins make red things fall. Then you'd have to explain why yellow, green, and purple things fall and why they fall in the same way as blue things. It is a lot simpler to say that gravity goblins make objects of every color fall.

This is not a philosophy lesson, or at least it is not a very good one. Please do notice, however, that the parsimony that drives science also drives software, as you will see in this chapter. In science, a theory acquires credibility when it best explains a number of related events without requiring complex juggling to accommodate special cases. Similarly, in software, an architecture works when it best supports a number of related applications without requiring complex juggling to fit special cases.

Nicholas Copernicus' explanation of a sun-centric planetary model eliminated endless and practically hopeless geometrics and computations that explained the movement of planets around the earth. At the time, everyone knew that the earth was at the center of the universe and that all motion was circular. Figure 7.2 illustrates the Aristotelian view of "the way things are" (or at

Figure 7.2
The Aristotelian Cosmos modeled the universe with the earth at its center. From Peter Apian, Cosmographia (1524). Source: Smithsonian Institution Libraries © 2000 Smithsonian Institution.

least should be), which was widely taught at the time of Copernicus. Aristotle (384–322 BCE) taught that heavenly bodies were part of "spherical shells of aether." These bodies moved in perfect spherical motion, neither speeding up nor slowing down. About 1200 CE, universities adopted Aristotle's cosmology despite some very difficult problems with the model: If the earth is at the center of the universe, and if heavenly bodies move around the earth in a perfectly circular and regular motion, why do some get dimmer and brighter? Why do some heavenly bodies speed up, slow down, and even stop? Impractical as Aristotle's model might have been, it fit well with medieval theology and eventually became intertwined with religious dogma [VanHelden00].

For those who actually wanted to study the stars (e.g., to predict star positions), a considerably more complex theory was applied. The theory developed by Claudius Ptolemy several hundred years after Aristotle's death, stretched, but did not question Aristotle's basic assumptions. Rather, the theory introduced several extraordinarily complex concepts, which we will not attempt to explain here, that accounted for the motions of heavenly bodies. Putting the sun at the center of the solar system, as advocated by Copernicus, not only made it possible to simplify astronomy, but it also removed the rationale for separating cosmology as a separate discipline [VanHelden00]. Needless to say, Copernicus' ideas were not always welcomed.

It is worth observing that Aristotle's cosmology was adopted not because it fit with reality, but because it supported the prevailing world view. Similarly, one can draw a comparison to an organization "choosing" an architecture that reflects or supports its current structure, even though that might not be the simplest solution. Just as separate disciplines of astronomy and cosmology evolved, organizations may create complex organizations and architectures to address separate concerns if opportunities to find simpler, common solutions are bypassed. This is especially noticeable in large organizations that end up forming many different groups, all of which deal with "architecture."

We suspect there is an unwritten rule that large bureaucratic organizations have at least two architecture groups. Each group appears to have responsibility for the corporate architecture, but neither group has sufficient authority or resources to do the job. Worse, political boundaries prevent the groups from coalescing around a single organization. The corollary to this rule is that when architecture groups don't accommodate all requirements or perspectives, more architecture groups form. Although this situation reads as satire, our observations match the conjecture.

If an organization exhibits skills such as simplification, partnering, and rhythm, sharing architecture over time can lead to minimizing code, documentation, and process. You're not reinventing new chunks of code, you are producing a common language that can be shared across the organization by engineers. Sharing can also lead to clarification, since it minimizes the risk of using similar terms to describe very different concepts. It goes without saying that sharing does not automatically produce these benefits. Given the state of affairs within many organizations, sharing can and does lead to bloating and other undesirable or disastrous results.

Don't Forget Common Sense

Minimization in the wrong hands can be downright dangerous. Well-intentioned "bottom-line" executives sometimes slash the architecture budget while demanding dramatic changes to the product line, saying, "We can work on the architecture later." By the time "later" comes around, things have gotten intolerably complex (See LOAN SHARK). Executives, managers, architects, and users must exercise intelligence. Intelligence implies a degree of self-honesty, without which simplification will never happen. Few ideas are more seductive than, "We can keep just the 'easy to do' parts of that feature" (see VENUS FLY TRAP).

PUTTING SIMPLIFICATION INTO PRACTICE: CRITERIA, ANTIPATTERNS, AND PATTERNS

The preceding sections describe how focusing the architecture on customer and business value is important in fulfilling the principle of simplification, and how clarifying an organization's structure, in turn, helps to clarify and minimize the architecture. The consequences of not simplifying the architecture—and defending it from unwarranted complexity as the product line evolves—can be severe. The architecture may not get used and it may become so complex that the architecture detracts value, rather than saving time and money.

The following criteria, antipatterns, and patterns provide guidelines and techniques that organizations can use to determine how well they simplify, clarify, and minimize themselves and their architecture.

CRITERIA

When simplification is working,

1. Developers continue to use the architecture over time, reducing overall cost and complexity.

2. The architecture group clearly understands the essential minimal requirements and builds them into core elements that are shared across one or more applications.

3. Long-term budget and action ensure that elements are removed from the core when

   - they are not shared, or add unnecessary complexity, and
   - there is a clear business case.

ANTIPATTERNS

CLONING illustrates what can happen when programmers are pushed to complete tasks quickly before they learn to use or respect the architecture. Instead of negotiating a change with the component owner, programmers copy and modify parts of the architecture and end up maintaining a lot more than they bargained for.

The pendulum antipatterns, BANYAN and ROOT BOUND, provide a visual image for organizations that swing back and forth, emphasizing simplification way too much or way too little. BANYAN, using the image of a Banyan tree with supporting tendrils growing down from its many branches, describes the consequences of building point solutions over time. ROOT BOUND, the image of an overgrown trunk with few branches, describes a condition in which an architecture or platform team builds in too many "nice-to-have" features or those that are unique to a single customer.

VENUS FLY TRAP illustrates how easy it is to be sweet-talked into adding just one "easy-to-do" feature when the stakes are very high.

LOAN SHARK describes how *not* to implement ARCHITECT ALSO IMPLEMENTS. The architect is moved onto a crash project to add a new set of features, generally for a very important customer. Just as a loan shark promises easy money now for grief in the future, an architect can get a project out of trouble today, but has no time to evolve the existing architecture.

PATTERNS

SLOW DOWN TO SPEED UP describes what to do when developers reject the use of architecture to keep up with schedule and get further behind as a result. The solution: ease up on the schedule and tighten up on the process.

MIGRATION PATH describes an approach to engaging a new user community by building a competency-enhancing bridge.

WHIRLPOOL WATCH is a method for selecting which architectural components need to be examined for rework by watching the degree of churn.

TABLE 7.1   *Mapping Criteria to Antipatterns and Patterns*

CRITERION— HOW YOU MEASURE	ANTIPATTERN— WHAT NOT TO DO	PATTERN— WHAT YOU CAN DO
Developers continue to use the architecture over time, reducing overall cost and complexity.	CLONING	SLOW DOWN TO SPEED UP
The architecture group clearly understands the essential minimal requirements and builds them into core elements that are shared across one or more applications.	BANYAN, ROOT BOUND, and VENUS FLYTRAP	MIGRATION PATH
Long-term budget and action ensure that elements are removed from the core when • they are not shared, or add unnecessary complexity, and • there is a clear business case.	LOAN SHARK	WHIRLPOOL WATCH

Criterion 1: Developers continue to use the architecture over time, reducing cost and complexity

Cloning

Slow Down to Speed Up

Now we come to the hardest part, getting the architecture used correctly. Use requires obtaining and sustaining the trust of managers and practitioners. Unless the architecture is used meaningfully over time, things will get very complex very quickly. When a clear common architecture vision is present, systems can even become simpler over time. Booch observes, "it is only through having a clear sense of a system's architecture that it becomes possible to discover common abstractions and mechanisms." He says, "Exploiting this commonality ultimately leads to the construction of systems that are simpler, and therefore smaller and more reliable" [Booch96].

Antipattern: CLONING

Alias: SEND IN THE CLONES

General Form.   You are a product manager or technical lead who is under pressure to quickly complete a task. There is already code in the architecture that provides similar functionality. So to complete the task quickly, your team creates a clone, an identical or very similar unit of software [Mayrand96].

Your team then adds to or changes the clone to meet your specific task requirements. However, now the duplicated code must be maintained. While cloning offers a means to respond quickly to pressure to develop new features, it often has far-reaching consequences. For example, if a defect is found in the original code, how can your organization ensure that the defect is fixed in all of the clones of code you made, as well as clones made by all of your colleagues?

Forces.   When a software product grows quickly in popularity, there isn't time to fully train new team members before asking them to build new features. Further, many development organizations use maintenance as a training exercise. Developers are often anxious to get on with something new and get out of the responsibility for maintaining what they have built. Further, organizations that develop but do not have maintenance responsibility for a component may not have incentives to write maintainable code.

Even where CODE OWNERSHIP is the rule, negotiating for changes to a component with another component owner may be both awkward and time-consuming [Coplien95]. Component owners may themselves be under crushing pressure to field product and may not have an incentive to respond to requests for new or changed features. When faced with tight deadlines, developers may copy and modify existing code rather than negotiate changes with the owner. If they do not understand the code thoroughly, they may copy more than they need.

Even though lines of code are a good indicator of maintenance cost, some organizations use lines of code as a productivity metric, encouraging rather than discouraging the practice of cloning. This results in a dramatic increase in lines of code and a corresponding and spiraling decrease in its understandability and maintainability.

Solution.   There are several points during a component's life cycle where you can avoid clones. Encourage engineers to seek changes from a component owner before cloning the component. You can incorporate heuristics about avoiding clones into coding style guides so that clones can be identified and removed during code reviews; these heuristics might allow for limited cloning if an appropriate justification is provided. Automated tools can also be used to identify clones, especially in large legacy systems [Mayrand96]. When clones are identified, there are a number of code refactoring techniques that can be applied to remove the duplicated code [Fowler99].

Rationale.   Duplicated code is hard to maintain and use. For example, if there are two versions of the same component, how does a user select the appropriate one? If there are subtle differences in two components, it can be difficult for the maintainer to know if revisions to one version of the component will be appropriate for the other variant. Changes that would have been localized without cloning may now require changes across a much larger portion of the system. All of this adds up to slower, more expensive maintenance. Unfortunately, since these additional costs are often not realized at the time the cloning occurs, and often not by the developer doing the cloning, the temptation to clone is strong. In one case the authors learned about, an audit of a trading floor application for a securities firm found over 1,000 implementations of the Black-Scholles option pricing algorithm, each with its own set of issues and dependencies. If organizations consciously manage the risk of cloning, they can create an environment in which clones do not lead to a deterioration of the architecture. However, doing this requires very serious effort and, often, "burnt-in" experience.

In one case, an audit of a trading floor application for a securities firm found over 1,000 implementations of the Black-Scholles option pricing algorithm.

Example.   Nortel had a complex software architecture for a digital switch that fell victim to the effects of cloning. At first, the business unit had set aside 10% of its R&D funding to build new technology and add capacity to the architecture, but business pressures in 1986 caused the shifting of these funds to other uses. The unit's vision for its architecture deteriorated, and by the late 1980s developers would clone rather than share architecture components. They reported an increased amount of code in the product line, which they interpreted as an increase in productivity [Cashin91]. However, by 1993, the time between releases had tripled to one-and-a-half years and defects became unacceptably high [Ziegler93].

When is This Antipattern a Pattern?   Sometimes cloning makes sense in the short-term, but a decision should be accompanied by action to mitigate the risk, such as tracking cloned components and planning to MERGE AFTER CLONING [Dikel97b]. In this case a common sequence of events is that a request is made to the component owner. He or she cannot do the work in the time allotted, but agrees that the capability does belong in the component (this is important since it preserves the architecture). The owner agrees to the cloning and the eventual merge. An organization may also decide to accept the risks of cloning, for example, if there are no plans to maintain the code for an extended period of time, or if there are conflicting schedules and the merge is an explicitly scheduled part of the plan. Lastly, if and when a decision to clone is made, an effort should be made to minimize the amount of code duplicated. The cloned code might be refactored as a separate component both to minimize duplication and to make tracking easier.

Related Antipatterns and Patterns.   MERGE AFTER CLONING provides a way to mitigate the risks of CLONING by providing a road map for reintegrating clones back into common components [Dikel97b]. Some of the techniques in the "Streamed Lines" pattern language may also be adapted for managing changes to code that has been cloned [Cabrera99].

Pattern: SLOW DOWN TO SPEED UP

Problem Statement.   How do you introduce an architecture-based solution to a team that has not yet learned to use or trust the architecture?

Context.   You are an experienced technical manager who needs to implement a series of new features on a tight schedule. You have selected an architecture for the product line. The chosen architecture would glue together individual work products and simplify the job of making them interoperate. However, none of the members of your newly formed team has experience with the architecture and most are used to building point solutions. There is not time to implement each feature independently and integrate them later.

Forces.   Using a mature architecture can reduce redundancy and complexity by ensuring that team members' work products fit with one another and with the work products of other teams. Moving to an architecture-based solution presents its own set of problems and risks. As such, it requires team members to be independent problem-solvers, rather than coders. Yet, without an understanding of the problem the architecture has been chosen to address, or when they are unsure the architecture will help them deliver on their assignments, developers are more likely to optimize around specific point solutions. Further, new team members are reluctant to admit what they are not sure about.

If a manager imposes a very tight schedule combined with the demand to follow an approach that is unfamiliar, developers are even less likely to follow. Instead, they are likely to cut corners from their current approach, or abandon it entirely. CLONING and other quick fixes often rush in to fill the void.

This can result in an even bigger mess than if no method were prescribed.

Solution.   Involve developers in the problem you have chosen the architecture to address and coach them through developing parts of the solution. Give the process a higher priority than the schedule. Direct developers to step through the architecture. Provide an expert resource to the team who has used the process before and who has a proven ability to modify the architecture or process to meet diverse problems. Check to verify that the process is followed in a systematic and serious way and that meaningful steps are being made towards delivering the product.

Result.   The development team implements the architecture successfully, albeit after a series of trials and errors. The architecture and its supporting processes are also likely to improve. The second and third products take significantly less time to implement than the first, and the envisioned benefits begin to kick in. The team delivers the set of products in a reasonable amount of time, yet each benefits from many of the improvements made. Configuration management headaches are reduced. Developers become believers, while the manager achieves her or his long-term objectives.

Consequences.   Using this pattern risks losing track of the goal of delivering a viable product. Developers may lose hope and focus and get wrapped up on process. Imposing an unfamiliar process may cause engineers to resent management. It is not unusual for a team of inexperienced engineers to believe that architecture or process is totally unnecessary for professionals like themselves. Developers may then subvert the process, using the process to absolve themselves of any responsibility for failure.

Rationale.   Slow Down to Speed Up describes how a manager can prevent engineers from missing the benefits of an architecture. This is accomplished by allowing developers to get their hands dirty understanding and solving the problem the architecture seeks to solve, and by insisting and verifying that developers follow the process even if it takes longer. This puts developers and management on the same side. If the architecture and process are sound, the developers are likely to save some time and effort, building their trust in using the architecture. If following the process and using the architecture discovers unexpected glitches and causes delays, valuable feedback will have been gained and the architecture will be improved.

Example.   An architect worked with two programmers who were learning to use ColdFusion to build a Web-based platform that supported three or four separate applications. Because they were unfamiliar with the technology, the architect tightly controlled their work, making very specific assignments and checking the resulting code. This resulted in an implementation that conformed closely with the architecture.

However, as the programmers learned more, they saw new and different ways of accomplishing their assignments. One programmer charged ahead using several new product features and delivered an entire application. While his work satisfied the requirements and pleased the customer who had requested it, his work did not fit with the architecture and could not be utilized by other applications. When the programmer left, no one could figure out the code he had written, and his work rapidly became an albatross. The architect and sponsor eliminated the programmer's feature set, and substituted off-the-shelf technology.

Realizing things had gotten out of control, the architect slowed things down and changed his approach, challenging his entire development team to solve the problems the architecture was built to address, and insisting that everyone agree to use a common solution before proceeding. Each developer took over one or more architecture components. This changed developers' view of the architecture from a top-down structure that only the architect understood, to a solution developers understood and improved.

Related Antipatterns and Patterns.   PAIRS OR BETTER TO OPEN describes the introduction of two or more people from a team that has been successful using an innovative process or technology, which helps in introducing technology into the receiving team. "Human nature being what it is, there is always credibility in numbers." A manager could use this approach to mitigate the risk of introducing the new architecture [Olson97].

Criterion 2: The architecture group clearly understands the essential minimal requirements and builds them into core elements

Banyan

Root Bound

Venus
Flytrap

Migration
Path

Simplification requires knowing the most important problems to solve. Without a clear, congruent architecture vision, simplification is very hard to do. A good vision lays the groundwork for simplification. Done correctly, the architecture vision defines a clear customer value, identifies a small set of problems the architecture can reasonably solve first to deliver this value, and lays out a path toward expanding that value over time. Effective anticipation, too, can avoid the bumps in the road that result from changes such as the unexpected release of new technology or the entry of new competition. Both can burden an architecture with requirements that may not fit with its existing structure.

Maintaining a clear understanding of the essential minimal requirements requires discipline. The architecture team and those who make promises on its behalf must ferret out really cool features that don't belong in the core and find other ways for customers to implement those features. When the requirements handed to the architect are too detailed and provide too much of the solution, the architect must push back to gain time to think about the "right" way to enable—but not necessarily implement—these requirements.

Pendulum Antipatterns

The following antipatterns describe two conditions in which efforts to simplify have gone too far. BANYAN describes the consequences of building point solutions over time. A point solution is often the simplest way to deliver a solution to a specific customer need (see Figure 7.3). ROOT BOUND describes a condition where an architecture or platform team builds in features that are unique to each individual product the platform supports, or could possibly support (see Figure 7.4). They are called pendulum antipatterns because the reaction to one often triggers a reaction that brings on the other (see Figure 7.5).

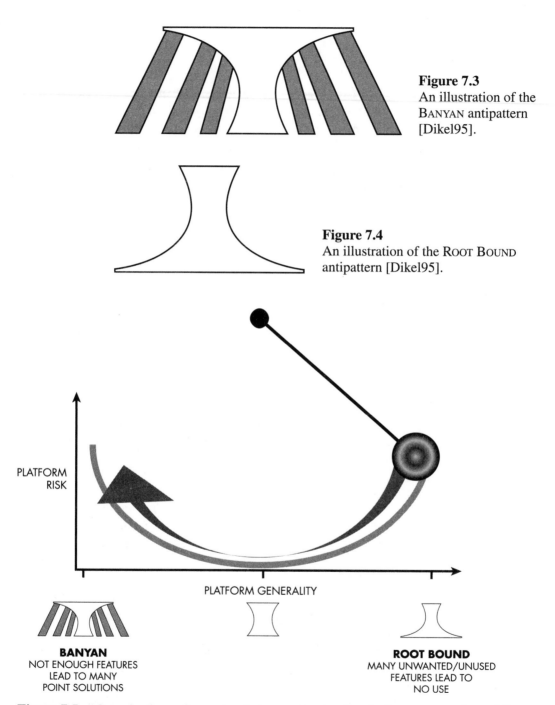

Figure 7.3
An illustration of the
BANYAN antipattern
[Dikel95].

Figure 7.4
An illustration of the ROOT BOUND
antipattern [Dikel95].

PLATFORM
RISK

PLATFORM GENERALITY

BANYAN
NOT ENOUGH FEATURES
LEAD TO MANY
POINT SOLUTIONS

ROOT BOUND
MANY UNWANTED/UNUSED
FEATURES LEAD TO
NO USE

Figure 7.5   Organizations often swing between starving the platform team and providing too many resources and not enough user validation.

Antipattern: BANYAN

General Form.   BANYAN describes the consequences of building point solutions over time. Your development team makes sure that each product it produces is the absolute simplest possible by building from scratch or CLONING a related product and fitting it to the problem at hand. You may get initial products to customers quickly, meeting their stated requirements; however, nothing is shared across products. As each product is maintained and upgraded, the BANYAN pattern begins to emerge. Individual products branch further apart. Since they are not strongly supported by a SHARED PLATFORM, each branch requires its own supporting structure, much like the branches of a Banyan tree, each of which is supported by numerous tendrils [Kane97]. BANYAN looks like it sounds, a martini glass with a huge bowl and a tiny bottom that is propped up so that it doesn't fall over (see Figure 7.3).

Forces.   Getting just the right product to market a month before the competition can mean the difference between gaining both market share and substantial profit and being an "also ran." Intense time pressures can drive management to ignore the benefits of building or even maintaining a SHARED PLATFORM. Breaking the development team into small independent groups, each focused on a separate market, and freeing each group from all constraints can get individual products to market quicker. However, building point solutions can result in spiraling complexity, maintenance costs that are out of control, and high defect rates. Crafting point solutions can also inhibit the ability to beef up capabilities by integrating other products. Experiencing severe consequences of BANYAN can lead executives and just about everyone else to head straight for the idea of a SHARED PLATFORM as the solution [Kane97]. Executives sometimes overreact and provide platform teams with lots of resources and too little direction.

Solution.   Consider merging chunks of core architecture that were modified to accommodate specific features back into the core as described in MERGE AFTER CLONING [Kane97]. Is it feasible? Is it desirable? Is it likely? In conducting the tradeoff analysis, consider the short-term and downstream consequences of BANYAN. Be careful to consider the possibility that rushing to build every envisioned product could burn up all resources before any products emerge. Recognize that time does not stop while the merger happens, so further cloning of the original code can occur. Without a serious commitment to get things back on to a single track, chaos is sure to ensue. If neither MERGE AFTER CLONING nor maintaining multiple products looks viable, reconsider using A FRAMEWORK TEAM to build a SHARED PLATFORM [Coplien95] [Kane97].

Rationale.   BANYAN is the result of too many point solutions and is often accompanied by CLONING. Too many short-term decisions are made to address immediate needs. The price for these decisions is higher maintenance costs and increased complexity. While this approach may lead to faster responses initially, in the long run this antipattern results in slower time-to-market. Controlling CLONING can help avoid creating a Banyan architecture, but once this antipattern has set in, duplicated code and capabilities need to be reigned in in order to reduce the accumulated complexity.

Example.   A development team supporting a portal framework for business-to-business applications with a growing customer base was challenged to adapt the portal to acquire data through XML rather than through calls to an SQLServer database. Team members went through their existing code and estimated there were four to five thousand queries scattered throughout. Faced with the prospect of adding XML calls to each query, then going back to add new calls for each new back end, they decided to put all data calls into one package. This resulted in a significant reduction in both effort and defects.

In the early 1990s, a product team was faced with a requirement to deploy a suite of development tools on two separate platforms before competitors could gain a foothold. In response, they decided to split into two separate groups that worked furiously to build features to a common set of requirements. No sooner had the teams fielded their products than several additional platforms emerged as critical targets along with a gaggle of additional requirements. The product manager's budget did not grow with the work, and the staff quickly realized they had passed their limits [Wilson96].

When This Antipattern is a Pattern.   In spite of sweeping government and industry reforms, there are still contracts and customer points of contact that encourage suppliers to build and maintain project-specific solutions. While this practice is often an antipattern in its own right, many vendors continue to reap significant profits by getting paid for inefficiency.

Related Patterns.   Both SHARED PLATFORM and FRAMEWORK TEAM are often driven into existence to prevent or remedy BANYAN [Kane97] [Coplien95]. As such, their forces overlap considerably. MERGE AFTER CLONING can in some cases be used to resolve the conditions described by BANYAN [Dikel97b]. The antipattern can result when an organization overcompensates for the ROOT BOUND antipattern.

Antipattern: ROOT BOUND

General Form.   With ROOT BOUND, your architecture or platform team builds in too many "nice to have" features or too many that are unique to each individual product the platform supports. Instead of providing a quick "one-off" feature for a customer, your colleagues build generics. As a result, way too much functionality is shared, and the platform is generally too big, too slow, and too late. Graphically, ROOT BOUND looks like what it sounds like, a martini glass with a huge bottom and a thimble-sized bowl (see Figure 7.4).

Forces.   Platform teams are often challenged to effect a merge of functions that are common across several existing products. Product development teams often insist on features that are unique to their product before they will give platform use serious consideration. On the other hand, the more product-specific features that are built into the shared platform, the less likely it is to meet the needs of any product team [Kane97].

Platform teams are sometimes initiated due to a strong, organization-wide reaction to disastrous consequences brought on by the BANYAN antipattern. Executives overreact to the situation and provide platform teams with lots of resources and too little market- or customer-focused direction. When platform teams are provided a liberal budget without a clearly defined delivery cycle, they may delay the task of prioritizing and scheduling features for upcoming releases.

Solution.   Keep product-specific features out of the platform by building or helping product teams to build product-specific modules that are not part of the architecture. Build a minimal shared set of features into the platform's plan and deliver the features on a regular release schedule according to their priority.

Rationale.   Organizations fall into ROOT BOUND when they lose focus on what is essential. Instead of building a core that is shared across the architecture, they try to build something that will satisfy all of the needs of all of the users of the architecture, even if those needs are not shared by the other users, or even if there is not an expected need for the capability. Only a focus on the core of the architecture can return the architecture to a balance.

When Antipattern is a Pattern.   An architect with extraordinary powers of anticipation and a good deal of luck can make a feature-laden platform work even when many of the features are unique to one or two supported products. This might be more likely when the supported products target closely related market segments in which any segment could demand any of the features at a moment's notice.

Example.   A large financial services company took what its management considered to be a great step by introducing a common architecture across its many operating units. A project team of the most brilliant and talented modeling experts money could buy began work on a common architecture. Rather than beginning with a few business units, the team resolved to progress toward deploying a single architecture. To accomplish this goal, they decided to build an all-encompassing common business model. Two years, hundreds of presentations, and thousands of pages later, the business model collapsed of its own weight, never to see daylight again. All efforts to actually get the organization to fit into the model failed.

Related Patterns and Antipatterns.   The antipattern can result when an organization overcompensates for the BANYAN antipattern.

Antipattern: VENUS FLY TRAP

Aliases: ADDING LITTLE OLE REQUIREMENTS IS SUCH SWEET SORROW

General Form.   Like many software developers, you are often sweet-talked into making architecture changes that you desperately want to believe are easy, though you know—or deeply suspect—the changes are extremely complex. Sometimes a demanding customer who expects but does not receive resistance inadvertently brings on this antipattern. You often see this antipattern in a competitive bid in which the customer has let it be known that low cost is going to be strongly considered, or late in the product release schedule when a competitor thrusts new features into the product space.

The product may be in a late stage of development and some unforeseen factor (the Internet, XML, wireless, etc.) that has been steadily growing in importance is suddenly seen as a "must-have" to make the release competitive. Against everyone's better judgment, new features are slammed in at the last minute to show that the organization is progressive and is tracking the latest developments. There is no time to do anything right, and the new features are almost universally regretted. They don't tend to last for more than one release, and if they do they often impose strangulating constraints on the architecture.

Forces.   Even organizations with solid data and estimation procedures can fall prey when they encounter situations they have never encountered before. Customers who talk about "Internet time" project a belief that Internet applications are different or that throwing out existing practices will result in a magical ability to meet compressed schedules with solid product. We really want to believe our manager or customer when they tell us we can separate the few bits they really want from "the hard stuff." In crunch situations there is often not enough time for developers to test their assumptions about products or objects they are expected to use. Without testing assumptions, it is easy to mistake a distant mountain for a small hill a mile away. When forced to estimate based on incomplete information, things can look a lot easier than they are. The alternative of compensating for uncertainty by estimating an order of magnitude more time than is apparent can be painful. The threat of losing business, or being in the doghouse with a boss or customer sometimes leads us to tiptoe into the old fly trap, our little voice screaming away. When we try to implement the solution we discover that implementing the easy parts means building a lot more.

Solutions.   Clarify the problem and solution before committing. Engage the customer in the clarification process so that he or she begins to see how complex the requirement is. Done right, this will protect the developer against low-bidding competitors who would rather not see the complexities right now, thank you.

Rationale.   Software developers—managers and architects included—tend to lean on the side of optimism, they believe "things will go as planned." In part, this is because software's complexities are often due to the sticky details that come from interacting with other software components, systems, and products. These elements appear stable and effective in the box, but become complex and problematic on integration.

Example.   A company designed a centralized case-tracking system for use in three sites. The designer calculated that the customer's ISDN connections would offer sufficient bandwidth. They centralized the database at the main site. When the product was installed, the designer learned, much to his horror, that bandwidth was severely constrained by the customer's network protocol.

Faced with the alternative of telling their customer to wait for a substantial redesign, the designer and project manager promised to build a "simple" replication scheme and synchronize the data daily. The problem was, every release of the replication system provided a new and unwelcome lesson. One year later, after spending over three times what the customer paid, the replication system still did not quite work.

The infamous baggage-handling system at the Denver International Airport is another good example of VENUS FLY TRAP antipattern (and perhaps many others as well). The new airport was to have begun operations in October 1993, but it did not open until February 1995. The primary reason for the delay was that the planned automated baggage-handling system was not ready, and the baggage system was essential to the operation of the airport. While baggage systems are an essential part of any airport's operations, the size of the new Denver airport required much better performance than conventional baggage systems. The delayed opening was estimated to have resulted in a loss of about $500 million. While automated baggage systems had been deployed in Atlanta and San Francisco, the system at Denver was much more complex [de Neufville94]. As reported in the *New York Times*:

> The Denver system represents a leap in scope, with 14 times the capacity of San Francisco's. It is the first such system to serve an entire airport. It is also the first where the carts will only slow down, not stop, to pick up and drop off bags, the first to be run by a network of desktop computers rather than a mainframe, the first to use radio links and the first system for oversized bags, which in Denver tend to be skis [Myerson94].

The contractor, BAE, had a world-class reputation and agreed to the work and to the crash schedule if there were no changes to the plans. As the CEO, Gene Di Fonso, said in 1994, "Who would turn down a $193 million contract? You'd expect a little trouble for that kind of money" [Myerson94]. However, there were changes to the plans. The system was initially planned for one airline, and the customer expanded the requirements to serve the entire airport.

The airport finally opened, but the automated baggage system was scaled back substantially. It only served one airline that used one of the three concourses. A slower conventional system with higher operational costs was used to serve the other airlines at the other concourses [de Neufville94].

While this example is of an entire system rather than just a software architecture, it is still instructive. The components of the system had worked individually on a smaller scale, but had never been integrated into such a large application before. Further, although the risks were visible at the earliest stages of the project, the customer's need for the system and the temptation of the project proved irresistible.

When is This Antipattern a Pattern?   When the risks are visible and jointly understood, both parties accept the risks because potential payoffs substantially outweigh the risks. The rule of thumb, according to several experienced architects, is that this antipattern may be a pattern when the payoffs outweigh risks by 3:1 or more.

Variation.   The customer inadvertently strong-arms suppliers to ignore risk and complexity in their bids. The customer's initial lack of understanding drives suppliers to make changes to their bids that are bad for everyone.

Related Antipatterns and Patterns.   DOORMAT describes a group lead that regularly caves in to any and all management demands [Rising98]. VENUS FLY TRAP is different from DOORMAT in that it can entrap even the senior leaders of the organization. VENUS FLY TRAP illustrates how easy it is to be sweet-talked into adding just "the easy-to-do" parts of a feature when the stakes are very high.

Pattern: MIGRATION PATH

Problem Statement. How do you engage a new user community in the use of a platform?

Context. You are an architect, and you would like to use your architecture to support a new and valuable application area. Succeeding in the new application area requires skills and perspectives that most current users don't possess. The user community that does possess the necessary skills is used to a different problem-solving approach than the one presented by the current platform.

Forces. People are threatened by change. Migration often requires multidimensional change (e.g., language could be one dimension; use of objects vs. procedural code another; relational vs. object database; distributed vs. centralized). The more dimensions there are, the harder it is to change. For example, a new project that only requires teaching the old developers a new language has a much better chance of succeeding than one that requires a new language and a new object paradigm. If the transition to a new technology involves changing so many dimensions that users feel they have lost the hard-won advantage of their current professional skills, traditional users will be unlikely to support the breakthrough technology. When new technology increases a user's grasp of his or her existing skills, users are much more like-

Habits die hard. Those stuck in them use new and powerful tools to do what they have done before in the same old way.

ly to adopt it. Habits die hard. Those stuck in them use new and powerful tools to do what they have done before in the same old way.

Solution. Choose a class of adopters that is most likely to expand the value of the architecture and work to make the architecture quickly understandable and usable to them.

Consider all of the classes of potential early adopters, looking at their skill sets and approach to solving problems. Determine which class is most likely to "get" or envision the breakthrough result and weigh this consideration as strongly as whether the class possesses the skills and knowledge necessary to implement the solution.

Provide migration paths for professionals who get the end vision but lack an important skill set; provide a simple way to get a basic set of results from the platform. Then, lead the users through progressively more specific uses of the platform.

Result.   A new type of application is opened very quickly through leveraging the knowledge and skills of the existing user community with the skills and vision of previously untapped classes of developers. People "trade up" their skill sets and deliver greater value using a new architecture.

Rationale.   Building a migration path makes a breakthrough technology competency enhancing to a target group and therefore accelerates their adoption and use.

Professionals that are familiar with existing software technologies may feel that a breakthrough technology will diminish the value of their skills as well as their standing within a group. Professionals to whom the breakthrough technology reaches out are more likely to feel that the value of their skills will be enhanced.

Consequences.   Investing in an approach to migrate a new class of platform users risks alienating existing users. The solution may also require the architect to enhance the competencies of the class of users that gets the vision while destroying and rebuilding competencies of users who don't get the vision. This approach can leave a supplier with less than critical mass and may lead to failure.

Example.   As the Web began to grow in popularity, Allaire Corporation recognized that most sites were static pages. Allaire made it easy for early Web users to develop interactive pages. These users were by necessity familiar with HTML, and they possessed a wide range of communication skills such as graphic arts, but by and large they did not possess database skills. These users had "gotten" how the Web worked and what it could do. On the whole, however, they knew very little about programming and database design. Allaire reached these users by building a fourth-generation language using HTML-like tags. In contrast, database providers targeted their products toward current users who had their hands (and pockets) full building client–server applications. Allaire users were able to field a large number of data driven applications and helped to demonstrate the viability of the Web for more than just brochureware.

As Web use became mature, Allaire users recognized their need for software and database skills. By then, the number and complexity of Web applications had grown significantly, and traditional database developers had become engaged by the Web. At that point, Allaire expanded into enterprise applications, bringing along its original users while engaging the traditional software engineers and database developers.

Loan Shark

 Whirlpool
Watch

Criterion 3: Long-term budget and action ensure that elements are removed from the core when 1) they are not shared, or add unnecessary complexity, and 2) there is a clear business case

Improving an architecture takes a regular investment of time and money. Regularity is really important because the times when executive or managers are least inclined to focus on architecture are very often the times when the architecture is most vulnerable. It is really tempting to pull the architect into a crash project to field a new feature and let the architecture fend for itself (see LOAN SHARK). Regular investment must be accompanied by adult supervision, or a ROOT BOUND situation will result.

At least one person must monitor the architecture, insist upon its maintenance, and take action to remove complexities that spring up. He or she must have substantial control of the architecture even though many such champions do not receive executive support or recognition for their efforts. This is a difficult thing to do. Often, a tantalizingly sweet idea puts additional features into the core in the first place. Then these features get a following. In organizations where simplification works, developers work to remove elements from the core because everyone is aware of the pain that a complex core brings and fights to keep it simple. When such a feature is removed, a wise provider can take steps to make sure that loyal customers can recover. Accomplishing this could result in a two-level architecture: a core and then some kind of "adaptation package" around it.

In order to remove nonessential elements from the core you have to know what not to get rid of. Knowing what not to get rid of means understanding the compelling value architecture adds to the products it supports and how it delivers that value.

Antipattern: LOAN SHARK

Alias: CAPTAIN ON DECK

General Form.   As a lead architect, you are charged with adapting and maintaining the architecture and are transferred to an all-out effort to implement a new feature-set. The features get implemented, but the architecture team is left without a pilot. Because there isn't time to make reasoned changes to the architecture, you create a specialized version of the existing architecture to solve the problem. As a result, the new feature does not fit with the current architecture. Management's promise to provide you with time and resources to fix the problem later can't be fulfilled because of the degree of effort needed to maintain a product that lacks conceptual integrity [Brooks82].

Forces.   Architects are easy targets when staffing gets low. The lead architect is a particularly good target because he or she may be the only person on the team who understands all the architecture lore and undocumented features—what can be done and where it will break. The architect has often "graduated" from the ranks of the development team and is seen as someone with the right skills to jump in and do what is unfortunately often characterized as "real work," as opposed to the more vaporous architecture stuff.

On the other hand, the lead architect may be the only person who can adapt the architecture to accomplish the very same new feature or requirement. Throwing the lead architect at the problem in a "code red" environment often forces the architect to make a specialized fix rather than enhance the architecture. This may cause the architect to leave, field a prototype solution, or make it impossible to maintain the legacy system.

Solution.   Split the lead architect's time between implementing the new feature and adapting the architecture by engaging the savviest engineer as lead for implementing the new feature. Allow the lead architect to guide the implementation while providing time and resources so that the architecture can adapt to the new requirements.

Rationale.   Moving the lead architect fully into a developer role before a replacement is fully capable is like going to a loan shark to payoff your creditors or a captain leaving his post unmanned to work on the deck. Without the lead architect's guidance, seemingly minor maintenance changes can have unanticipated and unpleasant consequences. Building significant new capabilities into the architecture presents an even greater risk. What often happens is that the architecture begins to lose value because its conceptual integrity degrades. Because expected delivery of new capabilities slips, users take architecture maintenance and development into their own hands or replace the architecture entirely.

Example.   A business-to-business Web company was preparing its baseline, next-generation platform. At the same time, the company's largest customer was getting ready to demonstrate to its customers and to Wall Street analysts a new product line that was based on the Web company's current platform. At the last minute, several components of the customer's roll-out needed adjusting. Guess what happened to the next generation architecture? The Web company's architect, who was also one of their best programmers, spent most of his time off-site at the customer's offices fitting outside components into the alpha version of his platform. As a result, the next-generation platform release and its hoped-for value were delayed more than six months.

When is This Antipattern a Pattern?   When the lead architect refuses to dirty his or her hands with implementation details and has insisted on an unworkable architecture, this may be the best solution. Putting the architect in the implementers' shoes might not solve the whole problem, but it would help the architect learn.

Related Antipatterns and Patterns.   CLONING can be a side effect of this pattern. Since the architect is no longer focusing on the architecture, groups relying on it may clone instead of waiting for architecture changes. This is not the best way to do ARCHITECT ALSO IMPLEMENTS [Coplien95].

Pattern: WHIRLPOOL WATCH

Problem Statement.   How do you know what to refactor—that is, what to remove from the core or simplify?

Context.   You are a product manager or technical lead for an architecture that is shared across several applications or products.

Forces.   When core components are too closely coupled with one another, one change affects a number of others. Changes in core components should be expected, particularly when they are heavily used by more than one application. When components are too tightly coupled with one application, new requirements from other applications can add unnecessary complexity.

Solution.   Observe the degree of churn for each component or subsystem over time. Those that churn the most are candidates for refactoring. Other monitoring strategies can also be applied, such as monitoring news and discussion lists for frequently requested components. This may also be a leading indicator of cloning.

Result.   In the hands of an experienced practitioner, this practice quickly identifies components and subsystems that are excellent targets for simplification, saving time and energy.

Consequences.   Any rule of thumb can be misapplied. High degrees of churn in a few components may be a good sign if other core components remain stable.

Rationale.   Measure and watch churn to identify components that are strong candidates for simplification. Churn may indicate a brittle and inflexible component, and so you should consider changing the component in some fundamental way. For example, churn may indicate popularity, so investigate further to understand the cause of the churn. While a high degree of use may not indicate complexity, it is a strong indicator that improvements will produce a high return on investment.

Churn may indicate a lack of sufficient generality or a high degree of coupling with other components or with applications. As a result, changes in some applications require a disproportionate amount of change in core components.

Churn may indicate unnecessary complexity. Complexity makes components hard to understand. When those who maintain the code are rushed, the changes they make may cause code size and complexity to grow very quickly. When this happens, apparently small changes call for lots of tweaking throughout the code of a complex component. In all these cases, focus on components with a significantly high degree of churn, and target your simplification efforts there.

Related Antipatterns and Patterns.   BANYAN describes the result of building many customized platforms that have the same parent. While much of the code is redundant, each change in each customized platform can affect the redundant code in a different way. If you looked at the customized platforms as a whole, you would see a lot of churn.

Example.   During a 1995 study of a Northern Telecom business unit, we interviewed programmers, architects, and several levels of management. The senior managers and practitioners whom we interviewed examined churn as a rule of thumb to determine which components were overly complex and/or needed maintenance [Dikel95].

SUMMARY

Simplification is widely recognized as essential to software success. It is even more essential to software architecture. The more products an architecture supports and the longer it supports those products, the more important simplification becomes.

Simplification requires effective organizational behaviors and individual skills. Keeping an architecture simple requires the tenacity to stay focused on minimal essential value and the skills to separate and deliver the architecture as a product that delivers that value and very little else.

Simplification is the intelligent clarification and minimization of both architecture and the organizational environment in which it is used.

Clarification means making a careful organizational analysis and working to adapt both organization and architecture to achieve and maintain alignment. Clarification also means digging to find the real requirements and spending the energy to fill them. Like clarification, minimization applies to both organization and architecture. As we can see from the writings of William of Ockham in the fourteenth century, minimization is not unique to software architecture. Nevertheless, a software organization that rejects these skills is subject to spiraling complexity, costs, and unwelcome surprises.

OTHER APPLICABLE PATTERNS AND ANTIPATTERNS

There are other patterns that can be used to put the principle of Simplification into practice, as well as antipatterns to avoid along the way. Table 7.2 lists organizational patterns and antipatterns cataloged in the 2000 edition of *The Patterns Almanac* [Rising00]. Table 7.3 lists antipatterns from *Antipatterns: Refactoring Software, Architectures, and Projects in Crisis* [BrownW98].

TABLE 7.2   *Organizational Patterns and Antipatterns That Can Shape Simplification [Rising00]*

AESTHETIC PATTERN [Coplien95]	MULTIPLE COMPETING DESIGNS [Weir98]
ARCHITECT ALSO IMPLEMENTS [Coplien95]	OWNER PER DELIVERABLE [Cockburn98]
BUFFALO MOUNTAIN [Coplien95]	PROBLEM-ORIENTED TEAM [Taylor99]
CONWAY'S LAW [Coplien95]	RECONSTRUCTION [Foote99]
DIVIDE AND CONQUER [Coplien95]	SIZE THE ORGANIZATION [Coplien95]
FORM FOLLOWS FUNCTION [Coplien95]	SKILL MIX [Cockburn96]
FUNCTION OWNERS/COMPONENT OWNERS [Cockburn98]	SOLO VIRTUOSO [Coplien95]
GENERIC UI, SPECIFIC UI [Cockburn96]	SPONSOR OBJECTIVES [Whitenack95]
GENERICS AND SPECIFICS [Cockburn96]	SUBCLASS PER TEAM [Cockburn96]
INFORMAL LABOR PLAN [Cuningham96]	SWEEPING IT UNDER THE RUG [Foote99]
MOVE RESPONSIBILITIES [Coplien95]	WORK SPLIT [Cunningham96]

TABLE 7.3   *Antipatterns That Can Derail Simplification [BrownW98]*

ARCHITECTURE BY IMPLICATION

AUTOGENERATED STOVEPIPE

BOAT ANCHOR

COVER YOUR ASSETS

CUT AND PASTE PROGRAMMING

TABLE 7.3   *(continued)*

DEAD END

FUNCTIONAL DECOMPOSITION

INPUT KLUDGE

LAVA FLOW

POLTERGEISTS

REINVENT THE WHEEL

SPAGHETTI CODE

STOVEPIPE SYSTEM

SWISS ARMY KNIFE

THE BLOB

WARM BODIES

PRINCIPLES AT WORK: THE ALLAIRE CASE STUDY

To be simple is the best thing in the world; to be modest is the next best thing. I'm not sure about being quiet.

—G.K. Chesterton, All Things Considered

INTRODUCTION

This chapter provides an illustrative case study of the VRAPS organizational principles for software architecture at work within Allaire Corporation. We examine each of the principles at work among the developers, users, and managers of Allaire's Web application architecture. For each principle, we provide a brief definition, a description of the value of the principle to Allaire, and several examples of practices we observed. We also recount what Allaire staff told us about how they tell that a principle is *not* in place.

Figure 8.1
Allaire founders, J.J. and Jeremy Allaire.

Why Allaire?

Allaire is a provider of Internet software products and services for companies building their business on the Web. Allaire provides an architecture that spans JRun (Java) and ColdFusion Web application servers, packaged applications (Allaire Spectra), and visual tools. As of this publication, Allaire counted more than 70,000 application server installations and a community of over 500,000 developers. Among its many customers, Allaire counts online companies Autobytel, Lycos, FAO Schwartz, and Williams-Sonoma, as well as the industrial firms Bank of America, Boeing, Kodak, Siemens, and United Parcel Service.

Allaire's future holds a number of the software architecture challenges we described in our study of Nortel [Dikel97a]. Simply put, if Allaire's architecture fails, the company and its customers will experience negative consequences. We selected Allaire as the focus for our case study for these reasons, and because the company was accessible and the authors were familiar with Allaire technologies and its customers.

The study of Allaire is an illustrative case study[1] that complements other case studies and research performed by the authors. While we wanted to test to see whether the VRAPS principles resonated with company founders, lead architect, senior managers, and engineers, we did not set out to irrevocably prove that the principles were the sole cause of Allaire's success, or that the principles were dogma within Allaire. Indeed, we observed that Allaire has experienced great successes as well as challenges, some of which did not directly relate to the architecture principles—for example, the availability of venture capital for Internet firms. In addition, the authors learned of cases where the lack of an organizational principle caused problems for Allaire architects.

The goal of our study, then, was to provide an illustration of how Allaire—in very specific terms—enacts the principles and what benefits and consequences result. To gain additional perspective, we spoke with partners who consult for Allaire and build products based on ColdFusion, and we spoke with industrial organizations that have adopted Allaire technology. At the time that we conducted most of the interviews for this case study, our focus was the ColdFusion product line. However, Allaire has been establishing a much stronger presence in the area of enterprise application development tools with new products and acquisitions such as Allaire Spectra, JRun, and the Web Dynamic Data Exchange (WDDX). We are able to gain insight into

---

[1] The General Accounting Office describes an illustrative case study as one that examines one or two instances and describes what happened and why [GAO90].

how Allaire has been able to extend the vision first established with ColdFusion and expand their customer base into these new markets.

Five Organizational Principles

This book articulates five principles that are key for the long-term success of software product line architecture. The principles transcend software engineering and management practices to provide software organizations with tools for cohesion and delivery of value. Table 8.1 summarizes the five principles and identifies the chapters where we describe the principles in detail.

TABLE 8.1   *The Five VRAPS Principles for Software Architecture*

Vision (Chapter 3) is the mapping of future value to architectural constraints as measured by how well the architecture's structures and goals are clear, compelling, congruent, and flexible.

Rhythm (Chapter 4) is the recurring, predictable exchange of work products within an architecture group and across their customers and suppliers.

Anticipation (Chapter 5) is the extent to which those who build and implement the architecture predict, validate, and adapt the architecture to changing technology, competition, and customer needs.

Partnering (Chapter 6) is the extent to which architecture stakeholders maintain clear, cooperative roles and maximize the value they deliver and receive.

Simplification (Chapter 7) is the intelligent clarification and minimization of both architecture and the organizational environment in which it functions.

What was Our Approach?

We first contacted Allaire in Fall 1998 and discussed the five VRAPS principles with Chief Technology Officer Jeremy Allaire. Jeremy was immediately enthused by the concept of organizational principles. He noted that social and organizational factors were very important to the company's success, and that both he and his brother, founder, Chairman, and Vice President J.J. Allaire, came from social science backgrounds. These backgrounds, Jeremy suggested, complement the company's strong engineering skills.

We based our approach for the study upon the reference model described in Chapter 2. We developed and used an interview protocol for each of the five organizational principles and conducted structured interviews among twelve Allaire employees, including the company's founders, chief architect, manager of partner relations, development managers, and several product engineers. We also interviewed customers and partners of Allaire. We conducted interviews at several levels within Allaire, as well as with external customers. This permitted us to triangulate our data, perform limited validation, and reduce the risk of bias.

We observed the Allaire ColdFusion architecture from two perspectives—first, as a software product line that is engineered, adapted, and packaged by the company; and, second, as a product that is used by its customers to develop Web applications. We saw evidence for each principle from both perspectives (see Table 8.2).

TABLE 8.2   *Exemplary Relations for Organizational Principles*

PRINCIPLE	INTERNAL PERSPECTIVE (E.G., ALLAIRE ENGINEER)	EXTERNAL PERSPECTIVE (E.G., WEB DEVELOPER)
Vision	What will customers need next year to leverage the Internet?	Will Allaire's Spectra help me to gain market share, or will it compete with me?
Rhythm	When do we need to train the support team in the new release features? Are there going to be enough QA staff when the product gets out of Alpha?	Will Allaire meet its ship date for version 5.0 in time for my use of the new search and indexing component for Linux?
Partnering	Can I trust that the ISAPI stub component will be modified correctly to run on IIS 5.0?	Will Allaire respond to my concern about multi-threaded Java integration?
Anticipation	Will we be wiped out by Microsoft's Windows 2000 release?	Is my investment in Allaire technology a good one? Will the product stay alive as I use new technologies?
Simplification	Can I produce a component to better fit Microsoft's SOAP?	Do I need to integrate other products to develop a solution? Can ColdFusion help me to manipulate binary objects?

About the Results

We organized our results around the five principles. For each principle there is a general discussion of how the principle was viewed at Allaire. We describe 2 to 3 practices used by Allaire to support the principle. We also list responses to the question "What are the warning signs that a principle is not in place?"

VISION: MAKING A GOOD VISION REAL

Definition and Description

We define vision as the mapping of customer value to constraints, as measured by the extent to which the structures, risks, and goals of the architecture are clear, compelling, congruent, and flexible (see Chapter 3). Allaire's entry into the Web application market in 1995 illustrates this point.

At the start, there was an individual need and a vision to address that need, or, as often seen by engineers, a vexing problem and some technical sweetness in its cure. J.J Allaire, a student at Macalester College in St. Paul, Minnesota, found that the technology to move information from a database to a Web page was extraordinarily complex and often fickle. As a result, it was very difficult to build business applications on the Web. At that time, the majority of Internet sites contained primarily static content. Several critics viewed the World Wide Web as 'flat' because much of it lacked the richness and utility that could be provided by data-driven applications, like electronic commerce, or workflow. There was a lot of content, but little form to make it useful. Robert Reid, in *Architects of the Web,* points out that "Indeed, the Internet in 1996 is analogous to air travel during its propeller era—neat but not particularly relevant to most activities, and limited to special uses, such as air-mail.... The most important impediment by far, is very simply a lack of useful

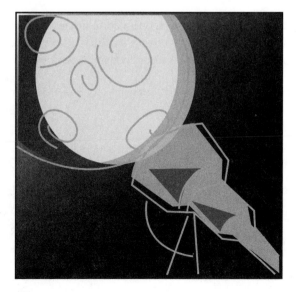

Figure 8.2
Allaire envisioned tools that made Web application development more accessible and simpler.

things to do!" [Reid97].[2] Once more, where there were tools with which to build Web applications, they were expensive to deploy because they required detailed knowledge of programming and required specialized code to connect the components of a typical application. Alternatively, applications could be built from the ground up with programming languages like PERL and C.

J.J. Allaire's vision and his first answer, which he developed from his college apartment, was to simplify data processing on the Web by applying the tag-based language used by Web page authors. These developers created Web pages with the Hypertext Markup Language (HTML). Allaire implemented HTML-like tags such as "<CFQUERY>" that handled the complexity of connecting to a database and returning a dataset to the Web application server. Thus, using ColdFusion Markup Language, a developer could extract and output data in a handful of lines, where other technologies require many more lines of code. For example, a CFML directive to print an HTML table with a list of camera products for an e-commerce site would require the following code:

```
<cfquery name="getproducts" datasource="catalogDB">
   select productid, productname, price
   from producttable
   where producttype = 'camera'
</cfquery>

<table>
<cfoutput query="getproducts">
   <tr><td>#productid#</td><td>#productname#</td><td>#price#</td></tr>
</cfoutput>
</table>
```

The CFML code resembled and operated in line with HTML statements. By comparison, an equivalent directive using the PERL scripting language required much more code, code that was less clear code to the majority of Web developers:[3]

```
open(SQLPLUS, "| (/opt/oracle/product/7.3.3/bin/sqlplus -s userid/password >
tmp/products.txt.$$)")

print SQLPLUS "set heading off\n";
print SQLPLUS "set pagesize 0\n";
print SQLPLUS "set linesize 1000\n";
print SQLPLUS "set newpage 0\n";
print SQLPLUS "set echo off\n";
```

---

[2] R. Reid, *Architects of the Web,* Copyright © 1997 Robert H. Reid, Reprinted by permission of John Wiley and Sons.

[3] The PERL example is derived from an actual application that was written about the time that ColdFusion was first gaining popularity.

```
print SQLPLUS "set feedback off\n";
print SQLPLUS "set verify off\n";
print SQLPLUS "set space 0\n";
print SQLPLUS "select productid, ':', productname, ':', price from
producttable where producttype = 'camera'";

close(SQLPLUS);

print "<table>";
$i = 0;
open(RETURNED, "<tmp/products.txt.$$")
while(<RETURNED>)
{
$i++;
chomp($_);
s/\s//g;
( $productid[$i], $productname[$i], $price[$1] ) = split/:/;
print
"<tr><td>$productid[$i]</td><td>$productname[$i]</td><td>$price[$i]
      </td></tr>\n";
}
close(RETURNED);
unlink "tmp/products.txt.$$"
print "</table>";
```

J.J. Allaire noted that "using a tag-based language to create computer applications was radical," compared to then-standard software engineering. But ColdFusion 1.0 quickly created a grassroots following in the Web-development community—composed of graphic artists as much as engineers—because it made Web application development accessible and much simpler. Allaire believed that ColdFusion, and the problem space he sought to fill, was the basis for a successful enterprise. He tested his vision and approach. "Early on," J.J. reported, "we conducted a number of participant observations to understand how our product fit" the needs of Web authors. Initial users and sponsors "got" the vision and, J.J noted, "helped to develop and define our initial product."

We were impressed by how well Allaire's vision fit Aligent's Dean Thompson's three-step process for defining a software architecture vision:[4]

1. Articulate a compelling customer value clearly and concisely.

2. Map the value to a small set of specific, solvable problems.

3. Translate these problems into a minimal set of constraints.

---

[4] See Chapter 3, "Vision," for more extensive discussion of Thompson's approach.

In 1995, visionaries like J.J. Allaire saw that the Internet was a technology and potential locus that could produce large-scale economic and social change.

Allaire clearly identified a compelling customer value. In 1995, visionaries like J.J. Allaire saw that the Internet was a technology and potential locus that could produce large-scale economic and social change. J.J. recollected that "from a social context, we realized that the Internet was going to be the core of a new Industrial Revolution. Everybody who founded this company believed they were participating in a revolution, the democratization of information, by providing developers, Webmasters, and designers the power to create Web applications." J.J. saw that in order for the Internet to deliver value, it had to become more accessible to application engineers and Web authors and provide the capability to deliver value such as that provided by standard business software and the media—entities that did not at that time operate on the Web.

Allaire mapped this customer need to a small set of specific, solvable problems. These problems centered on accessing and publishing database information on Web pages, which are written in HTML, and providing programming logic to handle user actions, such as security and updating databases. As the ColdFusion vision advanced, Allaire provided larger solution sets that addressed the needs not just of grass roots developers, but also of enterprise information systems. These problems were translated into a set of constraints that embodied the solution. The constraints offered by Allaire included a tag-based programming language that resembled HTML and that did not require significant development effort, especially for simple applications. It was also expected that the only operating system that would need to be supported would be Microsoft Windows NT. J.J. noted,

> There is a magical balance between structure and function. A vision exists that is implicit in the behavior of many individuals at Allaire. We work on identifying what that vision is, culling out what is happening, and identifying the implications of strategy on our product line. We work to cull out what customers do, what they want, what they need, to make our vision effective.

Practices to Project Architecture Vision and Keep It Alive

We sought to understand how the visionary communicated vision to those charged with building the product line and how he kept the vision alive. We learned of a range of practices used across the company to help spread the vision. In the sections below, we describe these practices (see Table 8.3).

TABLE 8.3 *Practices for Putting Vision into Place*

Evangelicalism (and a quiet priesthood)

Fiery debate (with respect)

Executive (and venture) alignment

Evangelicalism (and a Quiet Priesthood)

Allaire, like many companies offering advanced computer products, is evangelical in promoting its vision. Evangelicalism seems to expand the possibilities available to new users who fill in the details by building products using new ColdFusion technologies. Armed with Allaire's vision, developers take CFML and create new ways of doing and thinking for their organizations and customers. They see the change occur and learn what works and what does not. Allaire gains by observing the impact of this sharing and learning. Although the context is different, this practice appears similar to that of EVANGELIST and LOCAL LEADER [Manns00].

Allaire's senior executives—J.J., Jeremy, President and CEO David Orfao, and Director of Product Management Adam Berrey—frequently share their vision of how the Allaire product line is changing the world or, "democratizing the Internet." They offer imaginative new solutions that leverage the latest technology advances, such as, data syndication, Internet work flow management, and handheld wireless internet terminals. Allaire presents its vision directly to major customers and prospects, at trade shows, users groups and conferences, in the press, and across several media. Users groups, like the Washington, D.C.-based ColdFusion Users Group (CFUG), founded by FigLeaf Software's Steve Drucker, closely track Allaire's vision and its response to changing markets and technology. "We keep a close watch on Allaire and where it's headed, and where it says it is headed," Drucker reports, "because we make significant investments in where we are going based on Allaire's technology." Drucker's company has grown from under ten to nearly eighty employees in four years, based largely on its success working with ColdFusion and related Allaire technology.

Complementing Allaire's highly visible evangelicalism, senior Allaire engineers quietly offer to the public their views and vision for Allaire's technology through newsgroups, informal email, beta programs, white papers, and advanced seminars. This quiet priesthood, exemplified by Chief Architect Simeon Simeonov, is a wire that connects the engineers within Allaire who build the products with the customers who develop Web applications using Allaire technology. Without fanfare (but usually through structured channels),

Allaire engineers avail themselves to customer questions and product problems. "Much of our vision is set by understanding real world problems and selecting among customer needs," Director of Product Management Adam Berrey reports. "Sometimes these needs come through complex, obscure emails. Other times, they're on the front page of the *Wall Street Journal*."

Fiery Debate (with Respect)

Working in tandem with evangelicalism are practices that reduce the vision to tangible software architecture and code. We have observed in other high-tech companies that fiery debate plays a role in forging and communicating a software architecture vision. When focused on the architecture, and not on individuals, fiery debate seems to promote the best and brightest ideas. Jeremy Allaire noted, "People would be amazed to see some of our architectural debates. They seem incredibly hostile. People stand up and fight for what they think the vision should be, what a good technical decision is. They are absolutely passionate. Then they decimate their opponents, or they lose and retreat." Allaire continued, "We get absolutely fiery, then we build a consensus. At the end of the day, the architecture is better." Jeremy noted that the company could not have people who were lukewarm about what they do and why they do it, and still build a great product. Lack of fiery debate about a vision can lead to dead-end assumptions, lost time, and lost opportunities.

Balancing fiery debate, which is a controlled behavior, is a pattern we have observed at several high-tech firms. The heuristic is to "be nice." Respect for knowledge workers—architects, engineers, designers, and others—is a key lubricant for architecture and product line success. Fiery debate that is not driven towards consensus by social norms—or even formal moderation—can lead to organizational corrosion and software architecture breakdown.

Fiery debate that is not driven towards consensus by social norms—or even formal moderation—can lead to organizational corrosion and software architecture breakdown.

Translating the sharp edges of "fiery debate" into a vision at Allaire, we saw additional evidence of lateral integration, behavior that can further smooth spikes and promote consensus and organizational learning. (See sidebar, "Lateral Integration Promotes Vision," Chapter 3.)

Executive (and Venture) Alignment

Another key point for Allaire's keeping the vision alive is executive alignment. We have observed companies where new executive talent was added, often at the behest of venture capitalists, but the new executive was not aligned with the company's architectural vision or culture. At Allaire, we explored the company's transition from leadership by the founders, J.J. and Jeremy Allaire, to leadership by an outside executive, David Orfao, who was brought in to help Allaire accomplish a further stage of growth and its initial public offering. Orfao assumed his role as President and CEO of Allaire in October 1998, following senior executive positions with SQL, Inc., and Claris Corporation.

We asked J.J. and Jeremy Allaire about the addition of the company's CEO: "Has it made it harder to keep your vision?" Jeremy responded, "No. David Orfao is a tremendous leader, a human leader. He relies upon us for vision and understanding the market; [he is sensitive to the question] 'What are the core values we want to articulate?'"

As a cross-check, we asked Chief Architect Simeon Simeonov about the roles executives play in shaping architecture. Simeonov quickly noted, "We have hands-off, no-nonsense management, willing to give away a lot of control. When you are small, management has the physical ability to micromanage. This doesn't work. The manager needs to step back." We asked Simeonov about who made architectural decisions at Allaire. He responded, "I like to avoid the term, but there's something of a 'cult' factor involved: J.J. and Jeremy have the vision for the cult; I maintain the architecture, the high-level design, and work with developers [to implement the architecture]." We asked him who says, "That isn't right!" Simeonov responded, "As leaders, J.J., Jeremy, and I can stop an architecture feature just by saying 'No.'"

Orfao, we learned, has kept his hands off the ColdFusion architecture and focused on creating markets and ColdFusion-based products for those markets. When we described this behavior to a friend who manages Linux products for a large computer manufacturer, he noted "That's exactly right. ... It's a lot like Linux! Linus (Torvalds[5]) really rides herd over the core architecture and vision. He vetoes bad ideas, and keeps it clean." Torvalds does this in the face of diverse pressures to change elements of the core architecture.

Warning Signs Identified by Allaire Staff

► Simeonov noted, "You see immediate friction with the early Beta releases. Customers don't get what they expect, products don't work together, and things break." To avoid this, another Allaire developer said, "We release early and often. We really work hard to involve our customers and partners in the requirements definition process; and we have a fairly open beta program, with lots of incremental releases." Allaire's product

---

[5] Torvalds wrote the kernel of Linux, a free operating system that mimics the behavior of Unix.

development cycle typically includes alpha, multiple beta, and several candidate releases shared with selected partners and customers.

► Another warning sign that vision is broken cited by a senior developer was that "you can't get an agreement on an issue in a fairly short matter of time. It is a sign that people are deviating from the core. [This discussion session is] usually a brain dump, with no format." Another ColdFusion developer noted that when this happens, "At the end of the day, you feel further behind than when you started."

► Simeonov also noted that he knows vision is off when "someone sends around an article in a trade rag. You look at it, and you have no idea what it is about…. It's a warning that someone dropped the ball, that it's not on your radar screen." He continued, "If you read something and it jiggles your heart or turns it upside down, then you are behind on vision as well as architecture." We asked Simeonov how he responded to such difficulties. He reported, "Your architecture should let you respond very, very quickly. If it doesn't, you are in trouble—and you are going to work a lot to get it right."

As described below, vision needs to synchronize with release cycles. In this context, one senior Allaire engineer noted, "an example of vision being off is, if you don't have a huge number of outstanding issues and features towards the end of the software development cycle, then clearly you are missing something: Your vision does not extend beyond the current release." A vision must extend beyond what is being done now.

Rhythm—The Beat Goes On

Definition and Description

We define rhythm as the predictable execution of beat, movement, and process within an architecture group and across its customers and suppliers (see Chapter 4).

Sharing architecture is like an improvisational jazz ensemble. Each player in an ensemble is autonomous, but the performance of each musician is coordinated by cues exchanged among the musicians, as well as by the tempo, key, and style of the performance. While the basic elements of the performance may be written down or planned, many elements are performed by the musicians relying on their instinct, training, and spontaneous reactions. This

Figure 8.3
Rhythm helped Allaire maintain
a quick and productive pace.

interdependent and rapidly adaptive behavior can be particularly evident in the architecture of a fast moving "dot-com" Internet company like Allaire.

When the rhythm principle is in place and working, managers periodically reevaluate, synchronize, and adapt the architecture; architecture users have a high level of confidence in the timing and content of architecture releases; and explicit activities across product teams are understood and coordinated. At Allaire, we learned that rhythm helps people understand how their jobs are going to cycle. For example, product support, before the release, is in intensive learning mode; after the release, they are in heavy support mode. Then, shortly after the release, they are dealing mostly with easy initial questions; later the questions become more difficult and intense. Then, they start gearing up for the next release.

Practices that Help an Architecture Organization Stay in Sync

At Allaire and among external stakeholders, we observed that rhythm was a very significant factor in the firm's planning and executing of product line architectures, and we saw pain when rhythm was absent. The sections below describe three practices that help Allaire architecture developers and users stay synchronized with one another (see Table 8.4).

TABLE 8.4   *Practices for Putting Rhythm Into Place*

Steady effort

Iterative review

Defer and break-up

Steady Effort

We learned from Jeremy and J.J. Allaire that the company values a steady pace over the frantic exertions of many startups. Jeremy said,

We will never create a software development organization where you are continuously in a state of panic, working a hundred hours each week or worse.

—Jeremy Allaire

> We don't have a bunch of stressed engineers with empty cases of [high-caffeine] Jolt cola all over the place. Yet we have enormous productivity. We are not at all like a Silicon Valley start-up. We will never create a software development organization where you are continuously in a state of panic, working a hundred hours each week or worse. Talk to Jack Lull, our VP of Engineering. He has a very particular philosophy regarding rhythm.... Jack was the lead developer behind PowerBuilder. He works every day from seven AM to six PM, steady and consistently; he doesn't come in on the weekend.

The founders also attributed to this practice the ability to deliver a major release and knowing what to do on the following day.

Decency and work environment are additional factors. Susan Albers Mohrman has described the importance of the psychological contract between a company and its knowledge workers [Mohrman95][Mohrman97]. Jeremy Allaire noted that his company works to attain very, very high employee satisfaction—both through compensation issues like stock and by treating people as humans. "We're not like Silicon Valley, where people work crazy hours, and fall apart," Allaire said.

Iterative Review

Vision changes as architects and engineers gain experience by building products according to the vision, and as external competitive factors, new technology, or major opportunities change or enter upon the scene. We observed at Allaire and among several organizations that use ColdFusion a pattern of iterative review where the vision, almost like daily journalism, is the "first rough draft of history" that is captured in a product. The vision at first may not quite fit the product, and it adapts to new insights furnished by the hard reality of product development and implementation. The visionaries stay in touch with the product developers and map their articulations of the vision to development activity. This interaction among visionaries and developers (as well as marketers, and other members of the value chain) promotes alignment and reduces surprises when the product ships or when broad product needs shift.

Allaire sets its rhythm to produce an executable release, with function points delivered daily, according to a senior engineer. "We produce a daily build, and [we] manage very carefully what goes into shipping," he said.

Defer and Break Up

Allaire defers features with high technical and schedule risks and takes large features and breaks them into the appropriate sizes so they do not hold up release of key features. According to a senior engineer, "We do a daily 'smoke test' to see what breaks and what holds. We do frequent betas, particularly at the end of the product delivery schedule. We defer features and move them across beta releases, from beta to beta." We heard examples of specific negotiations between marketing and the development team, considering both the demand for features and the risks. "We maintain a list of features: There's the A-list, the B-list, and the C-list. We move features across the lists based on market priority and development schedule," he said.

Warning Signs Identified by Allaire Staff

One participant who worked in Allaire's Partners Program pointed out two warning signs.

First, he said we knew Rhythm was broken when, "We could see a dramatic shortage of people in a particular group." He also said that when you see "Any miscommunication [about the contents of a release] with customers. It is a sign that groups are not in sync." He cited as an example, the missed delivery date of the Not-For-Resale ColdFusion 4.0.

ANTICIPATION—PREDICT, VALIDATE, AND ADAPT

Definition and Description

We define anticipation as the extent to which those who build and implement the architecture *predict*, *validate*, and *adapt* the architecture to changing technology, competition, and customer needs (see Chapter 5).

Good software architectures can be expensive. They are best when they make a lot of money for a long, long time. To achieve that payoff, the organiza-

Figure 8.4
Allaire overcame challenges
to adapt their product line to
enter enterprise markets.

tion must make sure that the architecture meets the needs of many applications, including those that are probably not envisioned when the architecture is designed. This longevity has several implications. Assumptions made when the architecture was first developed may not be valid years later even though the architecture is still in use. Because of this, the organization must be able to anticipate and evolve the architecture. The architecture must be able to adapt to new technologies, standards, markets, and competitors. For example, Allaire initially assumed that ColdFusion would only need to support the Windows NT operating system, that Windows NT would be dominant and sufficient for the company's success. Later, the company saw that supporting Unix platforms would enable it to enter additional enterprise markets and provide an alternative to the complexity inherent in the Microsoft Windows NT OS. Allaire expanded its investment in the core architecture, rewriting basic components, and ported ColdFusion to several Unix environments. This allowed the firm to establish an additional technical foothold for its customers and supported the firm's evolving vision to become a leading enterprise Web application solution provider.

Since successful software architecture lives a long time, the architect should be able to predict the future, or at least be able to make reasonable guesses. The architect must consider how the architecture's customers could change, how the competitive landscape may shift and what the operating environment will be like in the future. Many plans are constructed on assumptions about what the future holds, but prediction means that assumptions are explicitly considered. Validation is necessary to test the assumptions that underlie the architecture. For example, do the customers actually want what is planned, and can the available technology do what the customers want? The reason that it is important to analyze these assumptions is that architects and their sponsors make many difficult decisions about the architecture, and very expensive mistakes may result if incorrect assumptions are not identified until the architecture is fielded.

The long-term success of the software architecture depends on adapting it to the assumptions identified and information gathered through prediction and validation. Adaptation is the adjustment of the architecture plans and the architecture itself to incorporate new features, compete in new markets, or survive in new environments. These adjustments can include not just the architecture itself, but also the plans, and even the overall vision of the architecture.

Practices to Maintain an Architecture's "Friction With the Future"

Allaire's Chief Architect Simeon Simeonov reported, "Anticipation is key. I like to work with an emphasis on future needs." The Web application technology space is changing so quickly that it is not a viable option to avoid the future. How does Allaire make this magic happen?

We learned that Allaire architects and product line architectures are driven by a number of active practices that help the company to anticipate the future and respond to change. These include the practices listed in the table below (see Table 8.5).

TABLE 8.5   *Practices for Putting Anticipation Into Place*

Marketing Requirements Document

Dogfooding

Marketing Requirements Document

The battleground for an Allaire product is captured and managed through the Marketing Requirements Document (MRD). The MRD "describes the target customers and their reason for needing this product, and then goes on to list the features of the product which address these customer needs. The Marketing Requirements Document (MRD) is the battleground where the answer to the question 'What should we build, and who will use it?' is decided" [Vixie99]. To check on anticipation, Allaire vice presidents, chief architects, and senior representatives from engineering, marketing, and customer support meet at least once a week to review development progress against the MRD, to consider new features to be added, features that may be deferred for a release or deleted from the MRD, and test assumptions about why something is being done. MRD review meetings are often passionate, filled with fiery debate.

Each department reduces elements of the MRD to specific, enactable components. For example, early in the cycle, the architect may prototype particularly complex or uncertain features to establish feasibility and review these with the MRD committee. Engineering draws up a clear schedule and assignment of commitments for the components that need to be built for each MRD requirement or a logical collection of requirements.

In addition, Simeonov, reported, "The Web application technology space is changing so quickly that you can't avoid planning for the future." However, Simeonov reported, too much focus on the future "may not scale to a larger environment or hierarchy." Large and longer-term projects, like a massive digital switch architecture, have less flexibility for change and need to adhere to longer-term standards and pathways.

> The thrashing that goes with having to do the latest thing can break an architecture. —J.J. Allaire

Dogfooding

New hires were regularly assigned to the Allaire Web site. They learned how to use the Allaire product and got an immediate and compelling feel for what Allaire's customers were going through.

Dogfooding is a term popularized by Microsoft that describes the idea that organizations that build products should also use and rely on those same products. The idea, he says, stems from the old marketing saw that dogfood manufacturers should "eat their own dogfood" [McCarthy95]. The hardware equivalent might be Boeing's engineers climbing aboard a new jetliner for its maiden flight.

We were told that new hires were regularly assigned to the Allaire Web site. They learned how to use the Allaire product and got an immediate and compelling feel for what Allaire's customers were going through. Allaire engineers used ColdFusion to build its next generation packaged system, Allaire Spectra. "Dogfooding helps developers to keep an appropriate friction with your product and its prospective future," an Allaire senior engineer told us. "This is a virtuous cycle. Allaire used the Web to promote its product. [You should] use the medium of your architecture to promote your architecture."

Figure 8.5
Allaire practiced Dogfooding—
They used their own products
to gain insights from their customers' perspective.

Warning Signs Identified by Allaire Staff

You are blind-sided by a competitor and trapped into quick decisions. One engineer described an example of this in the development of the ColdFusion 4.0 release:

> At the beginning of the 4.0 MRD, we had a huge number of potential areas to be investigated. We made guesses and assumptions about the competitive landscape. One was that remote application server code debugging would not become a high priority. At the Microsoft TechEd98 conference, which we attended, we saw that Microsoft did a similar analysis, but decided that remote debugging *was* a big issue, and made the feature a big splash at the conference. Allaire quickly elevated this massive feature, and made remote server debugging a "priority one" feature.... Microsoft drove us to make the assumption that this was a big deal for most developers. But this was not right. Most developers don't use it.

PARTNERING—LIFELINES

Definition and Description

We define partnering as the extent to which architecture stakeholders maintain clear, cooperative roles and maximize the value they deliver and receive. A stakeholder is a person or organization whose actions and ongoing trust are essential to establishing and sustaining the value of an architecture over time (see Chapter 6).

Stakeholders include engineers who build architecture components and customers who use the architecture to deliver value—and many parties in between. The "N-tier" architecture implicit in the Internet has made Web application development a highly cooperative venture. For example, developers rely upon standard feature sets for HTML and JavaScript implementation in order to build an interactive Web application, well-formed XML results when they pull data from a syndicated data source across the Internet; and consistent privilege management when they interact with the Web server. However, unlike mainframe or client-server architecture, today's Web developer has little—or no—control over these key architecture components.

Without serious, sober, and regular attention to both formal and informal relationships implicit in architecture, an organization has little chance of reaping the benefits of the common platform.

Without serious, sober, and regular attention to both formal and informal relationships implicit in architecture, an organization has little chance of reaping the benefits of the common platform. Instead of focusing on what that organization does best—e.g., building a server-side procedural language like ColdFusion—the organization would be confronted with an immense and intractable problem space.

Figure 8.6
Allaire established a strong partnership program with their developers.

Partnering provides a frame of reference for managing these relationships. In Chapter 6, we articulated key tenets of partnering to include building teamwork and commitment between parties, recognizing and supporting networked organizations that span tiers in an architecture, clearly understanding the value chain that spans from architecture definition to customer implementation and end-user needs fulfillment, and trust.

Trust is the most critical ingredient. It influences the likelihood that an architecture component will be used and whether, in fact, the product as a whole will deliver benefit. A product or component coming from a source that previously failed to meet expectations gathers dust and probably will not sell.

"Internal partnering contributes to our success by maintaining internal communications. Externally, partnering provides a development community around our tool," one senior Allaire engineer noted.

Practices That Support Partnering

Allaire recognized early on that "developers are Allaire's best business and sales resource." Allaire faced a potential show-stopping problem. Sales were limited by the available developer pool. A manager of Allaire partner programs noted, "Allaire's partner program drove the concept for the company's organization. The partnering program went a long way to resolve this critical problem. All the while the partners bought and developed products with Allaire software, they evangelized."

At Allaire we found a range of informal and formal practices that encourage partnering. These include formal contracts with Allaire "Partners" who serve as channels for delivery of products and technology, to informal relationship management within workgroups and across the company. Specific practices we observed include encouraging relationships and tracking commitments, having smart people, and leveraging what you know, as outlined in the following sections (see Table 8.6).

TABLE 8.6   *Practices for Putting Partnering Into Place*

Encourage relationships and track commitments

Hire smart people—who everyone agrees upon

You are what you know—a meritocracy

Encourage Relationships and Track Commitments

Everyone we spoke with at Allaire attributed a high value to internal and external trust. Like most companies, Allaire's stakeholders were usually spread across multiple departments—for example, user interface design, component development, integration, documentation, and training—and depended upon each other for knowledge and to fulfill commitments. Allaire had many formal and informal mechanisms to share and coordinate the vision for the architecture. For example, internal commitments were documented and tracked very explicitly. There were also brown bag lunches and quarterly seminars. At their biweekly product development group meetings, engineers and managers could check on commitments and consider new issues.

A Marketing Requirements Document (MRD) is formally managed to help assure consistency between the vision and marketing and development organization commitments. (See "Anticipation," above.) One engineer pointed out that Allaire has, "very consensus-oriented information processing and decision making—with a huge amount of email discussion. Things come up on the radar screen pretty early. We talk through issues at length and discuss them over email." The engineer commented that changes in vision are to be expected in the software development process. He noted, however, that "changes in direction have always been somewhat painful; but if you do them early [through clear communication] they are less painful." We have observed that email tends to flatten hierarchies where they don't fit and foster lateral integration. Allaire backs email with threaded discussion group tools ("Allaire Forums") that maintain an online journal of communications, both within the company as part of an Intranet and with external customers, over the Internet.

Hire Smart People, Who Everyone Agrees On

We were very interested in how the company hired staff to obtain what J.J Allaire described as "a magical balance between structure and function. A vision ... that is implicit in the behavior of many individuals...." "Trust," said Simeonov, "is the most important thing. Allaire was founded by a group of young people who know how to work with each other. They established trust with each other, across many wide-ranging debates, even debates that might sound like attacks but were accepted as a necessary part of the communications process—to learn."

Simeonov described the hiring process: "We set priorities at hiring time.... The hardest thing to decide is what you are looking for in a candidate. It's like research work, you need a strong hypothesis to filter useful from useless information, for what value that person is going to add." He elaborated,

"When we bring people in, the primary requirement is that the person is smart and willing to learn; [and he or she can] survive in a development culture that is not formal, that does not have a lot of documentation. That person needs to be able to make a decision in not very much time." Simeonov went on in rapid-fire sentences, "The person has to be able to accept communication, either negative or positive. This is key to Allaire's success. We have no formal metrics. You try to hire people that you know; you cannot always determine knowledge and smartness in just a few interviews. Knowledge of a particular technology is only important in the short term. It is generally quite irrelevant to success. Of course," he added, "you need [in the candidate] the general ability to be a good software developer."

> Allaire is very focused on the goal of shipping software that solves concrete customer problems. —Simeon Simeonov

We asked Simeonov about how an organization focuses such a sharp staff. He answered, "One thing that candidates must know is that we don't build software because we like to, we build software because we have a goal.... Allaire is very focused on the goal of shipping software that solves concrete customer problems." If staff don't want to focus on shipping software, then they should not be working at Allaire. "We are not an open R&D place. Knowledge of how technology becomes valuable is key, the software engineer's appreciation of the business value of software," Simeonov concluded. We were struck by how closely this insight mapped to the very serious value chain work performed by some of the largest computer companies.

Another requirement that we heard about from executives at Allaire was that all their employees must "get and be excited about the vision. They sign up to change the world." Indeed, everyone we interviewed at Allaire and among their many partners seemed to share the same basic vision—and most were passionate in describing the product line's future.

You are What You Know—A Meritocracy

We learned about and observed several practices that relate the abilities of the knowledge workers who design and implement software to the software architecture vision. If knowledge workers do not have expertise in core implementation technologies, the implementation of the software architecture vision will suffer—at times, the lack of efficiently translated and adopted vision can prove disastrous. Jeremy Allaire, Simeon Simeonov, and others we interviewed at Allaire noted that the company works very hard to hire and retain the best talents in the industry and to make sure that new hires fit very well with team and business needs. This makes it easier for the vision to "happen." They effectively put COMPENSATE SUCCESS into place [Coplien95].

Similarly, FigLeaf Software's Steve Drucker, a developer of ColdFusion products for organizations like Bell Atlantic and America Online, maintains aggressive recruitment and training programs to keep his workers' skills sharp. We wondered how leaders like Drucker retain such talented workers. Drucker wrote, "You teach them everything you know and you keep them learning. If they're out front, they won't leave."

We observed one practice we titled "You are what you know" at three Web development organizations that use ColdFusion to deliver business-to-business (B2B) applications. Software engineering organizations, often comprised largely of twenty- or perhaps thirty-somethings often seem to have little patience for folks who don't know the complex details that are necessary to build the latest product. These staffers work hard to always learn new things and increase their competencies. As a result, they are extremely valuable employees—and often very highly compensated.

This meritocracy of knowledge workers poses challenges to organizational principles, because the staff may not *get* the principles' importance. How do you communicate, for example, a vision, or the need to simplify to these gifted, essential staff—without restraining their creative charge, or making work appear as a hassle, and sending them across the street to the next hot job shop, a yet newer thing? We asked a question along these lines of Chief Architect Simeon Simeonov, and of other architects who build Web applications. Simeonov told us that helping developers to use architecture and document their products is a continuing challenge. He noted, "I try to give them tools that are easy to use and increase productivity and are cool—they use the latest technology." Simeonov described a semantic description language he developed that leverages XML to help make code products clearer and more self-documenting.

Warning Signs Identified by Allaire Staff

One participant that worked in Allaire's partners program pointed out that you know partnering is weak when, "…You see a particular complaint that gets repeated many times, in the Forums or elsewhere." He also said that of course you don't have partnering if, "Customers become disaffected and leave, [e.g.,] they go to ASP,[6] stop using ColdFusion because they are not succeeding.…"

---

[6] Microsoft's Active Server Pages.

SIMPLIFICATION—FINDING THE ESSENTIAL

Definition and Description

Simplification helps to reduce "the fog of software."

In Chapter 8, we define simplification as the intelligent clarification and minimization of architecture components, documentation, and process, and the organization in which they function. To turn a phrase of Carl von Clausewitz's,[7] simplification helps to reduce "the fog of software."

At Allaire, we saw simplification as core to the firm's initial market positioning as well as the company's product line architecture. Allaire entered the market and succeeded because the company made the task of developing applications on the Internet simpler and more accessible. In interviews with the company's founders, chief architect, managers, and several engineers, we found that the company's core products focused on simplification as a core value provided to customers.

J.J. and Jeremy Allaire both identified simplification as a core attribute of their product vision and understanding of the future of the Internet. Jeremy noted, "Simplicity is the essence of the Web. The software architecture of the Web itself is about simplicity. One reason we see that the Web is so popular today," he continued, "is that it is a reaction against complexity. What they did with Mosaic was to make it simple, so it could be easily learned." When thinking about simplification, Jeremy said that he was influenced by the work of Donald Norman. In *The Invisible Computer*, Norman wrote:

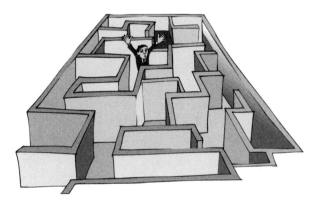

Figure 8.7
Simplification was at the core of Allaire's architecture and their market positioning.

---

[7] Clausewitz wrote of the "Fog of War" in his 1832 book, *On War* [Clausewitz32].

The personal computer is perhaps the most frustrating technology ever... Its complexities and frustrations are largely due to the attempt to cram far too many functions into a single box that sits on the desktop. The business model of the computer industry is structured in such a way that it must produce new products every six to twelve months, products that are faster, more powerful, and with more features than the current ones. The result is that the entire industry is trapped by its own success, trapped into a cycle of ever-increasing complexity from which it cannot escape [Norman98].

Practices that Support Simplification

A focus on simplicity has been a hallmark of Allaire products. ColdFusion was built around the idea that building interactivity into the Web should not require complex programming skills. Later efforts, such as WDDX, were built on the premise that developers did not need to master the complexity of all of XML in order to solve meaningful problems with the technology. We found that there were many practices within Allaire that enabled the firm to maintain this focus on Simplification (see Table 8.7).

TABLE 8.7   *Practices for Putting Simplification Into Place*

Just Enough Documentation
Keep the Core Clean
Feature Focus

Just Enough Documentation

We found that the engineering process at Allaire kept many specifications and designs informally. Email, and a high degree of collaboration among small teams, enabled the engineering teams to propose, review, and make decisions very efficiently. One engineer reported that to introduce a design change, "a simple note to articulate a product area" was needed, and "then there's a period of discussion and debate, and we're done. It is the responsibility of the people who are coding to do detailed design." Teams were kept small so that this lightweight approach to documentation and process could be effective.

Keep the Core Clean

While we did not find evidence of unnecessary features being removed from the core to fight complexity, we did find that Allaire had a strong focus on avoiding unneeded baggage being introduced to the core of the product. As one engineer described the approach, "Simplification is not an issue of removing complexity. It's how do you avoid the morass." Allaire would define the features for a particular release in a Marketing Requirements Document. They would then strip it down to the minimum to meet requirements.

Sometimes the features in the core of the ColdFusion product would be extended with what Allaire called Fuel Packs, essentially custom tags that enabled added functionality. This approach kept complex features out of the core. Some of these Fuel Packs would prove very popular, and then they might be migrated to the core. An engineer pointed out that the practice gave Allaire "a way to deliver value without putting everything in the core."

Feature Focus

Allaire appeared to be especially strong at finding the essential features for solving problems of their customers. We have already described how ColdFusion addressed the problems of Web developers who wanted to create more interactive sites. Another tool developed at Allaire, Web Distributed Data Exchange (WDDX), further illustrates this focus on the minimal features needed to solve the customer problems. WDDX is an application of the eXtensible Markup Language (XML). XML is a markup language for describing structured information and is gaining momentum in a variety of applications. For example, it is being used as a protocol for application integration. Unlike HTML, it is useful for separating the description of content on the Web from the presentation information. One of the strengths of XML is its extensibility. XML is extended with complementary standards for styling, linking, and querying XML documents, and it has also been extended to exchange information in many different application domains by defining Document Type Definitions (DTD) to describe the information being exchanged.

Chief Architect Simeonov saw that XML could be valuable to ColdFusion developers, but the very flexibility of XML made it challenging to apply easily. ColdFusion, and many other Web application developers, use structured information stored in databases, and they use HTML to display this information on the Web, although transporting this data from the database to Web browsers often required clunky code. Simeonov saw that XML could be used as the markup for this structured data and could allow it to be consistently used by application code running on both the server and the browser. However, without somehow simplifying XML, he realized that most developers would not be able to use it to solve this problem.

Simeonov created WDDX. Like other application domain XML extensions, the first part of WDDX is a DTD. The DTD describes application-level data structures. In addition to the DTD, WDDX also includes a WDDX-specific application interface. Unlike other general-purpose XML APIs like DOM or

SAX, the WDDX is specifically designed for creating and extracting XML documents based on the WDDX DTD. The API is available through an open-source license for many languages including ColdFusion, Javascript, Java, and Perl. Some of these implementations were developed by Allaire, while other versions were implemented by other developers. While this API sacrifices some of the flexibility of XML, it is easier to use because it is focused on solving the specific problem of transporting database results across Web applications. To enable simplification of Web application development, Simeonov wrote, "WDDX lets developers achieve XML data mapping (a) without their knowing any XML, and (b) without their having to write any custom code for data conversion. When you use WDDX, you don't have to worry about XML at all. With one line of application code you can convert your data to XML and with one line of application code you can get data back from the XML" [Simeonov00].

Warning Signs Identified by Allaire Staff

One engineer pointed out that, "When you start worrying about handling as work-arounds numerous special cases, you've probably blown it as far as simplification." For example, the ColdFusion parser used to be very forgiving about supporting certain types of constructs that created ambiguities. Similarly, the Netscape browser became less accommodating with respect to syntax variants it would accept, and of course XML has very strict syntax requirements. Trying to manage all of these syntax variations introduced a significant amount of complexity to the product.

SUMMARY

Allaire is a leading firm that was founded by J.J. Allaire with a compelling vision for making the Web more interesting and useful by providing application development platforms. The firm has grown from being the provider of choice for grassroots Web developers into a full-fledged enterprise information systems vendor, and they have gone from a small privately held start-up to a publicly traded corporation. As the firm has gone through these changes, software architecture has continued to be a foundation upon which the firm's success has been built. Their success helps illustrate how the principles described in the VRAPS model can help organizations achieve and sustain long-term success. The study also illustrates how the principles can be applied in the fast-paced world of Internet software development.

Case Study: Building and Implementing a Benchmark Using VRAPS

Architects work in ways that allow them to accomplish their dual mission of designing technically possible and organizationally feasible products.
                                          —Rebecca Grintner [Grintner99]

Overview

This case study illustrates how we applied benchmarking to address several compelling problems in understanding the relationship between organization and software architecture. We used the VRAPS Model, described in Chapter 2, as a basis for a multi-company benchmark. This chapter presents the experience from this benchmark, aiming to share both the instruments and processes we developed, lessons we learned, as well as some results. By reading this chapter, you can learn how to apply and gain insights into the model. Further, you can reuse or adapt both the templates and the process to observe, analyze, and understand other organizations.

When we began our study, there was a fair amount of literature on how to build an architecture, but very little research into how to keep the architecture alive. We had seen many projects fail in spite of impressive technical horsepower. When we asked recognized and accomplished leaders to describe practices that were most critical to their software reuse and architecture success, we heard about a surprising number of nontechnical practices. Our earlier case studies had identified several organizational factors that apparently drove architecture success [Wilson96][Dikel97a]. To mature this understanding, we needed to engage a broad set of organizations that were recognized for their success in software architecture. To address the following problems to achieve our goal:

► How do you capture an exemplary practice in an area you do not yet fully understand?
► How do you ensure that those who might adopt the practice have enough information to decide when and where the practice is appropriate?
► How do you compare performance across organizations?

Transferring best practices is a sobering challenge.

Transferring well-understood practices so they take hold and deliver positive results can present sobering challenges. To capture and compare organizational practices and results in the areas of software architecture, we developed five templates and built processes to collect and present information. These templates incorporate what we have learned from our research into technology transition, practice capture, and benchmarking. They also reflect much trial-and-error learning across over 100 benchmark interviews.

BENCHMARKING PROVIDED A FRAMEWORK

Just before we began work on the benchmark, we had completed a case study in which we tested an initial set of hypotheses about organizational principles that led to architecture success [Dikel97a]. We knew that in order to strengthen our work, we would have to build a model and test it in a wider group of organizations that were recognized for their successful use of software architecture. We decided to structure our research as a benchmark because it allowed us to test and improve our model while providing participants the ability to compare sensitive practices, strengths, and perspectives. Robert Camp's working definition for benchmarking provided a guideline for our work. He wrote, "Benchmarking is the search for industry best practices that lead to superior performance" [Camp89].

Camp's definition focuses on practices. Camp explains that an organization can only improve performance if it changes its practices, or methods, of performing business processes. To effect this change, people who are slated to adopt a new approach must identify the most effective practices and understand how, why, and in what context they are used. After these practices are identified and understood, metrics should be derived [Camp89]. Our work corresponds with the first seven of Camp's ten benchmarking process steps. Benchmark participants handled implementation for themselves (see Figure 9.1).

We used the VRAPS Model as a basis to measure and compare architecture-related organizational skills and developed a series of questions to gauge these skills' effect on business drivers. To gain consistent information during short visits and across many interviews, we designed and used a series of templates. Templates expedited data collection, enabling us to quickly characterize the organization and the business context in which the architecture was developed and used. The templates enabled us to gather broad as well as detailed data about principles. Using this approach we captured exemplary practices along with the problems they addressed and the critical context in which they were applied. After we completed these templates, we used them to obtain participant review and clearance and used them again to present the data in a graphical and intuitively sensible way. Templates also served to "blind" the survey data while preserving its context.

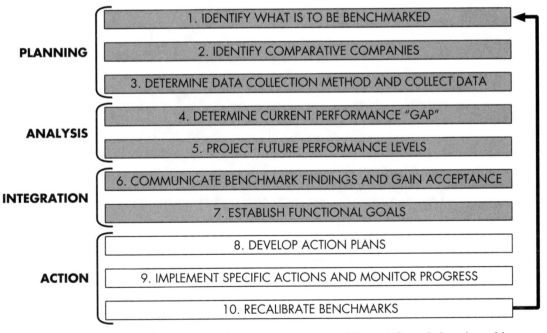

Figure 9.1   Our approach mapped to the first seven steps of Robert Camp's benchmarking process. Source: © 1989 ASQC Quality Press, R. Camp, *Benchmarking: The Search for Industry Best Practices that Lead to Superior Performance.* Used by permission.

The template approach yielded the following benefits:

▶ *It engaged the interview subject*—We produced and validated the templates with the subject. This increased the subjects' comfort level and sense of ownership.
▶ *It increased data consistency*—The templates and processes kept our interviews focused and regular while allowing the interviewer flexibility to vary the question sequence to match the flow of the interview.
▶ *It decreased the time it took to validate interview notes and clear them out of non-disclosure*—We are not sure why, but templates get cleared much more quickly than interview scripts. Perhaps because people have a clearer picture of what the end product will look like.

We built five basic templates, which are described in Table 9.1.

TABLE 9.1   *Templates and the Types of Data They are Designed to Collect*

TEMPLATE	TYPE OF DATA
Survey Template	Interview subject's role, perspective on architecture, and overall view of organizational strengths and weaknesses with respect to the principles
Organization Background and Context Template	Environment in which the architecture team and its products functioned
Architecture Overview and Return on Investment Template	Business unit or product line manager perspective
Principle Template	Specifics about each principle
Practice Template	Exemplary practices

Survey Template

The purpose of the survey template was to introduce our study and define what we meant by architecture and the principles, to gain a quick picture of the subject and the subject's role, and to provide a broad-based cross check on in-depth interviews on each of the principles (see Figure 9.2).

As a rule, we went over the quick survey with each interview subject. Our initial benchmark revealed a strong need to spend time with each interview subject communicating what we meant by architecture, describing each

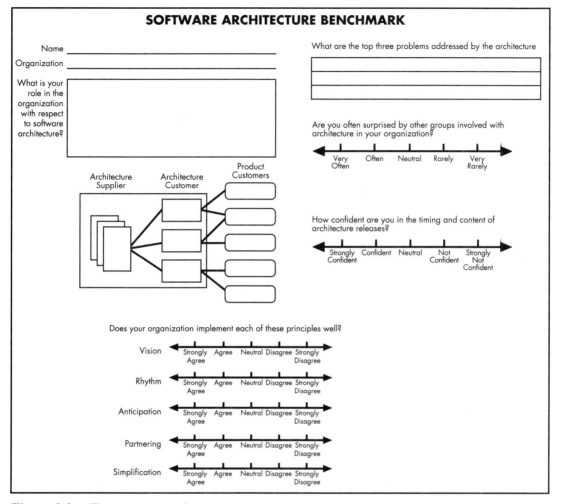

Figure 9.2 The survey template.

of the principles, and relating our study goals. A back-of-the-envelope calculation told us that time constraints would limit in-depth interviews on each principle to too small a number to allow us to triangulate our data, that is, to compare our data across the organization to ensure consistency. We developed the survey template to address both of these needs.

The survey template addressed several concerns. Our tests told us that there was a lack of alignment on what people meant when they said "architecture"—even within the same organization. We used the survey to graphically describe an architecture team in relationship to its users and their customers, relate their organization to our graphic, and graphically define the scope of our questions. We asked subjects to rate their organization's strengths and weaknesses. In the process we asked the participant to point out where he or she fit. We also described the principles and checked to make sure the subject understood them. We then asked the participants to rate how well their organization practiced each principle. We asked more detailed questions about the principles using other templates. The survey template also allowed us to ask participants to list the top three problems that were addressed by the architecture, which we used to assess how well the perspectives of the participants were aligned.

Organization Background and Context Template

We used the organization template to capture an understanding of the environment in which the architecture team and its products functioned. We filled in the template with our point of contact and then confirmed the answers with the business unit manager. The template contained questions about the business unit's distinguishing characteristics, size, process maturity, customer environment, and typical project characteristics (see Figure 9.3).

Architecture Overview and Return on Investment Template

The architecture overview template sought to capture the perspective of the business unit or product line manager. As such, it asked about key business drivers, how the organization viewed architecture success, how it measured results, and whether success was achieved. The template also captured specific data about investment and return (see Figure 9.4). This template was effective in documenting measurable results. It also helped uncover very interesting insights about the sponsor's vision and approach.

Principle Template

The principle template was core to our benchmark. We used this template to capture specifics about each principle. We targeted interview subjects by asking our points of contact at each site to select two or more people for each principle who came to mind when our contact thought about the principle. We also requested that the two subjects represent different perspectives (e.g., developer and senior manager).

Because we broke out each principle into actionable criteria, we were able to gain a fine-grained picture of the subject's observations about the way each principle was practiced, as well as the depth and breadth of its use. (See

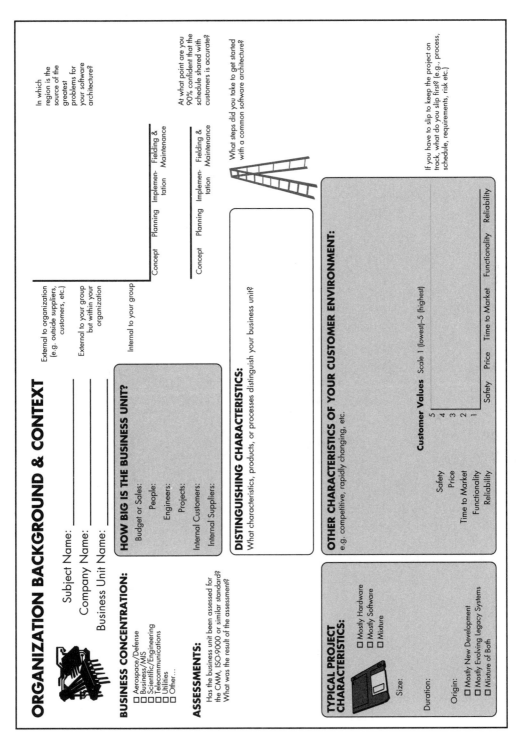

The following text appears within the template:

ORGANIZATION BACKGROUND & CONTEXT

Subject Name: _____

Company Name: _____

Business Unit Name: _____

BUSINESS CONCENTRATION:
☐ Aerospace/Defense
☐ Business/MIS
☐ Scientific/Engineering
☐ Telecommunications
☐ Utilities
☐ Other...

ASSESSMENTS:
Has the business unit been assessed for the CMM, ISO-9000 or similar standard? What was the result of the assessment?

HOW BIG IS THE BUSINESS UNIT?
Budget or Sales:

People:

Engineers:

Projects:

Internal Customers:

Internal Suppliers:

External to organization (e.g. outside suppliers, customers, etc.)

External to your group but within your organization

Internal to your group

| Concept | Planning | Implemen-tation | Fielding & Maintenance |

| Concept | Planning | Implemen-tation | Fielding & Maintenance |

In which region is the source of the greatest problems for your software architecture?

At what point are you 90% confident that the schedule shared with customers is accurate?

What steps did you take to get started with a common software architecture?

DISTINGUISHING CHARACTERISTICS:
What characteristics, products, or processes distinguish your business unit?

OTHER CHARACTERISTICS OF YOUR CUSTOMER ENVIRONMENT:
e.g. competitive, rapidly changing, etc.

Customer Values Scale 1 (lowest)–5 (highest)

	5	4	3	2	1
Safety					
Price					
Time to Market					
Functionality					
Reliability					

Safety   Price   Time to Market   Functionality   Reliability

TYPICAL PROJECT CHARACTERISTICS:
☐ Mostly Hardware
☐ Mostly Software
☐ Mixture

Size:

Duration:

Origin:
☐ Mostly New Development
☐ Mostly Evolving Legacy Systems
☐ Mixture of Both

If you have to slip to keep the project on track, what do you slip first? (e.g., process, schedule, requirements, risk etc.)

Figure 9.3   The organization background and context template.

ARCHITECTURE OVERVIEW AND RETURN ON INVESTMENT

Subject:

Company:

Business Unit:

What is the single biggest benefit of your software architecture?

What was the most compelling reason to invest in software architecture?

Is there a story that contrasts what it was like before the software architecture was adopted compared to now?

How do you explain your software architecture investment to your boss or board of directors? (draw a picture if you'd like)

How will the software architecture enable the business unit to address these key areas of performance in the future?

What are the top three business unit's key drivers; that is, strategically important areas of performance?

How do you assess these key areas of performance?

What percentage of the total cost in your organization is expended on software architecture?

What investments have you made in software architecture? How large were they?

How many products are supported by the business unit?

What percentage of those products are supported by a common software architecture?

How does software architecture fit with other improvement efforts?

How many years has your software architecture been in place?

How many years did it take you to reach a positive return on investment?

10
8
6
4
2

Years   ROI

WHAT IMPROVEMENTS HAVE YOU MEASURED?

Intermediate Indicators of Success, e.g., defects, break-even point, rework required, cost, productivity, employee stress and morale, gate slippage, churn, etc.

Measure	Before	After	Interval

Long-Term Indicators of Success, e.g., cycle-time, quality, customer satisfaction, Return on investment, marketshare, etc.

Measure	Before	After	Interval

Using software architecture, is your organization better able to take risks and seize opportunities?

Strongly Agree   Agree   Neutral   Disagree   Strongly Disagree

Using software architecture, has your organization improved product performance?

Strongly Agree   Agree   Neutral   Disagree   Strongly Disagree

Figure 9.4 The architecture overview and return on investment template.

Table 9.2 for a complete list of criteria.) We learned how the practice was implemented, what kinds of results were attributed to the practice, and how these results were measured. The template also captured warning signs, obstacles to implementation, and special considerations.

TABLE 9.2 *Detailed Listing of Criteria Used on Principle Templates [Dikel97e]*

Vision:

1. Architecture suppliers' and architecture customers' practitioners "see" the same picture of architecture components and know who "owns" those components (e.g., could they all draw a similar diagram of the architecture and associate owners with components?).

2. Architecture vision aligns with the architecture customer's mission goals. Similarly, each person who is critical to the delivery of the architecture's value sees how what he or she does supports the activities of each other person in the chain.

3. Architecture suppliers' and architecture customers' practitioners (developers) "see" the most important problems the architect seeks to solve with the architecture (e.g., could they all name the top three such problems?).

4. When architecture suppliers' and architecture customers' practitioners use the architecture for its envisioned purpose, they are rewarded. (We are looking for situations where using the architecture would bring negative consequences.)

5. Architecture suppliers' and architecture customers' practitioners trust that the shared vision reflects the actual components, connectors, and constraints.

6. The architecture is explicitly discussed when changes to the products it supports are evaluated and enacted (e.g., changes to requirements and design).

Rhythm:

1. Architecture customers and suppliers have a high level of confidence in the timing and content of architecture releases.

2. Explicit activities are coordinated via rhythm with no explicit communication.

3. Architecture releases are scheduled and incorporated into product plans.

4. Features with high technical risk are considered for deferral, and large features are broken up into the appropriate level of granularity so they do not hold up release of key features.

5. Regular software builds (e.g., weekly or daily) are compiled and tested before the next scheduled build.

6. Rhythm permeates organizations related to the architecture (e.g., marketing, sales, engineering, etc.).

Anticipation:

1. Architecture capability is regularly enhanced to respond to (a) Anticipated risks and requirements of customers and their customers, (b) Market-driving standards and evolving technology, and (c) Strategic business direction.

2. Enhancements are tested to see if they achieve their technical and business goals.

3. Architecture is called out in the line of business strategic plan.

TABLE 9.2   *(Continued)*

	4. Technical and business risks and opportunities are evaluated through a quick cycle of development (e.g., products are delivered to targeted customers to verify that the way risks and opportunities were addressed actually meets their needs).
	5. Architecture regularly enables architecture customers to achieve their mission goals (e.g., enhance their competitive position).
	6. Road map shows major evolutionary changes to architecture and how they feed into customers' product development efforts.
	7. Current customers' plans are consistent with road map.
Partnering:	1. Clear contracts between architecture customers and suppliers specify rewards and penalties.
	2. Penalties and rewards are perceived as compelling and "real."
	3. Customer conflicts are resolved by a clear mechanism (e.g., a shared risk/opportunity model and/or strategic business plan).
	4. Architect is aware of customers' current and future business needs and risks.
	5. Rules of social conduct encourage partnering to solve a common goal.
	6. Suppliers hear of customer needs earlier and earlier.
Simplification:	1. Architecture supplier clearly understands the essential minimal requirements and builds those into the core elements.
	2. Stakeholders agree on top three priorities for the architecture.
	3. Major simplification takes place when there is a strongly agreed to business case.
	4. Elements are removed from the core if they are not shared, or add unnecessary risk or complexity.
	5. Developers are encouraged and rewarded for solving multiple problems that result in simplifying the architecture with a single solution, even when some of the problems are from an external product group.
	6. Processes and documentation that do not add value are removed or trimmed.
	7. Code growth for the product family is stable or linear.
	8. Churn for the product family is stable over time.

The principle template has four sections that capture information about the criteria, results, rules of thumb, and implementation details (see Figure 9.5).

1. *Criteria*—The template provides five to seven criteria, each of which provides operational definitions of how the principle is enacted. For each criterion, the template captures what the organization does to implement

it. To gauge the extent to which the criterion is practiced, we asked subjects to rate against two scales. The first scale question asked, "Do you practice this exactly as stated?" The second asked, "Is this practice done for all products supported by the architecture?"

2. *Rationale and Results*—This section requests for a before and after story about the principle. It also asks about the principle's contribution to overall success, how this contribution was measured and the degree of confidence the subject has in the measure.

3. *Rules of Thumb*—This section probes for observations and approaches. It includes questions about whether the subject can tell the if principle is not in place or is coming unglued and what obstacles they faced when introducing the principle. This was one of our favorite sections because it elicited some great insights from the practitioners that we interviewed.

4. *Implementation Details*—This section seeks to draw out implementation experience by focusing on implementation phase, on forces, and on specific steps the organization takes to implement the principle.

Figures 9.6 and 9.7 shows the principle template with additional detail.

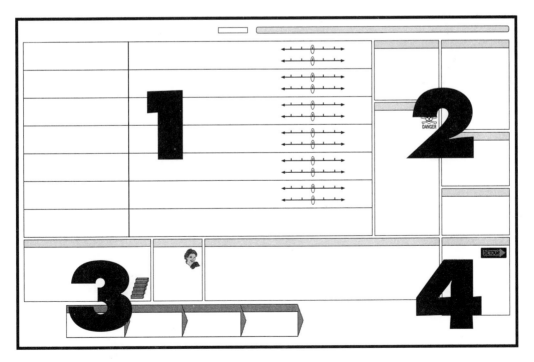

Figure 9.5   Sections of the principle template.

ANTICIPATING, TESTING, AND ADAPTING   INTERVIEW 1

OPERATIONAL DEFINITION	WHAT IS DONE TO IMPLEMENT THIS ITEM?
Architecture capability is regularly enhanced to respond to (1) Anticipated risks and requirements of customers and their customers, (2) Market-driving standards and evolving technology, and (3) Strategic business direction	
Enhancements are tested to see if they achieve their technical and business goals	
Architecture is called out in the line of business strategic plan	
Technical and business risks and opportunities are evaluated through a quick cycle of development (e.g., products are delivered to targeted customers to verify that the way risks and opportunities were addressed actually meets their needs)	
Architecture regularly enables architecture customers to acheive their mission goals, e.g., enhance their competitive positions	
Road map shows major evolutionary changes to architecture and how they feed into customers product development efforts	
Current customers plans are consistent with road map	

STEPS

What steps does your organization take to get started with this?

WHO

Who is responsible for

FORCES

Are there special considerations necessary for implementing the principle at any of these stages?

CONCEPT   **PLANNING**   **IMPLEMENTATION**

Figure 9.6   The principle template (left side).

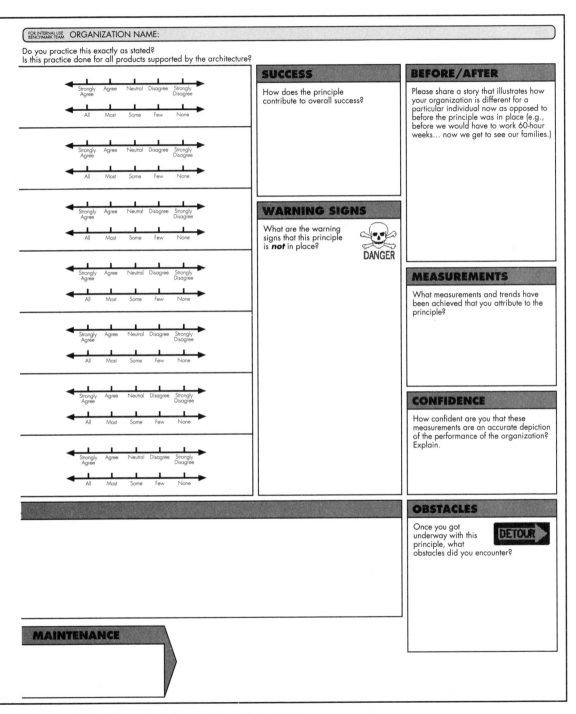

Figure 9.7 The principle template (right side).

Practice Template

The practice template is designed to guide you through the difficult process of extracting exemplary practices. Capturing practice always turns out to be a lot harder than it seems. The template was derived from one we developed for a benchmark of software reuse practices [Wilson96]. If you have ever had the opportunity to try to capture practice, you probably have experienced pitfalls such as:

► *The fire hose*—being left with your head spinning after getting a stack of briefing charts and/or process diagrams, and several hours of presentations. You're not sure whether you heard about one practice or fifty, what problems they solved, or who could use them.

► *The gap*—sitting down to write up a number of practices and discovering that each covers a different set of questions about the practice. One has a lot of step-by-step guidance about how to do the practice but doesn't contain a thing about why they adopted it; one has a lot of data about when and where to use the practice but no data about why it was adopted.

► *The iceman or woman*—being unable to engage an introverted subject and ending up with a practice like "do domain analysis" with little additional detail.

► *The blank stare*—presenting the practices you just collected to a group of people who can't figure out why they should care.

We designed the practice template to avoid problems such as these. The template structures data collection into the following five main sections. As you will see, the template also provides a quickly readable presentation vehicle (see Figure 9.8).

1. *Background*—Beginning in the upper left corner, the template collects descriptive information about the practice to answer the questions: What is the practice? Where can I find more detail? What resources are available? What types of people are needed to use and manage the practice?

2. *Maturity*—The center of the template records information about the extent and type of use of the practice. It seeks to answer questions such as: Does this practice have a track record in large-scale projects? How do I know it is based on experience, and not just theory? How important to project success has the practice proven to be?

3. *Rationale and Result*—The upper right corner of the template captures insights into why the practice was used in the first place, i.e., what specific problems it solved. It also captures benefits ascribed to the practice.

This data is designed to help the reader determine answers to questions such as: Will the practice solve my problem? What can I expect to happen? What is the economic story?

4. *Constraints*—The lower right corner of the template records comments and experiences from implementation and use of the practice. Reading this section, a project manager and users can identify pitfalls or what infrastructure may be needed to make the practice successful. What will be my investment? What do I need to consider or do to make it work? What other things do I need to be aware of?

5. *Applicability*—The lower left corner of the template describes information to determine the applicability to a specific organizational situation. This can help the decision maker or implementer decide if the practice is valuable for a particular environment. Does it apply to my situation? How would this practice fit with other initiatives I currently am sponsoring?

Figures 9.9 and 9.10 show the practice template with additional detail.

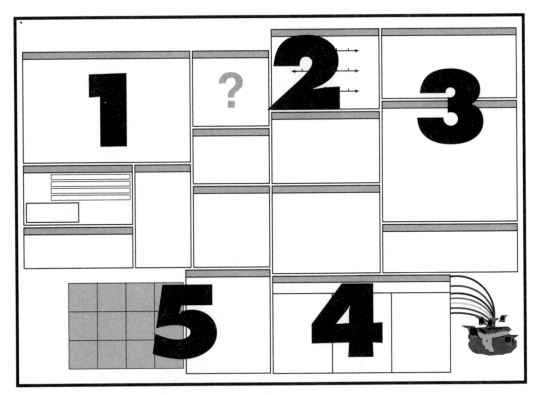

Figure 9.8   Architecture practice template layout

SOFTWARE ARCHITECTURE BENCHMARK

ORGANIZATION: PRACTICE NAME: INTERVIEW SUBJECT:

PRACTICE DESCRIPTION

What is the practice, and what steps are involved?

MORE INFO?

Where should you go for more information on this practice?

?

REWARDS

How are people rewarded for participating in the practice? Is it a regular part of the culture?

PRIMARY PRACTICE PARTICIPANTS

USERS

MANAGERS

SPONSORS

Other key roles

These questions draw from Bowers, Barbara, Whole Customer Planning—Segmented by Roles, Hewlett-Packard, 1994.

FIT

Did you use the practice to satisfy the requirements of a capability model? (e.g., Baldridge, CMM, etc.) If so, which ones, and how did they fit?

WHERE TO USE PRACTICE

MISCELLANEOUS

How does the practice fit other improvement efforts?

In what areas are the problems/drivers that are affected by this practice?

External to organization (e.g., outside suppliers, customers, etc.)

External to your group but within your organization

Internal to your group

Concept   Planning   Implementation   Fielding & Maintenance

CONTEXT

Draw a picture that describes the context of the practice. How does it fit with other efforts and drivers in your organization?

Figure 9.9   The practice template (left side).

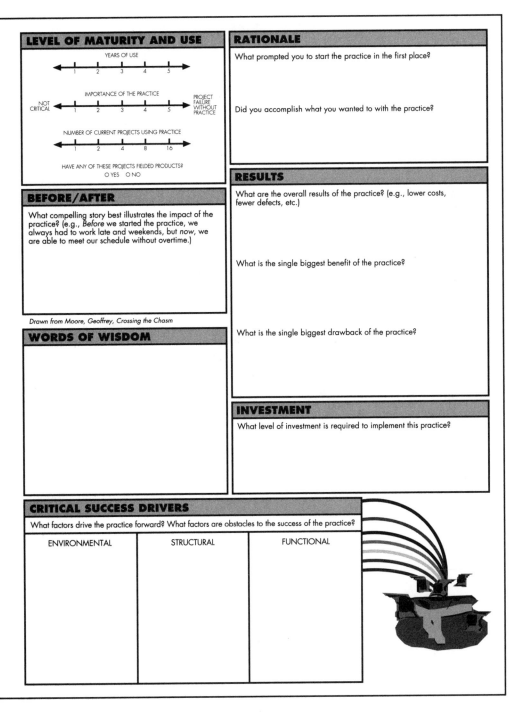

LEVEL OF MATURITY AND USE

YEARS OF USE

1 2 3 4 5

IMPORTANCE OF THE PRACTICE

NOT CRITICAL 1 2 3 4 5 PROJECT FAILURE WITHOUT PRACTICE

NUMBER OF CURRENT PROJECTS USING PRACTICE

1 2 4 8 16

HAVE ANY OF THESE PROJECTS FIELDED PRODUCTS?
O YES O NO

BEFORE/AFTER

What compelling story best illustrates the impact of the practice? (e.g., *Before* we started the practice, we always had to work late and weekends, but *now*, we are able to meet our schedule without overtime.)

Drawn from Moore, Geoffrey, Crossing the Chasm

WORDS OF WISDOM

RATIONALE

What prompted you to start the practice in the first place?

Did you accomplish what you wanted to with the practice?

RESULTS

What are the overall results of the practice? (e.g., lower costs, fewer defects, etc.)

What is the single biggest benefit of the practice?

What is the single biggest drawback of the practice?

INVESTMENT

What level of investment is required to implement this practice?

CRITICAL SUCCESS DRIVERS

What factors drive the practice forward? What factors are obstacles to the success of the practice?

ENVIRONMENTAL	STRUCTURAL	FUNCTIONAL

Figure 9.10   The practice template (right side).

*We found that
even organizations
that had earned a
CMM level 3 or
won the Malcolm
Baldrige Award
had not fully artic-
ulated some prac-
tices that were
key to architecture
success.*

The practice template lent itself well to teasing out critical information about a practice and addressing the problems stated above. We found that even organizations that had earned a CMM level 3 or won the Malcolm Baldrige Award had not fully articulated some practices that were key to architecture success. Separating these practice descriptions from mounds of detail often required perseverance along with practiced use of the template. We began by asking the subject to describe the practice. Often, the answer would be something like, "Develop an architecture vision," or "Do domain analysis." We would spend a little time extracting a few more details, then go to another section asking questions like, "What prompted you to start the practice in the first place?" These additional questions helped the subject and us see the practice from a different perspective.

By inquiring about the problem the practice sought to address and results attained, the interview subject would often sharpen their description of the practice. Similarly, as we moved through other sections and learned where the practice originated, how it fit with other practices and critical success drivers, the subject often thought of new things to say about the practice. We also utilized the templates' range of easy to thought-provoking questions. When the subject would seem overwhelmed with a question, we could move to a simple question like "How many years has the practice been in use?" As a result, we were able to capture a more complete, more relevant, and certainly more interesting understanding of the practice.

HOW WE CONDUCTED THE BENCHMARK

We did the research in two phases. First, we developed a workable, coherent vision by writing a value proposition, developing a research plan and supporting documents, and engaging participants. Second, we obtained and made sense of information through conducting interviews, reviewing research results, and adjusting our approach. For this study, we were not involved in the implementation of benchmark results within participant organizations.

Getting to a Workable Vision

Getting to a workable vision that balanced benefits and contributions for all benchmark partners took several iterations. We realized we would have to engage participant organizations that were widely recognized for leadership in software architecture. As such, we were faced with the challenge of aligning the benchmark plan so that we could deliver compelling value to each participant while fulfilling our goal. As illustrated in Figure 9.11, we cycled through

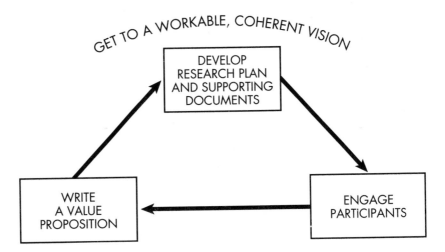

Figure 9.11   Getting to a workable coherent vision was an iterative process.

writing and revising our value proposition and research plan and talking with partners until we achieved a balance.

After several iterations, we developed a value proposition that resonated with sponsors, managers, and practitioners. Elements of value included:

► *Comparing partners to competitors and other leaders*—VRAPS Model enabled comparison of actions and transfer of experience while blinding proprietary data.
► *Helping to predict and avoid unwelcome surprises*—Findings illustrated how and why gaps in adhering to principles increase risk.
► *Capturing, packaging, and defending what the organization is doing right*—Essential practices and patterns of social behavior and personal contributions can easily be overlooked in the midst of strong growth or change. By making them explicit and documenting their value, these practices and patterns and their supporters were better acknowledged and supported.
► *Providing real-world solutions to common challenges*—Templates provided the right level of information to make an informed decision about adopting the practice and to know where to go to get more information.

Similarly, as we learned more about the situations and requirements of study participants, we adapted our research plans to accommodate specifics, such as organizational size and geographic distribution.

About Benchmark Participants

We selected participants who had significant investments in software architecture, and who had also been successful with these investments. For many of the groups, the focus was on a particular business unit. In at least one case, the focus was on the group responsible for the architecture of their enterprise information systems. The four partners' business units ranged from $30 million to $4 billion in revenue, and employed several hundred to more than a thousand engineers. Their applications included business information systems, workflow management, telecommunications and network management.

Conducting the Interviews

A typical benchmark consisted of several days of preparation, two days on site and a follow-up visit ending in a debriefing. As is customary when conducting site visits, we asked that a point of contact be assigned who could orchestrate our visit. We worked with them to make sure they understood the nature and objectives of our work. Once this was accomplished, we worked to get a nondisclosure in place and provided summary information for review and distribution.

After reviewing the principles with our contacts, we asked that they identify the person or persons who most completely embodied each principle and arrange an interview with that person. To realize this objective, we asked our contacts to ensure that our interview schedule included the chief architect, one or more programmers, and first- through third-level managers and directors. We also asked for a brief meeting with the business unit or product line manager.

Using the five templates, we collected and validated data with subjects and cleared them out of nondisclosure. We interviewed over 40 subjects within the four partners' organizations, collecting more than 65 templates.

BENCHMARK RESULTS AND LESSONS LEARNED

We learned a great deal from conducting the benchmark. We uncovered a number of practices that solved not-so-obvious problems encountered with software architecture. These practices are described in patterns throughout this book. Besides the practices, we found that the VRAPS principles resonated

The VRAPS principles resonated with the participants we interviewed.

with the participants we interviewed. We also gained a greater understanding about how the principles related to each other. Lastly, we learned many lessons about conducting benchmarks such as this one.

Principles Resonated

We found that the principles engaged the interview participants, and that many had already given thought to the ideas represented by the principles. Nearly everyone interviewed said that they thought that the principles contributed to their overall success with software architecture. Unlike some models that are viewed skeptically by practitioners, when we identified weaknesses in an organization's use of one of the principles, the participants appeared to take these observations seriously.

Many of the participants had heuristics that they used as measurements and warning signs for their organizations. For example, for the principle of Rhythm, one organization measured the amount of overtime work by engineering teams to give an indication of when their pace was askew. Another watched the rate at which problem reports were recorded, especially as a release date neared.

When we found strong resonance, our confidence in the validity of specific principles and practices increased. The principle template enabled us to collect evidence of resonance while examining how each criterion of each practice was enacted across participating organizations.

Principle Relationships

One of the goals of the benchmark was not only to validate the VRAPS Model, but also to better understand the relationships among the principles. There were several surprising results.

Partnering was Weakest

Although there was one organization for which Partnering was the strongest principle, overall the organizations in the benchmark ranked themselves lowest in Partnering. We had not expected to find such disconnects. The Partnering criterion stating "Clear contracts between architecture customers and suppliers specify rewards and penalties" was rated among the weakest and least widespread by the participants. For example, one internal architecture customer reported, "There is no contract [between architecture customers and suppliers]. There are no rewards if they deliver and no penalties for not delivering. There is no pressure felt by the architects [if they do not deliver]."

No Principle Dominated

We had thought that we might find that organizations gained strength in some principles before others. However, we found no such progression. In fact, each organization in the benchmark appeared strongest in a different principle (see Table 9.3). It seems that for organizations looking to improve their use of software architecture, there is not a particular principle with which their initial efforts should be focused.

TABLE 9.3   *Each Organization was Strongest in a Different Principle*

ORGANIZATION IDENTIFIERS	STRONGEST PRINCIPLE
1	Partnering
2	Vision
3	Anticipation
4	Simplification

Anticipation and Simplification Were Coupled

We had expected to find relationships between the principles, but the two most pronounced ones surprised us. First, we found that when Anticipation was strong, Simplification was also strong, and when Anticipation was weak, so was Simplification. We don't know what causes the relationship, but we suspect that there is a feedback between the two. In two of the participants, Anticipation and Simplification were the two strongest principles. In another organization, these were the two weakest principles. Organizations that are better at Anticipation appear better able to determine the minimal, essential characteristics of their architecture. Organizations that are good at Simplification are better able to commit the resources to test and validate their assumptions about the evolution of their architecture.

Rhythm and Vision Were Coupled

We were even more surprised by the relationship between Rhythm and Vision. We found that when Rhythm was strong, Vision was also strong; and when Vision was weak, so was Rhythm. We suspect that sharing a strong vision is important for successfully putting Rhythm into place. An engineer at an organization whose Vision and Rhythm were fairly weak, said, "One of our most important architecture customers (a highly successful product line) never put our architecture components into their product plans. This realization happened for different people at different times." The lack of a shared vision and effective rhythm resulted in disconnected planning. Without the common purpose and direction provided by Vision, getting implicit coordination of Rhythm would be difficult to achieve.

Lessons Learned

Leading Organizations Cared a Lot About Practice and Context

One sponsor told us that the opportunity to observe us collecting practices was by itself worth the time, cost, and effort associated with the benchmark. We had found in previous benchmarking efforts that often the practices that were most critical to success had not been documented, and that organizations valued capturing these practices [Wilson96]. We found that this was the case during here as well.

Self-Assessments Help Prioritize

"Degree-to-which" scales told us more about a participant's culture and subject's management level but were not helpful in comparing across organizations. Some groups appeared to have said practices, but were tough critics, and did not rate themselves highly. Other groups rated themselves strong across the board in spite of obvious weaknesses in their organization. However, the ratings correlated well with relative strengths of the principles within each organization.

Enterprise Architectures Required a Modified Approach

One of the benchmark participants was seeking to deploy an enterprise architecture across a large and complex organization. Their architecture-related issues were almost an order of magnitude more diverse than those of the other benchmark participants. With such a large architecture, we found that the benchmark needed to be more tightly focused on a particular piece, or broken into several different groups. We found pockets within the organization that appeared to have exemplary skills in the use of the VRAPS principles and that spoke of compelling results. Other pockets had more difficulty maintaining legacy architectures. For the benchmark to aid an enterprise architecture effort most effectively, these pockets need to be profiled as well as the organization as a whole.

SUMMARY

We found that measuring and comparing organizational performance in the area of software architecture was not easy. The VRAPS Model combined with the template-based process we developed enabled us to make significant progress capturing exemplary practices while gaining and sharing a better understanding of organizational factors in software architecture. The templates enabled us to capture a rich set of information detailing when and where these practices would be most productive and where they would not. We hope that sharing our methods and results will save others time and serve as a framework for future learning.

QUICK REFERENCE TABLE: PRINCIPLES, CRITERIA, ANTIPATTERNS, AND PATTERNS

PRINCIPLE	DEFINITION AND CRITERION—WHAT IT IS; HOW YOU MEASURE	ANTIPATTERN— WHAT NOT TO DO	PATTERN— WHAT CAN YOU DO
VISION:			
Vision is the mapping of future value to architectural constraints as measured by how well the architecture's structures and goals are clear, compelling, congruent, and flexible.			
Criterion 1	Architect's vision aligns with what his or her sponsors, users, and end customers are trying to accomplish.	ANTIGRAVITY MODULE	FRONT-END ALIGNMENT
Criterion 2	Practitioners trust and use the architecture.	TREND SURFER	GENERATIVE VISION
Criterion 3	Tacit knowledge about architecture and components is visible and accessible to users.	FOLLOWING ORDERS	ROTATION
RHYTHM:			
Rhythm is the recurring, predictable exchange of work products within an architecture group and across their customers and suppliers.			
Criterion 1	Managers periodically reevaluate, synchronize, and adapt the architecture.	KILLER FEATURE	RELEASE COMMITTEE

Principle	Definition and Criterion—What it is; How you measure	Antipattern— What not to do	Pattern— What can you do
Criterion 2	Architecture users have a high level of confidence in the timing and content of architecture releases.	SHORT CUT	DROP PASS
Criterion 3	Explicit activities are coordinated via rhythm.	BROKEN LOADS	SYNCHRONIZE RELEASES

ANTICIPATION:

Anticipation is the extent to which those who build and implement the architecture predict, validate, and adapt the architecture to changing technology, competition, and customer needs.

Principle	Definition and Criterion	Antipattern	Pattern
Criterion 1	Architecture capability is regularly enhanced to respond to • anticipated risks and requirements of architecture customers and their customers • market-driving standards and evolving technology • changes in strategic business directions.	MISSING PIECE	PILOT
Criterion 2	Technical and business risks and opportunities are evaluated through quick cycles of review and development.	BLEEDING EDGE	ARCHITECTURE REVIEW
Criterion 3	Features, budgets, plans, or schedules are adapted when it is recognized that critical estimates or assumptions are incorrect.	TUNNEL VISION	OUTSOURCE

PARTNERING:

Partnering is the extent to which architecture stakeholders maintain clear, cooperative roles and maximize the value they deliver and receive.

Principle	Definition and Criterion	Antipattern	Pattern
Criterion 1	The architect continually seeks to understand who the most critical stakeholders are, how they contribute value, and what they want.	PHONE DOESN'T RING	KNOW THY STAKEHOLDERS

PRINCIPLE	DEFINITION AND CRITERION—WHAT IT IS; HOW YOU MEASURE	ANTIPATTERN— WHAT NOT TO DO	PATTERN— WHAT CAN YOU DO
Criterion 2	Clear, compelling agreements exist between stakeholders.	LIP-SYNCHING	RECIPROCITY
Criterion 3	Both policies and informal rules of social conduct enforce cooperation.	PERSONAL TIME	NO SURPRISES and PROMOTE THE NETWORK

SIMPLIFICATION:

Simplification means the intelligent clarification and minimization of both architecture and the organizational environment in which it functions.

Criterion 1	Developers continue to use the architecture over time, reducing overall cost and complexity.	CLONING	SLOW DOWN TO SPEED UP
Criterion 2	The architecture group clearly understands the essential minimal requirements and "builds" them into core elements that are shared across one or more applications.	BANYAN, ROOT BOUND, and VENUS FLY TRAP	MIGRATION PATH
Criterion 3	Long-term budget and action ensure that elements are removed from the core when • they are not shared, or add unnecessary complexity, and • there is a clear business case.	LOAN SHARK	WHIRLPOOL WATCH

ANTIPATTERN AND PATTERN SUMMARIES

Antipattern Summaries

DESCRIPTION	PRINCIPLE
ANTIGRAVITY MODULE is an antipattern in which the vision of the stakeholders is aligned by planning a component to satisfy all of the competing interests with minimal compromise and maximum optimism. The problem with such alignment is that the resulting component generally runs a lot better on the view graph projector than it does in real life.	Vision
BANYAN illustrates the consequences of too much minimization—quickly building point solutions without spending the time or resources to consolidate and simplify the ever-expanding branches of code. The pattern is illustrated by the image of a Banyan tree with roots growing downward to support its many branches. Banyan represents one extreme adapted in the name of simplification. ROOT BOUND, its sister antipattern, represents the other extreme. Together, we refer to them as the Pendulum Antipatterns.	Simplification
BLEEDING EDGE illustrates what can happen when architects get their users to buy into an immature technology without considering their users' customers.	Anticipation
BROKEN LOADS can happen when an organization has tried to implement regular builds, but the builds frequently fail to compile or pass automated tests. This represents a breakdown of coordination.	Rhythm

Antipattern Summaries

DESCRIPTION	PRINCIPLE
CLONING illustrates what can happen when programmers are pushed to complete tasks quickly before they learn to use or respect the architecture. Instead of negotiating a change with the component owner, programmers copy and modify parts of the architecture and end up maintaining a lot more than they bargained for.	Simplification
FOLLOWING ORDERS results when developers become too application-focused and do not create common solutions for problems shared by other architecture users even at the users' request.	Vision
KILLER FEATURE is what happens when an organization becomes so focused on getting one feature to market that the internal rhythm is disrupted. Even if the feature is delivered, the organization may be blind-sided by competition because of the single-minded focus on getting the feature to market. It is an example of what happens when the management does not regularly reevaluate and adapt the architecture.	Rhythm
LIP SYNCHING shows what happens when an architecture team avoids taking the necessary action to arrive at a clear contract with their high-visibility users. When these users lose interest, discussions often continue. However, the discussions lose substance and generally waste everyone's time.	Partnering
LOAN SHARK describes how *not* to implement ARCHITECT ALSO IMPLEMENTS. The architect is moved onto a crash project to add a new set of features, generally for a very important customer. Just as a loan shark promises easy money now for grief in the future, an architect can get a project out of trouble today, but sow the seeds of future problems. The architect has no time to evolve the existing architecture.	Simplification
MISSING PIECE describes the "Oh Shoot!" experience of finding that an obvious feature has been left out. Everyone has been so enmeshed in the release's powerful new features, they have overlooked capabilities that users cannot do without.	Anticipation
PERSONAL TIME describes what can happen when an engineer's proposal to modify a component to make it useful to other groups is met with a mixed message—"You can do it, but on your own time."	Partnering
PHONE DOESN'T RING shows what happens when the architect hears what his users want but misses the part about what he or she has to do to make it valuable to those users.	Partnering
ROOT BOUND paints a visual picture of what an architecture or platform team builds when they build too much into the core—putting in, for example, too many "nice-to-have" features, seeking to support too many disparate products or building in customer-specific solutions. The goal is to simplify the task of building and maintaining solutions. The resulting architecture is too complex to incorporate into products. ROOT BOUND conjures a picture of an overgrown, bottom-heavy trunk with few branches. The pattern represents one extreme behavior adopted in the name of simplification. BANYAN, its sister antipattern, represents the other extreme. Together, we refer to them as the Pendulum Antipatterns.	Simplification

Antipattern Summaries

DESCRIPTION	PRINCIPLE
SHORTCUT can happen when the organization tries to maintain a regular beat of releases by taking shortcuts in the organization's process. This antipattern compromises the quality and content that users expect from the architecture.	Rhythm
TREND SURFER describes a situation in which the vision is not well established, so the direction of the architecture changes frequently in response to competitive and customer pressure. The vision is never stable enough to be effectively shared.	Vision
TUNNEL VISION portrays what happens when plans for architecture development and implementation do not change as evidence mounts showing that their underlying assumptions and estimates are completely off the mark.	Anticipation
VENUS FLY TRAP illustrates how easy it is to be sweet-talked into adding just one "easy-to-do" feature when the stakes are very high.	Simplification

Pattern Summaries

DESCRIPTION	PRINCIPLE
ARCHITECTURE REVIEW outlines how to organize and execute a focused, expert assessment of a developing architecture designed to uncover high-impact problems and opportunities, such as assumption conflicts, and existing solutions that could be reused.	Anticipation
DROP PASS examines how organizations can maintain a beat by moving less critical features to later release cycles. By maintaining the rhythm, this pattern gives users more confidence on the timing of architecture releases.	Rhythm
FRONT-END ALIGNMENT calls for the executive driving an architecture investment to take an active role in maintaining the vision and to protect the vision from short-term pressures.	Vision
GENERATIVE VISION reflects the recognition that the architect is not always the source of the architecture vision. The architect helps establish a vision that users can flesh out and bring to life.	Vision
KNOW THY STAKEHOLDERS illustrates using value chain to identify, actively listen to, and gain the commitment of key stakeholders.	Partnering
MIGRATION PATH describes an approach to engaging a new user community by building a competency-enhancing bridge.	Simplification

Pattern Summaries

DESCRIPTION	PRINCIPLE
NO SURPRISES is based on the premise that partners should avoid surprising each other, and the pattern helps build an environment in which partnering can thrive.	Partnering
OUTSOURCE illustrates how to adapt when your customers demand new standards or technologies that are not part of your current or planned core capabilities. OUTSOURCE provides guidance on when and how to select an existing third-party component, or partner with a supplier whose best interests are served by building a solution you can use.	Anticipation
PILOT builds on a proven technology transition technique to introduce and get the kinks out of a new architecture. The pattern illustrates how to select an initial product or application.	Anticipation
PROMOTE THE NETWORK describes an approach to granting promotions based not just on an individual's technical skills and experience but also his or her ability to make effective and ethical use of informal networks.	Partnering
RECIPROCITY describes behavior that is essential to building relationships strong enough to support the common, successful use of software architecture.	Partnering
RELEASE COMMITTEE describes an approach for coordinating the parties involved in releasing a new architecture. The pattern illustrates a way for managers to reevaluate, synchronize, and adapt an architecture during the final stretch of an architecture's release.	Rhythm
ROTATION calls for people who work with architecture to be rotated to work in different areas of the architecture. This gives them both a direct understanding of more of the architecture and an opportunity to develop their informal networks.	Vision
SLOW DOWN TO SPEED UP describes what to do when developers reject the use of architecture to keep up with schedule and get further behind as a result. The solution—ease up on the schedule and tighten up on the process.	Simplification
SYNCHRONIZE RELEASES is a technique for extending the notion of rhythm beyond an organization's boundaries. This pattern provides a way to synchronize the activities of the architecture team and their users.	Rhythm
WHIRLPOOL WATCH is a method for selecting which architectural components need to be examined for rework by watching the degree of churn.	Simplification

REFERENCES

[Akroyd96]   M. Akroyd, "AntiPatterns: Vaccinations against Object Misuse," Object World West, San Francisco, 1996.

[Alexander77] C. Alexander, S. Ishikawa, and M. Silverstein, *A Pattern Language*. New York: Oxford University Press, 1977.

[Allaire99]   J. J. Allaire, "Scalability on the Web," http://alive.allaire.com, as viewed on January 29th, 1999.

[APG00]   IEEE 1471-2000: IEEE Recommended Practice for Architectural Descriptions of Software Intensive Systems.

[Apple99]   "Apple Updates Public Source License," press release April 19th, 1999, http://www.apple.com/pr/library/1999/apr/19opensource.html, as viewed on July 11th, 1999.

[Appleton97]   B. Appleton, "Patterns and Software: Essential Concepts and Terminology," *Object Magazine Online*, May 1997, v3 n5; also available at http://www.enteract.com/~bradapp/docs/patterns-intro.html.

[ASQ00]   American Society for Quality web site glossary page, http://www.asq.org/abtquality/definition.htm, as viewed on August 19th, 2000.

[Bass98]   L. Bass, P. Clements, R. Kazman, *Software Architecture in Practice*. Reading, MA: Addison-Wesley, 1998.

[Beale97]   S. Beale, "Amelio Carves a New Apple," *Macworld*, June 1997.

[Beck00]   K. Beck, *Extreme Programming Explained: Embrace Change,* Reading, MA: Addison-Wesley, 2000.

[Beedle99]   M. Beedle, M. Devos, Y. Sharon, K. Schwaber, J. Sutherland, "Scrum: A Pattern Language for Hyperproductive Software Development," *Pattern Languages of Program Design 4*. N. Harrison, B. Foote, H. Rohnert, eds., Reading, MA: Addison-Wesley, 1999.

[BIDM95]   1420.1-1995 IEEE Standard for Information Technology—Software Reuse—Data Model for Reuse Library Interoperability: Basic Interoperability Data Model.

[BIDM96]   1420.1a-1996 IEEE Guide for Information Technology—Software Reuse—Data Model for Reuse Library Interoperability: Asset Certification Framework.

[BIDM99]   1420.1b-1999 IEEE Trial-Use Supplement to IEEE Standard for Information Technology—Software Reuse—Data Model for Reuse Library Interoperability: Intellectual Property Rights Framework.

[Blice98]   D. Blice, Personal Communication with Dave Dikel, November 25th, 1998.

[Booch96]   G. Booch, *Object Solutions: Managing the Object-Oriented Project*. Reading, MA: Addison-Wesley, 1996.

[Bowers96]   B. Bowers, G.Moore, 1996 National Quality Symposium and Quality Forum XII.

[Box79]   G. Box, "Some Problems of Statistics and Everyday Life," *Journal of the American Statistical Association*, v74 n365, pp. 1-4.

[Box99]   G. Box, Personal communication with David Kane, November 25th, 1999.

[Brand94]   S. Brand, *How Buildings Learn: What Happens After They Are Built*. New York: Viking Books, 1994.

[Bredemeyer00] D. Bredemeyer, *Architecting Process*. http://www.bredemeyer.com/pdffiles/ProcessGuide.PDF as viewed on March 26th, 2000.

[Britannica00] *Britannica.com*, http://www.britannica.com/bcom/eb/article/printable/6/0,5722,56716,00.html as viewed on May 3rd, 2000.

[Brooks82]   F. P. Brooks, Jr., *The Mythical Man-Month: Essays on Software Engineering*. Reading, MA: Addison-Wesley, 1982.

[BrownW98]   W. Brown, R. Malveau, H. McCormick, T. Mowbray, *Antipatterns: Refactoring Software, Architectures and Projects in Crisis*. New York: John Wiley & Sons, 1998.

[BrownS98]   S. Brown, K. Eisenhardt, *Competing on the Edge*, Cambridge, MA: Harvard Business School Press, 1998.

[Cabrera99]   R. Cabrera, B Appleton, S. Berczuk, "Software Reconstruction: Patterns for Reproducing Software Builds," *Pattern Languages of Programming,* 1999, August 15–18, 1999.

[Camp89]   R. Camp, *Benchmarking: The Search for Industry Best Practices that Lead to Superior Performance*. ASQC Press, Milwaukee, Wisconsin, 1989.

[Cane85]   A. Cane, "Who's partnering in the R and D stakes." *Financial Times (London)*, Financial Times Limited, July 28, 1985.

[Cashin91]   P. Cashin, "BNR Remains at Forefront of Computing Technology," *Telesis*, July 1996, v92, pp. 73–75.

[Charette89]   R. Charette, *Software Engineering Risk Analysis and Management*. New York: Intertext Publications, 1989.

[Charette93]   R. Charette, "Management by Design," *Software Management*, October 1993, pp. 5–11.

[Charette97]   R. Charette, "Managing Risk in Software Management," *IEEE Software*, May/June 1997, v14, n3, pp. 43–50.

[Chase73]   W. Chase and H. Simon, "Perception in Chess." *Cognitive Psychology*, v4, n1, January 1973, pp. 55–81.

[Clayton86]   M. Clayton, "Series on Corporate Partnering," *Christian Science Monitor,* The Christian Science Publishing Society, April 15–16, 1986.

[Clausewitz32] C. von Clausewitz, *On War,* 1832.

[Cockburn96]   A. Cockburn, "Prioritizing Forces in Software Design," *Pattern Languages of Program Design 2.* J. Vlissides, J. Coplien, eds., Reading, MA: Addison-Wesley, 1996.

[Cockburn98]   A. Cockburn, *Surviving Object-Oriented Projects: A Manager's Guide*, Addison-Wesley, 1998.

[Conway68]   M. Conway, "How Do Committees Invent," *Datamation*, April 1968, v14, n4, pp. 28–31.

[Cooper94]   R. Cooper, "Debunking the Myths of New Product Development," *Research Technology Management*, July/Aug. 1994, v37, n4, pp. 40–50.

[Coplien95]   J. Coplien, "A Development Process Generative Pattern Language," *Pattern Languages of Program Design.* J. Coplien, and D. Schmidt, eds., Reading, MA: Addison-Wesley, 1995.

[Coplien00]   J. Coplien, Personal Communication with David Kane, July 17th, 2000.

[Cornwell96]   P. Collins Cornwell, "HP Domain Analysis: Producing Useful Models for Reusable Software" in *Hewlett-Packard Journal*, August 1996, v47, i4.

[Costello96]   E. Costello, "Warner Brothers Cartoon Companion," 1996, http://www.spumco.com/magazine/eowbcc viewed on August 31st, 2000.

[Couger88]   D. Couger, "Motivating IS Personnel" *Datamation*, September 15th 1988.

[Crabb98]   D. Crabb, "Apple Reveals its Mac OS Strategy—Again!," *Macweek*, May 21st, 1998, v12, i20.

[Crotty96]   C. Crotty, "Systems: Opal Opens Up OpenDoc," *Macworld*, July 1996, v13, n7, p. 39.

[Cunningham96] W. Cunningham, "EPISODES: A Pattern Language of Competitive Development," *Pattern Languages of Program Design 2.* J. Vlissides, J. Coplien, eds., Reading, MA: Addison-Wesley, 1996.

[Cunningham99] W. Cunningham, R. Gabriel. "The History of Patterns." *Pattern Languages of Programming 1999*, August 15th–18th 1999.

[Cusumano95]   M. Cusumano, *Microsoft Secrets: How the World's Most Powerful Software Company Creates Technology, Shapes Markets, and Manages People*. New York: Simon & Schuster, 1995.

[Delano97]   D. Delano, L. Rising, "Introducing Technology into the Workplace," Pattern Languages of Programming, 1997, Washington University Technical Report 97-34.

[Delano98]   D. Delano, L. Rising, "Patterns for System Testing" *Pattern Languages of Program Design 3*. R. Martin, D. Riehle, F. Buschmann, eds., Reading, MA: Addison-Wesley, 1998.

[de Neufville94] R. de Neufville, "The Baggage System at Denver: Prospects and Lessons," *Journal of Air Transport Management*, v1, n4, 1994, pp. 229–236.

[Dikel93]   D. Dikel, J. Lichtenstein, J. Rosoff, et. al., "TRILLIUM Case Study: A Commercial Example of a Software Supplier Capability Assessment Model that Encourages Effective Software Reuse," Produced for Defense Advance Projects Research Agency STARS program under contract to IBM Federal Systems Company, Report Number 05021-002, September 1993.

[Dikel95]   D. Dikel, D. Kane, S. Ornburn, J. Wilson "Software Architecture Case Study: Organizational Success Factors," *ARPA STARS*, December 1995.

[Dikel97a]   D. Dikel, D. Kane, S. Ornburn, W. Loftus, J.Wilson, "Applying Software Product-Line Architecture," *Computer*, August 1997.

[Dikel97b]   D. Dikel, C. Hermansen, D. Kane, R. Malveaux, "Organizational Patterns for Software Architecture," *Pattern Languages of Programming,* 1997, Washington University Technical Report 97-34.

[Dikel97c]   D. Dikel, D. Kane, "Organizational Principles For Software Reuse", *WISR8: 8th Annual Workshop on Software Reuse* http://www.umcs.maine.edu/~ftp/wisr/wisr8/wisr8-summary/principles.html and http://www.umcs.maine.edu/~ftp/wisr/wisr8/wisr8-summary/principles-long.html as viewed on October 17th, 1999.

[Dikel97d]   D. Dikel, D. Kane, "Principles of Software Reuse Working Group," *Reuse 97*, Principles of Software Reuse Working Group http://www.nplace.wvhtf.org/reuse97/DKane/index.htm as viewed on October 17th, 1999.

[Dikel97e]   D. Dikel D. Kane, M. Carlyn, J. Wilson, Software Architecture Benchmark (SAB) Model and Protocol, U.S. Department of Defense Advanced Research Projects Agency (DARPA) Software for Adaptable, Reliable Systems (STARS) Program, 1997.

[Dowat89]   S. Dowat, "Partnering continues to get high marks from both sides, purchasing managers and distributor execs see pretty much eye to eye on the value of working together," *Purchasing,* April 20, 1989.

[Dyer96]   J. Dyer, "How Chrysler Created an American Kieretsu," *Harvard Business Review,* July-August 1996, v74, n4, pp. 42–56.

[Eigen93]   L. Eigen, J. Siegel, *Dictionary of Political Quotations*. MacMillan Publishing Company, New York, 1993.

[Eisenhardt98]   K. Eisenhardt, S. Brown, "Time Pacing: Competing In Markets That Won't Stand Still," *Harvard Business Review*, March-April 1998, v76, n2, pp. 59–69.

[Fafchamps94]   F. Fafchamps, "Organizational Factors and Reuse," *IEEE Software*, Sept. 1994, v11, n5, pp. 31–41.

[Foote99]   B. Foote, J. Yoder, "Big Ball of Mud," *Pattern Languages of Program Design 4*. N. Harrison, B. Foote, H. Rohnert, eds., Reading, MA: Addison-Wesley, 1999.

[Fowler99]   M. Fowler, *Refactoring*. Reading, MA: Addison-Wesley, 1999.

[Fukuyama95]   F. Fukuyama, *Trust: The Social Virtues and the Creation of Prosperity*. New York: Simon and Schuster, 1995.

[Fukuyama97]   F. Fukuyama, A. Shulsky, *The "Virtual Corporation" and Army Organization*. RAND, 1997.

[Gamma94]   E. Gamma, R. Helm, R. Johnson, J. Vlissides, *Design Patterns*, Reading, MA: Addison-Wesley, 1994.

[GAO90]   U.S. General Accounting Office, *Case Study Evaluations*. GAO/PEMD-91-10.1.9, November 1990.

[Gartner99]   L. Gartner, "The Rookie Primer," Radcliffe Rugby Football Club, http://www.hcs.harvard.edu/~radrugby/rookie_primer.html as viewed on August 1st, 1999.

[Gates96]   B. Gates, *The Road Ahead: Completely Revised and Up-To-Date*. New York: Penguin Books, 1996.

[Gersick88]   C. Gersick, "Time and Transition in Work Teams: Toward a New Model of Group Development," *Academy of Management Journal,* 1988, v31, n 1, pp. 9–41.

[Gersick89]   C. Gersick, "Marking Time: Predictable Transitions In Task Groups," *Academy of Management Journal*, July 1989, v32, n2, pp. 274–309.

[Gersick91]   C. Gersick, "Revolutionary Change Theories: A Multilevel Exploration of the Punctuated Equilibrium Paradigm," *Academy of Management Review*, January 1991, v16, n1, pp. 10–37.

[Gersick94]   C. Gersick, "Pacing Strategic Change: The Case of a New Venture," *Academy of Management Journal*, February 1994, v37, n1, pp. 9–45.

[Gibbs96]   W. Gibbs, "Software's Chronic Crisis," *Scientific American*, September 1994, v271, n3, pp. 86–95.

[Gilb93]   T. Gilb, D. Graham, *Software Inspection*. Reading, MA: Addison-Wesley, 1993.

[Grady97]   R. Grady, *Successful Software Process Improvement*. Saddle River, NJ: Prentice Hall PTR, 1997.

[Grinter99]   R. Grinter, "Systems Architecture: Product Designing and Social Engineering," *Proceedings of the ACM International Conference on Work Activities Coordination and Collaboration*, February 22–25, 1999, San Francisco, CA, pp. 11–18.

[Halverson99]   L. Halverson, D. Kane, S. Lilly, et al., "Brown Bag Conferences: Supersizing a Tried-and-True Method to Introduce Technology." Object Technology Centers 1999.

[Harrison96]   N. Harrison, "Organizational Patterns for Teams," *Pattern Languages of Program Design 2*. J. Vlissides, J. Coplien, and N. Kerth, eds., Reading, MA: Addison-Wesley, 1996.

[Hecker00]   F. Heckler, "Setting Up Shop: The Business of Open-Source Software," http://www.hecker.org/writings/setting-up-shop.html, revision 0.8, updated June 20th, 2000, viewed on September 2nd, 2000.

[Iansiti93]   M. Iansiti, "Real-World R&D: Jumping the Product Generation Gap," *Harvard Business Review*, May-June 1993, v71, n3, pp. 138–147.

[Jacobson97]   I. Jacobson, M. Griss, P. Jonsson, *Software Reuse: Architecture, Process, and Organization for Business Success*. ACM Press, New York 1997.

[Javasoft00]   "The Java Servlet API, Industry Momentum" http://java.sun.com/products/servlet/industry.html, as viewed on July 21st, 2000.

[Kahney99a]   L. Kahney, "Apple Defends Open-Source Move," *Wired News*, March 17th, 1999, http://www.wired.com/news/print_version/technology/story.19233.html?wnpg=all.

[Kahney99b]   L. Kahney, "Apple Lifts License Restrictions," *Wired News*, April 21st, 1999, http://www.wired.com/news/print_version/technology/story.18515.html?wnpg=all.

[Kane97]   D. Kane, W. Opdyke, D. Dikel, "Managing Change to Reusable Software," Pattern Languages of Programming 1997, Washington University Technical Report 97-34.

[Kotler86]   P. Kotler, "Megamarketing," *Harvard Business Review,* President and Fellow of Harvard College, March/April 1986.

[Kruchten98]   P. Kruchten, *The Rational Unified Process*, Reading, MA: Addison-Wesley, 1998.

[Lague97]   B. Lague, D. Proulx, J. Mayrand, et al., "Assessing the Benefits of Incorporating Function Clone Detection in a Development Process," *Proceedings of the 1997 International Conference of Software Maintenance*.

[Lawrence69]   P. Lawrence, J. Lorsch, *Developing Organizations:Diagnosis and Action*. Reading, MA: Addison-Wesley, 1969.

[Lilly00]   S. Lilly, "How to Avoid Use-Case Pitfalls," *Software Development Magazine*, January 2000.

[Locke96]   K. Locke, "Rewriting *The Discovery of Grounded Theory* After 25 Years?," *Journal of Management Inquiry*, v5, n3, September 1996, pp. 239–245.

[Macweek97]   "Warnock Says Adobe Committed to Rhapsody," *Macweek*, March 21st, 1997, v11, i12.

[Maggio96]   R. Maggio, *The New Beacon Book of Quotations by Women*. Boston, MA: Beacon Press, 1996.

[Magretta98]   J. Magretta, "The Power of Virtual Integration: An Interview with Dell Computer's Michael Dell." *Harvard Business Review*, March-April 1998, v76, n2, pp. 72–84.

[Manns00]   M. Manns, L. Rising, "Evolving a Patterns Culture," Fifth European Conference on Pattern Languages of Programs, July 5–9, 2000

[Mayrand96]   J. Mayrand, C. Leblanc, E. Merlo, "Automatic Detection of Function Clones in a Software System Using Metrics," *Proceedings of the 1996 International Conference of Software Maintenance.*

[McCarthy95]   J McCarthy, *Dynamics of Software Development: "Don't Flip the Bozo Bit" and 53 More Rules for Delivering Great Software on Time.* Redmond, WA: Microsoft Press, 1995.

[McConnell96]   S. McConnell, "Best Practices: Daily Build and Smoke Test," *IEEE Software*, July 1996, v13, n4, pp. 143–144.

[McLendon96]   J. McLendon, G. Weinberg, "Beyond Blaming: Congruence in Large Systems Development Projects," *IEEE Software*, July 1996, v13, n4, pp. 32–43.

[Mohrman95]   S. A. Mohrman, S. Cohen, A. Mohrman, Jr., *Designing Team-Based Organizations: New Forms for Knowledge Work.* San Francisco: Jossey-Bass, 1995.

[Mohrman97]   S. A. Mohrman, R. V. Tenkasi, J. Colpin, P. Greenberg, "A Practical Framework for Organizational Learning: Learnings from a Study of Organizations in Transition," Seminar Notes, Center for Effective Organizations, Marshall School of Business, University of Southern California, November 12, 1997.

[Mohrman98]   S. A. Mohrman, J. A, Galbraith, E. E. Lawler III, et. al., *Tomorrow's Organization: Crafting Winning Capabilities in a Dynamic World.* San Francisco: Jossey-Bass, 1998.

[Moore65]   G. Moore, "Cramming More Components Onto Integrated Circuits," *Electronics*, April 19, 1965, v38, n8, pp. 114–117.

[Moore91]   G. Moore, *Crossing the Chasm: Marketing and Selling Technology Products to Mainstream Customers.* New York: Harper Business, 1991.

[Morgan86]   G. Morgan, *Images of Organization.* Newbury Park, CA: Sage Publications, 1986.

[Muoio99]   A. Muoio (Ed.), "Unit of One: The Art of Smart," *Fast Company,* July-August 1999, p. 98.

[Myerson94]   A. Myerson, "Automation Off Course in Denver," *New York Times*, March 18th, 1994, D1–D2.

[Norman98]   D. Norman, *Invisible Computer: Why Good Products Can Fail, the Personal Computer Is So Complex and Information Appliances Are the Solution.* Cambridge, MA: MIT Press, 1998.

[Oakes99]   C. Oakes, "Netscape Browser Guru: We Failed," *Wired News*, April 2nd, 1999, http://www.wired.com/news/print_version/technology/story/18926.html?wnpg=all.

[Olofson99]   C. Olofson, "Start the Day with Coffee and a Scrum," *Fast Company,* February-March 1999, i22, p. 60.

[Olson97]   D. Olson, "Breaking Up is Hard to Do," Pattern Languages of Programming 1997, Washington University Technical Report 97-34.

[Olson98]   D. Olson, "Patterns on the Fly," *The Patterns Handbook.* L. Rising, ed., New York: Cambridge University Press, 1998.

[Parisi99]   P. Parisi, "Weapons of Mass Entertainment," *Wired*, March 1999, v7, n3, pp. 122–123.

[Parnas76]   D. Parnas, "On the Design and Development of Program Families," *IEEE Transactions on Software Engineering*, March 1976, v2, n1, pp. 1–9.

[Passell97]   P. Passell, "Economic Scene: Is China's Latest Move to Capitalism Real?," *New York Times*, September 18, 1997.

[Perens99]   B. Perens, W. Akkerman, I. Jackson, "The Apple Public Source License—Our Concerns," http://perens.com/APSL.html as viewed on July 11th, 1999.

[Pogue97]   D. Pogue, "The Desktop Critic," *Macworld*, August 1997, v14, n8, pp. 205–206.

[Porter85]   M. Porter, *Competitive Advantage: Creating and Sustaining Superior Advantage.* New York: The Free Press, 1985.

[Porter98]   M. Porter, *Competitive Advantage: Creating and Sustaining Superior Advantage: With A New Introduction.* New York: The Free Press, 1998.

[Prahalad90]   C. Prahalad, G. Hamel, "The Core Competence of the Corporation," *Harvard Business Review*, May-June 1990, v68, n3, pp. 79–91.

[Raymond99]   E. Raymond, *The Cathedral and the Bazaar: Musings on Linux and Open Source by an Accidental Revolutionary*, Sebastopol, CA: O'Reilly & Associates, 1999.

[Reid97]   R. Reid, *Architects of the Web: 1,000 Days that Built the Future of Business.* New York: John Wiley & Sons, Inc., 1997.

[Rising98]   L. Rising, *The Patterns Handbook,* Cambridge University Press, 1998.

[Rising99]   L. Rising, "Customer Interaction Patterns," *Pattern Languages of Program Design 4.* N. Harrison, B. Foote, H. Rohnert, eds., Reading, MA: Addison-Wesley, 1999.

[Rising00]   L. Rising, *The Pattern Almanac 2000.* Reading, MA: Addison-Wesley, 2000.

[RSC99]   Reuse Steering Committee, http://www.asset.com/rsc, as viewed on October 17th, 1999.

[Sabherwal99]   R. Sabherwal, "The Role of Trust in Outsourced IS Development Projects," *Communications of the ACM*, February 1999, v42, n2, pp. 80–86.

[Senge90]   P.M. Senge, *The Fifth Discipline.* New York: Doubleday, 1990.

[Senge94]   P. M. Senge and A. Kleiner (eds), *The Fifth Discipline Fieldbook : Strategies and Tools for Building a Learning Organization.* New York: Doubleday, 1994.

[Sessions99]   R. Sessions, "A Lesson from Palm Pilot," *IEEE Software*, January-February 1999, v16, n1, pp. 36, 38, ©1999 IEEE.

[Shaw97]   R. Shaw, *Trust in the Balance: Building Successful Organizations on Results, Integrity, and Concern*. San Francisco: Jossey-Bass Publishers, 1997.

[Sherman97]   E. Sherman, "Developers Split on Adoption of Rhapsody OS," *Macweek*, May 19th, 1997, v11, i20.

[Simeonov00]   S. Simeonov, "XML for B2B Integration," *XMLJournal.com*, v1 i2, available at, http://www.sys-con.com/xml/archives/0102/simeonov, viewed on June 22nd, 2000.

[Simos95]   M. Simos, R. Creps, C. Klingler, L. Lavine, "Organizational Domain Modeling (ODM) Guidebook," Version 1.0, *Informal Technical Report for Software Technology for Adaptable, Reliable, Systems (STARS)*, STARS-VC-A023/011/00, Contract Number F19628-93-C-130, March 1995.

[Simos96]   M. Simos, "Organizational Domain Modeling (ODM): Domain Engineering as a Co-Methodology to Object-Oriented Techniques," *Fusion Newsletter*, v4.4, October 1996.

[Sitwell65]   E. Sitwell, *Taken Care Of*, New York: Simon & Schuster, 1965.

[Smith87]   K. Smith, D. Berg, *Paradoxes of Group Life: Understanding Conflict, Paralysis, and Movement in Group Dynamic*. San Francisco: Jossey-Bass, 1987.

[Stasek93]   J. Stasek, "Partnering, Keeping Contracts out of the Courtroom, *Contract Management Magazine*, November 1993, pp. 26–29.

[Swartz96]   J. Swartz, "Clarisworks to Support OpenDoc," *Macweek*, February 16th 1996, v10, n8.

[Taylor99]   P. Taylor, "Capable, Productive and Satisfied," *Pattern Languages of Program Design 4*. N. Harrison, B. Foote, H. Rohnert, eds., Reading, MA: Addison-Wesley, 1999.

[USCF99]   US Chess Federation web site, http://www.uschess.org, as viewed on November 7th, 1999.

[VanHelden00]   A. Van Helden, E. Burr, "The Galileo Project," http://es.rice.edu/ES/humsoc/Galileo as viewed on May 3rd, 2000.

[Vixie99]   P. Vixie, "Software Engineering," in *Open Sources: Voices from the Open Source Revolution*. O'Reilly & Associates, 1999.

[Weinberg98]   G. Weinberg, *The Psychology of Computer Programming: Silver Anniversary Edition*. New York: Dorset House, 1998. www.dorsethouse.com.

[Weir98]   C. Weir, "Patterns for Designing Teams" *Pattern Languages of Program Design 3*. R. Martin, D. Riehle, F. Buschmann, eds., Reading, MA: Addison-Wesley, 1998.

[Whitenack95]   B. Whitenack, "RAPPeL: A Requirements-Analysis Process Pattern Language for Object-Oriented Development," *Pattern Languages of Program Design*. J. Coplien, and D. Schmidt, eds., Reading, MA: Addison-Wesley, 1995.

[Wilson96]   J. Wilson, D. Dikel, D. Kane, M. Carlyn C. Terry, E. Cavanaugh, D. Johnson, "Software Reuse Benchmarking Study: Learning from Industry and Government Leaders," sponsored by U.S. Department of Defense, Software Reuse Initiative, January 1996. Available online at http://dii-sw.ncr.disa.mil/reuseic/lessons/benchmark/html as viewed on October 17th, 1999.

[Ziegler93]   B. Ziegler, "What Really Happened at Northern Telecom," *Business Week*, August 9, 1993, n 3331, pp. 27–28.

INDEX

related antipatterns and patterns, 166
Ptololmey, Claudius, 177

Q

Quality, 77
    as an element of Rhythm principle, 74
    deterioration, 77f
QuickTime Server, 148

R

Rational Unified Process (RUP), 41–42
    and architectural review, 121
Raymond, Eric, 148
Reality *see* Vision
RECIPROCITY, 140, 155–157, 166
    examples, 157–158
    related antipatterns and patterns, 158
REDEFINE THE RULES, 90
Refactoring *see* Simplification
Reid, Robert, 205
RELEASE COMMITTEE, 81
    vs. configuration control board, 86
    example, 87
    mitigating effects of DROP PASS, 91–92
    as a pattern of a Rhythm criterion, 85–87
    related patterns and antipatterns, 87
    see also REPRESENTATIVE RELEASE COMMITTEE
        variation
Release cycle
    regular release schedules as examples of tempo,
        75, 79f–80f
    release gate and Rhythm principle, 8
    and Rhythm in Allaire example, 78
Release plan, 87
REPRESENTATIVE RELEASE COMMITTEE variation, 86, 87
Reuse98, 36
Reuse Steering Committee (RSC)/Reuse Library
Interoperability Group (RIG), 36, 105–106
Rhapsody *see* Apple/NeXT acquisition
Rhythm, 8, 73–74, 202, 212
    antipatterns that can derail Rhythm, 98t
    in benchmarking case study, 250–251
    coordinating activities across groups, 92
    criteria, 80, 82, 82t, 88, 92
    definition, 74
    drive to closure, 78

elements, 74, 96
    see also Content; Quality; Tempo
    importance, 78, 96–97
    misapplication example, 10, 11f
    organizational patterns/antipatterns that can shape
        Rhythm, 97t–98t
    patterns and antipatterns, 81, 82t
    and taking charge, 79, 79f, 80f
    and temporal framework, 25, 74
    time-pacing, as an effective strategy, 82
    transition management aid, 78, 97
Rising, Linda, 28, 92
Risk, list, 10
    management, and "no surprises" policy, 164
    and prototyping, 116
ROOT BOUND, 189, 195
    antipattern as a pattern, 189
    example, 190
    as a pendulum antipattern, 179, 185, 186f, 188
    related patterns and antipatterns, 190
ROTATION, 51, 52, 166
    example, 68
    as a pattern of a Vision criterion, 65–68
    related antipatterns and patterns, 68–69
    spirals vs. flat rings, 67
RUNNING ON EMPTY *see* BLEEDING EDGE

S

Savely, Bob, 35
SAX (Simplified API for XML), 228
SCHEDULE CHICKEN, 85, 87, 90, 123
SCRUM MASTER, 50
SCRUM MEETING, 50
Scrum method, 49–50
Senge, Peter, 40, 41, 55
Servlet API, 102–104
ServletExec *see* Unify eWave
SHARED PLATFORM, 187, 188
SHORTCUT, 81
    as an antipattern of a Rhythm criterion, 88–89, 88f
    example, 89
    as a pattern, 89–90
    related antipatterns and patterns, 90
    see also REDEFINE THE RULES
SHOW PERSONAL INTEGRITY, 144
SIDE PIECE, 114
Simeonov, Simeon, 209, 211–212, 217–218, 222–224

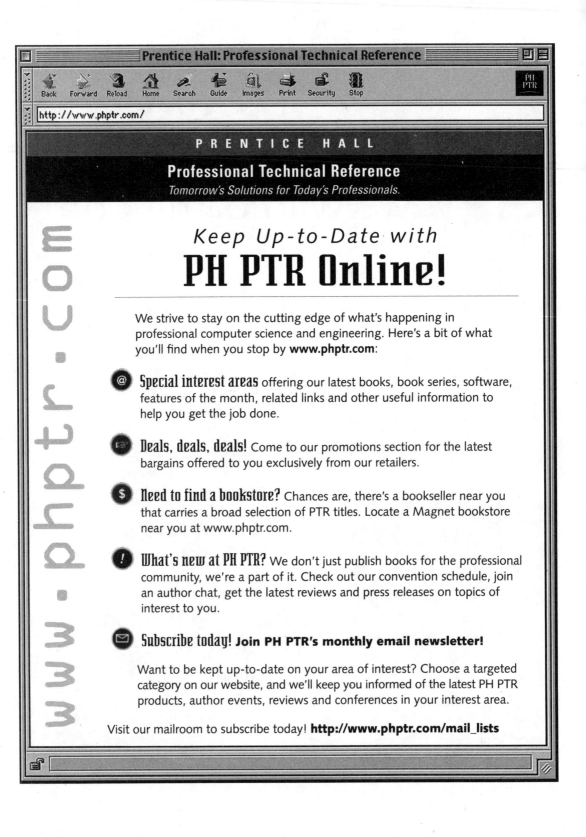